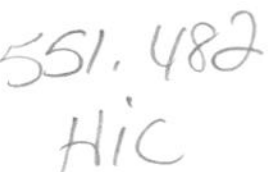

THE POND BOOK

A Complete Guide to Site Planning, Design, and Management of Small Lakes and Ponds

THE POND BOOK

A Complete Guide to Site Planning, Design, and Management of Small Lakes and Ponds

John Stephen Hicks

Fitzhenry & Whiteside

Published in Canada by Fitzhenry & Whiteside, 195 Allstate Parkway, Markham, ON L3R 4T8
Published in the United States by Fitzhenry & Whiteside, 311 Washington Street, Brighton, Massachusetts 02135

10 9 8 7 6 5 4 3 2 1

Fitzhenry & Whiteside acknowledges with thanks the Canada Council for the Arts, and the Ontario Arts Council for their support of our publishing program. We acknowledge the financial support of the Government of Canada through the Canada Book Fund (CBF) for our publishing activities.

Canada Council for the Arts Conseil des Arts du Canada

Library and Archives Canada Cataloguing in Publication
Hicks, John Stephen
The pond book : a complete guide to site planning, design and management of small lakes and ponds / John Stephen Hicks.
Includes index.
ISBN 978-1-55455-160-6
1. Ponds. 2. Ponds--Design and construction. 3. Pond ecology.
I. Title.
GB1803.2.H53 2012 551.48′2 C2011-902774-7

Publisher Cataloging-in-Publication Data (U.S.)
Hicks, John Stephen.
The pond book: a complete guide to site planning, design and management of small lakes and ponds / John Stephen hicks.
[216] p. : col. photos., maps ; cm.
Includes index.
Summary: Explore the wide variety of pond ecosystems and their function: topographic and soil requirements, design and construction techniques, wildlife management, fish species and their cultivation, local bylaws affecting pond maintenance, algae and plant control, parasite problems, chemical and physical parameters of water sources, and water control and erosion devices.
ISBN: 978-1-55455-160-6 (pbk.)
1. Pond life. 2. Pond ecology. I. Title.
574.526322 dc23 QH541.5.P63H535 2011
Printed and bound in Canada by Friesens Corporation

DEDICATION

This book is primarily dedicated to my father who built our pond and who spent many years trying to improve it. It is also dedicated in fond memory of our two pets, Mousse and Daisy, whose lifelong interest was exploring its perimeter and inspecting its inhabitants. The York Environmental Stewardship Council, whose work spirited my decision to undertake the book, deserves a dedication for their patience in awaiting a long-sought volume to use in their landowner assistance programs. And last but not least, I dedicate the book to my wife whose patience was unlimited, and who spent many sun-filled days without companionship, awaiting the book's completion.

Contents

Foreword

For years, my family home was perched on the western shoreline of Grenadier Pond in High Park, Toronto. With only a minute's walk down a path to good fishing, I spent many afternoons after school along the pond's western shoreline. Its diverse habitat was well populated with game and pan fish. Although it had a weedy bottom, the pond's water was clear enough along the shoreline for me to see the flash of bluegills and other sunfish in the depths. We called the pond the "Grennie," and it was there that my passion for the environment grew and my journey toward an outdoor profession commenced. An old man who lived by the pond for many years taught me the essentials of locating fish in their habitat and showed me how to make split bamboo rods. His green skiff, complete with his small terrier, was always out in the middle of the water when I went to fish. My friend knew every nook and cranny of the Grennie. He was an environmentalist way ahead of his time and could always catch a good-size pike or smallmouth bass. One side of Grenadier Pond flanked High Park, the other, the Village of Swansea. In the fifties, this was still wilderness to a teenage boy with a fishing rod. My friend taught me much about things absent from my high school biology course; he was constantly concerned about pollutants entering the pond at a time when little attention was given toward the sustainability of environmental systems.

The north end of Grenadier Pond during the early sixties, looking toward High Park.

Later, I took up fly fishing, largely because I wanted to master the skill involved in using the tackle, and also because it is a subtle form of the sport, with

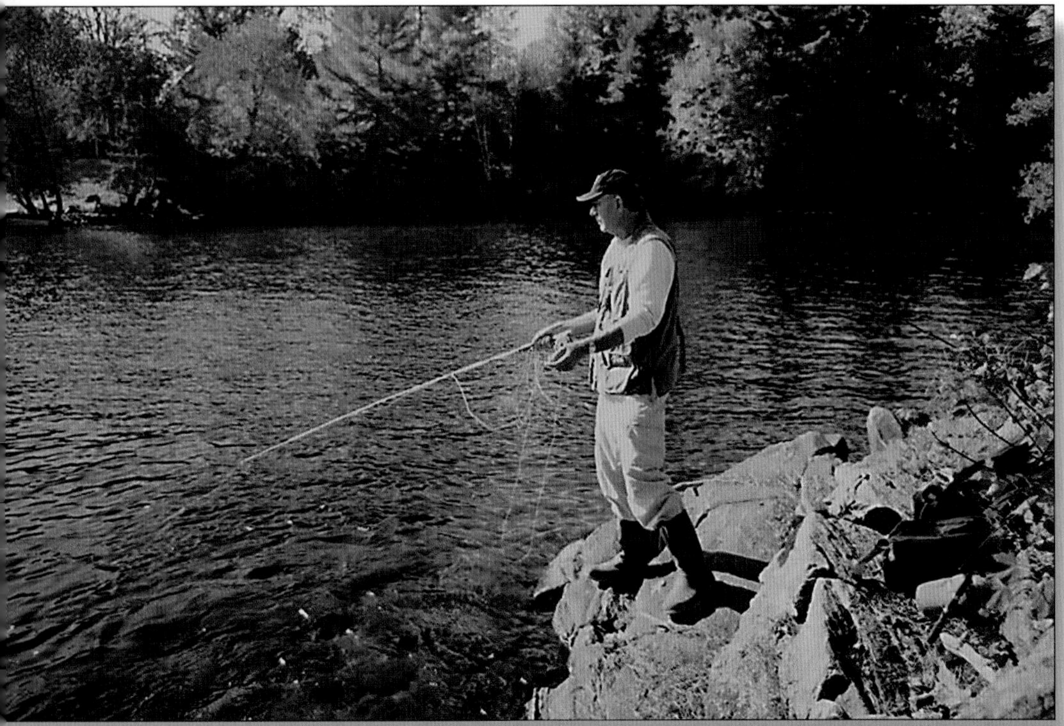

The author fly fishing in one of his favorite places—the Gull River at Elliot's Falls, just north of the town of Norland, Ontario.

low environmental impact. I focused upon tributary streams north of the Oak Ridges Moraine in Ontario and tracked brooks well up into their source areas. I often followed creeks that were only a foot or two wide as I searched for trout under grass-lined banks or in the occasional woodland or on-stream pond. I carried an early series of national defense maps in order to locate and follow abandoned railways or rights-of-ways for access into streams and ponds situated in the middle of concessions. I enjoyed many days on the banks of these waterways noticing the diversity of plant and animal life, and I began to see the relationship between various vegetation types and site conditions. My interest in the complexity of streams and ponds began at an early age, rather unconsciously, alongside my search for fish habitats.

During my youth, many good fly-fishing rivers and rural streams in southern Ontario were slowly deteriorating under development pressures, which contributed both bacterial pollution and phosphates from septic-bed systems and sewage-treatment-plant outfalls. It wasn't long before the best of my accessible streams and on-stream ponds began to experience some form of pollution, altering their fragile environments. The first indication of excess phosphate contamination was always the appearance of green algae, genus *Spirogyra*, attached to submerged rocks in streams or gathered around the littoral areas of ponds. My old trout habitats slowly began to contain more chub and sucker species, while the trout began to disappear.

Soon, career responsibilities took precedence over my earlier passion for fishing, and my travels turned to fieldwork and studies relevant to forestry and further to landscape planning. However, I never forgot the Grennie and its impact. Wherever and whenever I traveled, I always searched for such transparent waters, bountiful supplies of fish, and plant diversity as I had discovered in the Grennie. Even today, as I advance into my senior years, I have a mental image of the shoreline and weedy depths of that pond as if I had seen it just yesterday. It leaves me with as warm a mood as it did over fifty years ago on a sunny afternoon after school with my cherished fly rod.

Introduction

During the sixties, my father acquired a twenty-acre (8.09 ha) parcel of marginal land, a former mink farm and residual pasture from a larger farm lot. At first, I felt that the site was not a worthwhile purchase, being a worn-out pasture with little landscape appeal and requiring a great deal of effort to improve its diversity. Within a year or so, I had convinced my father to plant the property in a contract with Lands and Forests under the Woodlands Improvement Act. In 1962, the marginal upland portion of the property was planted in a mixture of white pine, red pine, white spruce, and larch, on five-foot centers.

In addition to his reforestation effort, my father decided to dig a large pond in a low area just outside the limit of a wetland bog forest. Knowing there was enough water at that location seemed to be sufficient evidence for a successful pond (small pools of water existed between muck patches and wetland grasses). With expectations of a clear and deep pond, my father proceeded to locate a contractor.

This site selection turned out to be somewhat of a mistake in the long run. My father hired a dragline operator and work proceeded quickly: an enormous muddy crater was created and slowly filled with water, apparently from spring-fed sources. There was little soil investigation, and it appeared to me that my father had initially encountered a few feet of peat, then a mucky soil type (Lyons loam) which even-

The pond immediately after construction, before its perimeter was graded out smooth.

tually ended at a blue-clay base about 5 ft. (1.53 m) down. The contractor placed some of the clay around the proposed pond, forming a dam for at least half its western perimeter (the site being on a subtle hillside which sloped from east to west). The final depth of the pond at the center was to be 10 ft. (3.05 m). The entire exercise was essentially a cut-and-fill operation on a gentle slope, forming a dam 6 ft. (1.83 m) high on the western or downhill perimeter, with an additional excavation of about 5 ft. (1.52 m) in the center portion.

As final topsoil, the contractor spread an excessive amount of the extra peat around the top of the dam, forming what turned out to be a dusty, loose soil which would not hold turf but was very suitable for goldenrod and weeds. The pond filled up quickly with aquamarine-tinted water (due to clay particles from the blue-clay bottom)—which seemed delightful. After quite a long period of time, the water cleared, the clay particles settled, and we began to level and seed the perimeter. The next spring, the pond margins began to grow *Equisetum* (horsetail), initiating a long process of plant succession that effected a slow but deliberate transition from pond back to swamp. This transformation, due largely to improper site selection and poor construction methods, ultimately resulted in a pond management problem. Thus, after we had taken over the property, it was obvious that our pond had become a good example of what not to be done in

Above: For a few years after construction, the pond my father built was left as a wildlife pond stocked with smallmouth black bass.

Our clear pond showing dock and storage shed, with canoe alongside, following completion of our country home in 1988.

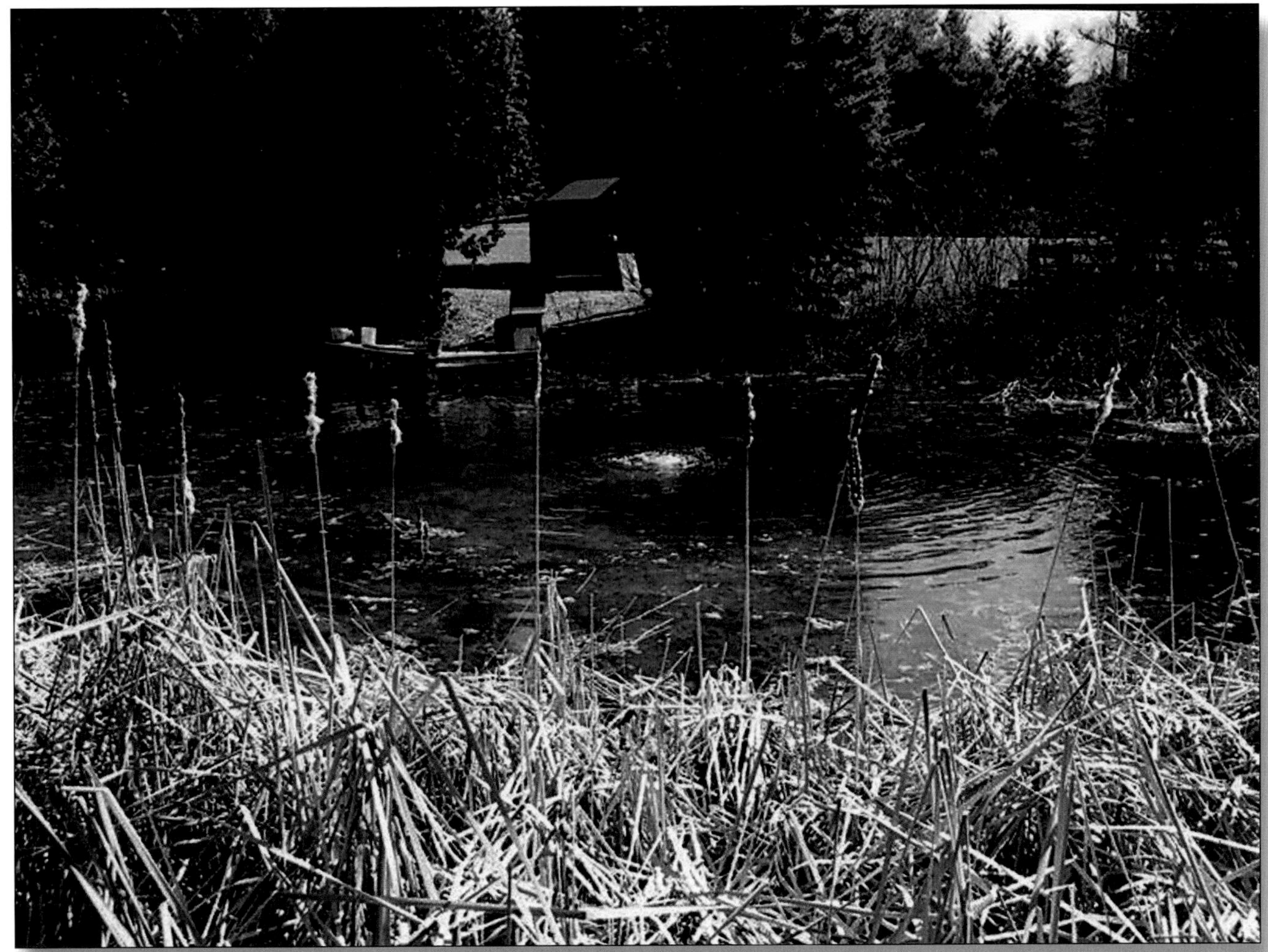

construction and how important soil/site conditions are in pond location and design.

The principles described in this book cover all aspects of pond design, planning, and management, all of which are dependent upon a solid understanding of soil/ site conditions. These conditions predict the final chemical and biological characteristics of the pond and the degree of management required. This book provides essential guidelines to landowners who wish to design and construct a pond; it will also give present pond owners management or design techniques to solve existing pond problems. It should also be helpful to landowners who want to enhance existing ponds for fish habitat, wildlife habitat, or landscape appeal.

This photo taken in 2010 illustrates how our pond—showing definite signs of transition—is attempting to revert to its original swamp condition.

Chapter One
Reasons for Constructing a Pond

Landscape Appeal

Henry David Thoreau, in *Walden*, describes a lake (or pond) thus: "…the landscape's most beautiful and expressive feature. It is earth's eye: looking into which the beholder measures the depth of his own nature. The fluviatile trees next the shore are the slender eyelashes which fringe it, and the wooded hills and cliffs around are its overhanging brows."

Throughout *Walden*, Thoreau refers to the advantages of a pond as a psychological medium, adding an extra dimension to one's life: "It is well to have some water in your neighborhood, to give buoyancy to, and float the earth." I suspect the "buoyancy" Thoreau refers to also applies to the enhancement of human spirit.

Selecting an aesthetically pleasing pond site visible from your home will improve your overall landscape. The chosen location should also be compatible with its surrounding landscape. A pond perched on a high piece of ground in the open never appears natural; it is also impossible to sustain without a liner or other artificial means. A pond serving as a transitional feature between wet meadow and wetland forest edge looks more as if natural forces created it. A forest or even a hedgerow behind the pond provides a link to another natural feature, improving its natural setting. The treatment of materials excavated from a dug-out or embankment pond is also of utmost importance. Nothing looks more unfinished and unnatural than mounded perimeters never graded out. Nature rarely, if ever, creates mini drumlins scattered every which way around a body of water. Ultimately, such an area becomes unmanageable, and usually ends up weed-infested, because the perimeter cannot be cut effectively. Many ponds I have visited seem to end up unfinished looking because the owner lacked either aesthetic sense or an appreciation of natural landforms. The selection of a site that allows exca-

A pond can be the most beautiful and expressive feature of your overall landscape, great crystals on the surface of the earth reflecting the clouds and trees that surround it.

A fringe of emergent aquatic plants attracts wildlife to this beautiful pond on the Pefferlaw Brook, Ontario.

vated soils to be spread out is an expense saved, since trucking the material elsewhere is an added cost.

Once constructed and graded out, any pond benefits from planting—preferably with flora indigenous to the area—which draws attention to the water as a landscape feature or focal point on the property. A pond also serves as a natural greenhouse where a variety of wetland plants can be introduced, expanding the diversity of plant life on your land. You can spend relaxing hours sitting by your pond, reading or writing, immersed in a serene, private ecosystem. Perhaps a pond on your landscape can serve as a memorial garden, created to contemplate those who have passed away. Carefully planted, with the addition of natural perch stones or a bench, a pond can offer a place to retreat to when you are in need of privacy and reflection. A fountain operating on a pump system can add the sound of falling water, which induces relaxation. Such is our own pond; its small monument, tiger lilies, and sundial form a memorial garden quite reserved from the rest of the managed areas of our landscape and offer a peaceful escape from reality, as well as a tribute to my parents.

Of all the reasons for constructing a pond, its aesthetic benefit is rarely talked about. I believe this quality ranks as the most immediate and also the most lasting.

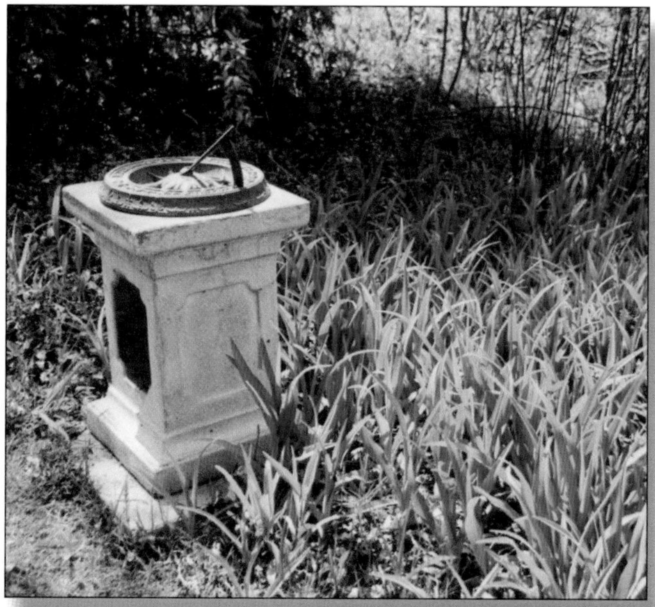

Monument and memorial plaque on the shore of our pond, complete with sundial and a thick bed of tiger lilies.

A large buck visits the edge of a wildlife pond. [Photo by Ivan Foster, Pefferlaw, Ontario]

Waterfowl and Wildlife Habitat

Ponds are major attractors of wildlife. Migrating waterfowl use them as nesting sites in annual flights south, and again on the way back north. You will find that many of the species that nest in your pond return year after year. Upland game species also find ponds essential as watering places and will visit your pond on a regular basis early in the morning or in the evening, often creating pathways which emerge from a nearby forest or farm woodlot. Pond shorelines and connecting buffer areas can be planted to create a more diverse habitat around the water and provide some cover for interested animals.

Many landowners and golf course managers fail

Canoeing on a large pond or small lake can provide many hours of exploration and relaxation.

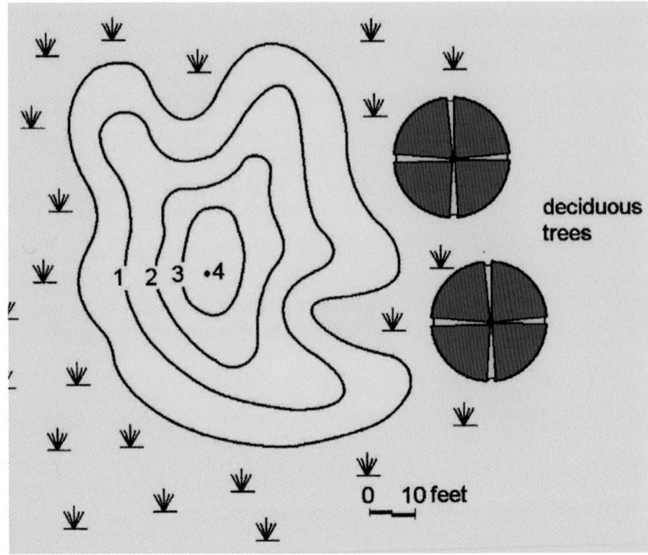

Figure 1.1 Ponds with an irregular shoreline and shallow depth create conditions attractive to wildlife. Planting native grasses and a few deciduous trees provides more habitat.

to manage their ponds for wildlife, even though the natural habitat around these ponds is often already initiated and will provide a good starting point for enhancement. The key to wildlife diversity is creating a wide variety of habitat, including groundcover, intermediate, and canopy levels around your pond.

Any new pond owner should first consider his/ her primary goals—nature appreciation, fishing, swimming, etc.—some of which might conflict with maintaining a wildlife pond. Ponds designed for waterfowl, for instance, are usually no more than 3-4 ft. (1-1.2 m) deep with low, sloping banks and mucky bottoms, making them unsatisfactory for wading or swimming use. These ponds provide the landowner with wildlife-viewing and photographic opportunities. Wildlife nesting structures for species such as mallard ducks, wood ducks, purple martins, bluebirds, etc., can be added to your pond, aiding in insect removal, and, to some extent, aquatic weed control.

The shallow near-shore area around wildlife ponds, called the *littoral* zone, contains diverse habitats preferred by many species. These near-shore zones are easily degraded by human activities such as grass-cutting, dumping of fill, or removal of emergent vegetation such as cattail. Depending on the level of nutrients in it, a wildlife pond will have moderate to dense aquatic weed growth, making it unsatisfactory for swimming if that is the primary objective of the pond owner. Wildlife ponds should also have a somewhat irregular shoreline to create shallow slopes and depths around the pond margin. All these features of a wildlife pond, coupled with its shallowness, make it a poor fish pond.

Recreational Value

Depending on water quality, depth, and access, your pond might offer swimming, boating, and fishing opportunities. Landscaping, whether natural or artificial, can turn the pond environment into a place for picnics, contemplation, and relaxation. A pond used for swimming might exclude the opportunity for supplying wildlife habitat, except in rare cases where a large pond provides both. Swimmers prefer deeper, cleaner water with a solid bottom of sand or fine gravel. Ponds that meet these criteria are usually rare—typically, natural circumstances produce a soft, muddy, benthal zone of the type found in wildlife ponds. If your pond is to be used primarily for swimming, it should have a gently sloping shore in at least one area of its perimeter, with a sand or fine-gravel bottom. A pond bottom of clay or muck usually discourages swimmers, who are uncomfortable standing in "ooze." Likewise, swimmers like to see where they are swimming, and murky, silt-laden water prevents identification of what is underfoot and obstacles underneath or ahead. Excess turbidity in water is another reason for concern.

If your pond is unsuitable for swimming, its natural qualities can still provide a good recreation outlet for canoeing, kayaking, bird-watching, or fishing. We will address fishing ponds, which generally require an area of 0.5-1 ac. (0.2-0.4 ha), in a separate section. Ponds of over 5 ac. (2.02 ha), although magnificent, should be carefully considered before undertaking, as they require costly construction and maintenance procedures.

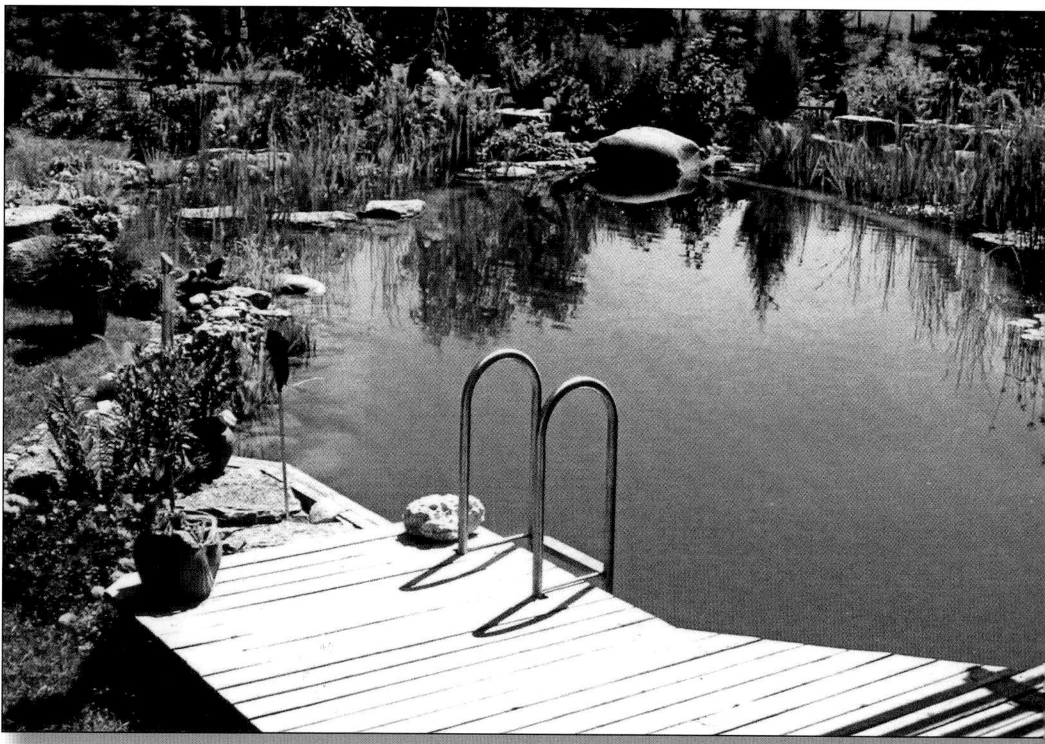

An example of a natural swimming pond where aquatic plants maintain good water quality. [Courtesy of Biotop Natural Swimming Pools]

Natural Ponds Designed for Swimming

Who wouldn't want to swim in a natural pond free from chlorine additives, cement edges, scupper drains, and pool covers? Natural swimming ponds are increasingly popular in Europe and are now

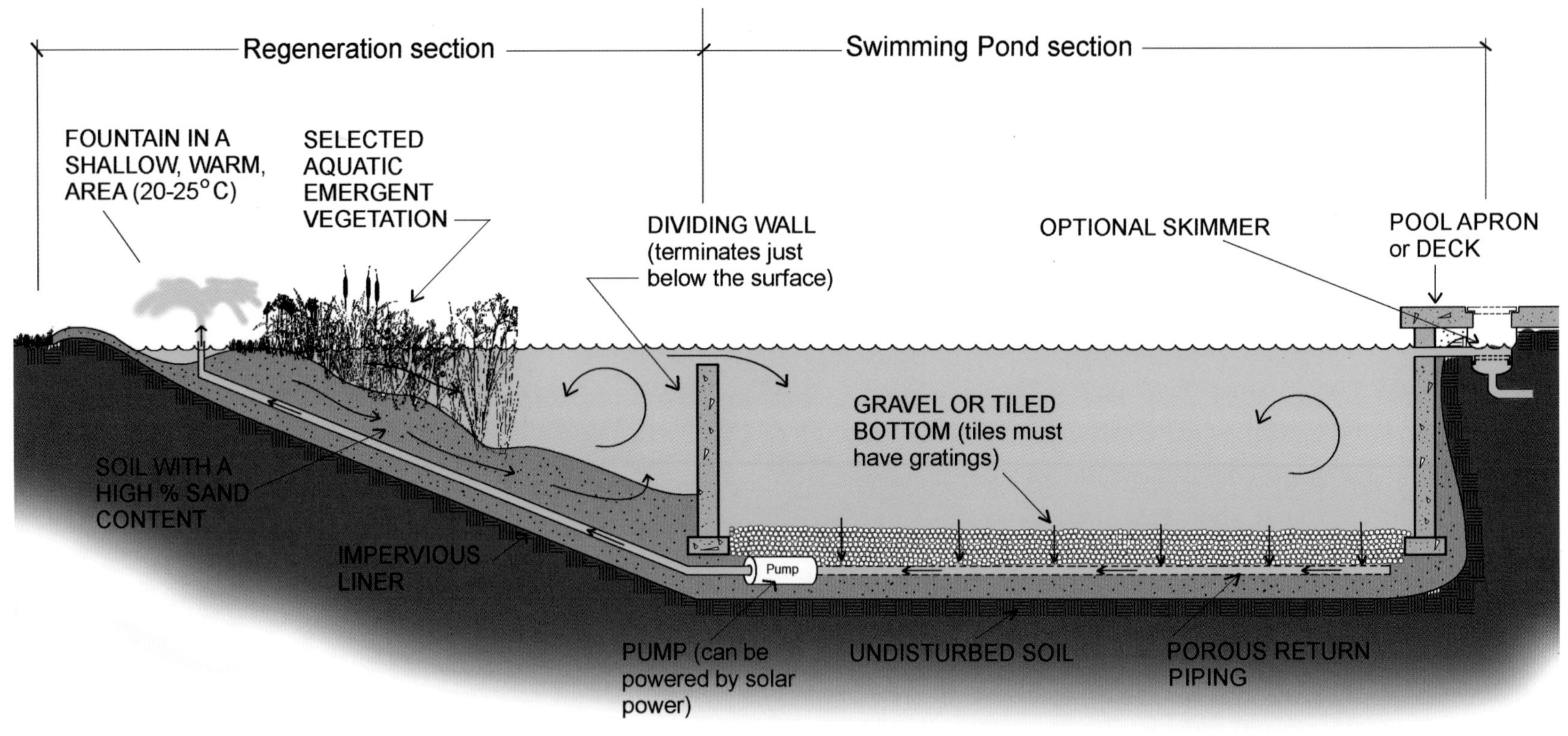

Figure 1.2 Cross-section of a natural swimming pond [Courtesy of GardenVisit.com, The Garden Landscape Guide, *"Construction of Natural Swimming Pools"]*

being installed in North America. Although they look natural, these ponds are, in fact, carefully constructed. The key to maintaining their clean water is continuous natural filtering by marginal plants in a gravel bed, aided by pumps and aeration devices. These specialized ponds are constructed with a wall that separates the deeper swimming area from a shallow vegetative area. This wall rises from the bottom of the pond to within one or two inches below the water surface. A circulating pump passes water between the two areas continuously. After the water has passed from the swimming pond to the planted pond, a skimmer removes debris. At this point, the roots of the aquatic vegetation absorb nutrients that would otherwise create undesirable algae growth. The pumping system is engineered to draw water through the plant roots down into the gravel bed and out into the swimming-pool portion. This circulation system must be kept running at all times, a parallel to the requirement for pumping water continuously through a filter in conventional pools.

A popular misconception is that natural swimming

ponds can be created from existing dug-out ponds. Swimming ponds must be graded properly and lined with expensive synthetic liners. Polyvinyl chloride (PVC) liners seem to be the most desirable, but require seam-welding expertise to install. The two halves of the system—swimming pond and aquatic-plant filter bed—should be of the same surface area in order to function efficiently. Once installed, the liner is overlaid with 4-5 in. (10-12.7 cm) of fine gravel, and the gravel bed in the vegetated pond is mixed with a suitable growing medium. The vegetated pond also carries an aeration system and piping which sucks the water through the plant roots via the circulating pump. Once-a-year cleaning is sufficient for these ponds, which require no chemical treatment. Fish and waterfowl are unfortunately prohibited in these ponds as they add pollution to the system. These ponds offer an experience similar to swimming in a lake.

Livestock Watering

Clean water is as important as forage to livestock, and a good pond is an asset in pastures or ranges. Providing ample watering places in pastures encourages more uniform grazing, as animals move between various pond sites. This prevents overgrazing on any one particular area and reduces the associated soil erosion, trampling, and contamination. A pond on any one site must meet the requirements of livestock using the surrounding grazing area. Having more than one pond over an extensive pastureland helps

LIVESTOCK	GALLONS PER ANIMAL PER DAY
Beef cattle and horses	12 to 15
Dairy cows	15
Dairy cows + barn water	35
Hogs	4
Sheep	2

the farmer carry out pasture improvements on sites reserved for rehabilitation. The table above illustrates the average daily consumption of water by various livestock and will serve as a guide for estimating water-quantity requirements.

To maintain good water quality, the owner must keep animals from wandering into the pond or from trampling its banks into a muddy, polluted morass. Using a wind-driven pump to fill troughs, with the pond fenced off completely, provides the best approach. Drainage from the stock-watering area should be directed away from the actual pond, and the pond shoreline should be planted to stabilize the soils and provide a good buffer/filter for any run-off that might enter it.

Domestic

In my own situation, water from my wildlife pond has been pumped effectively for the irrigation of my gardens and lawns and for other domestic uses. Pond water is also an indispensable aid in cleaning my lawn-tractor deck, which becomes clogged with grass clippings from trimming the meadows. Using precious well water would have been out of the question. Added nutrients from the pond provide any fertilization the landscape needs without the addition of commercial product—I have never needed to fertilize my lawns.

When the long roadway into my pond site was under construction, I buried both outdoor electric wire and hose lines (separately) underneath the road fill in a location suitable for hooking up to the future house site. A pump house constructed on the pond deck was built just large enough to accommodate the pump and aerator. A half-horsepower electric centrifugal pump was installed with no tank, the idea being to supply water directly from the pump pressure when needed. The pump supplied only enough pressure to lift the pond water about 10 ft. (3.05 m) over a 200 ft. (61 m) distance. I regretted later that I had not installed a heavier-duty outdoor wire over the distance, one which would have allowed a higher horsepower pump with more pressure.

The water pump and aerator in our small pump house by the pond. The timer on the left controls the aerator beneath it, and the water pump lies next to it.

I suggest a No. 10-gauge buried wire as a minimum, since you never know just what your future needs will be. My water intake holds a screened foot valve placed on the end of the 2 in. (5 cm) intake line, about 2 ft. (0.61 m) underwater. The foot valve prevents any water from seeping back into the pond, maintaining a constant "head" of water in the lines above the pump. This assures easy start-up with no requirement for pump priming. An instant flow of water is always available with the flick of a switch. Do remember that all switches and junction boxes on the line should be ground-fault protected.

My system is engineered to be switched over to a fountain in the pond center by means of a "Siamese valve" on the hose line. This provides many hours of enjoyment as we sit by the pond, and also delivers a small measure of aeration and circulation. In addition to providing irrigation the landscape needs, return flow from our lawns leaches back down through the naturalized pond perimeter, cleaning the water as it does so. Thus, we've established a miniature water cycle, one which aids both pond and landscape.

Commercial

Water-quantity requirements for commercial irrigation are greater than those of any of the uses discussed so far. The amount of water available throughout the growing season limits the area that can be irrigated from any pond. A pond's capacity must be pre-calculated during the design stage in order to avoid excessive water loss due to excessive or too extensive an application. As an example, a 3 in. (7.62 cm) depth of water applied over an acre will require approximately a pond with a volume of 81,000 gallons (308,000 L). Because of these large water requirements, irrigation from ponds is usually only realistic for high-value crops on small acreages (usually less than 50 ac. or 20.23 ha). The calculated storage capacity of a pond used for irrigation depends upon several factors which are inter-related:

- Water requirements for the crop to be irrigated
- Effective precipitation expected during the growing season
- Efficiency of irrigation method
- Losses due to evaporation, transpiration, and seepage
- Predicted flow rate into the pond

Top: A local river, the Maskinonge, in spring condition before its draw-down from water-taking (for irrigation) and from poor land-use management practices.

Bottom: The same section of river suffering from drought, aggravated by water-taking for specialty crop irrigation. Only one storage pond was present along this section of river, and thus, little storage capacity was available for drought conditions. Fish and waterfowl suffer immensely when this happens. [Courtesy of Roland Peacock]

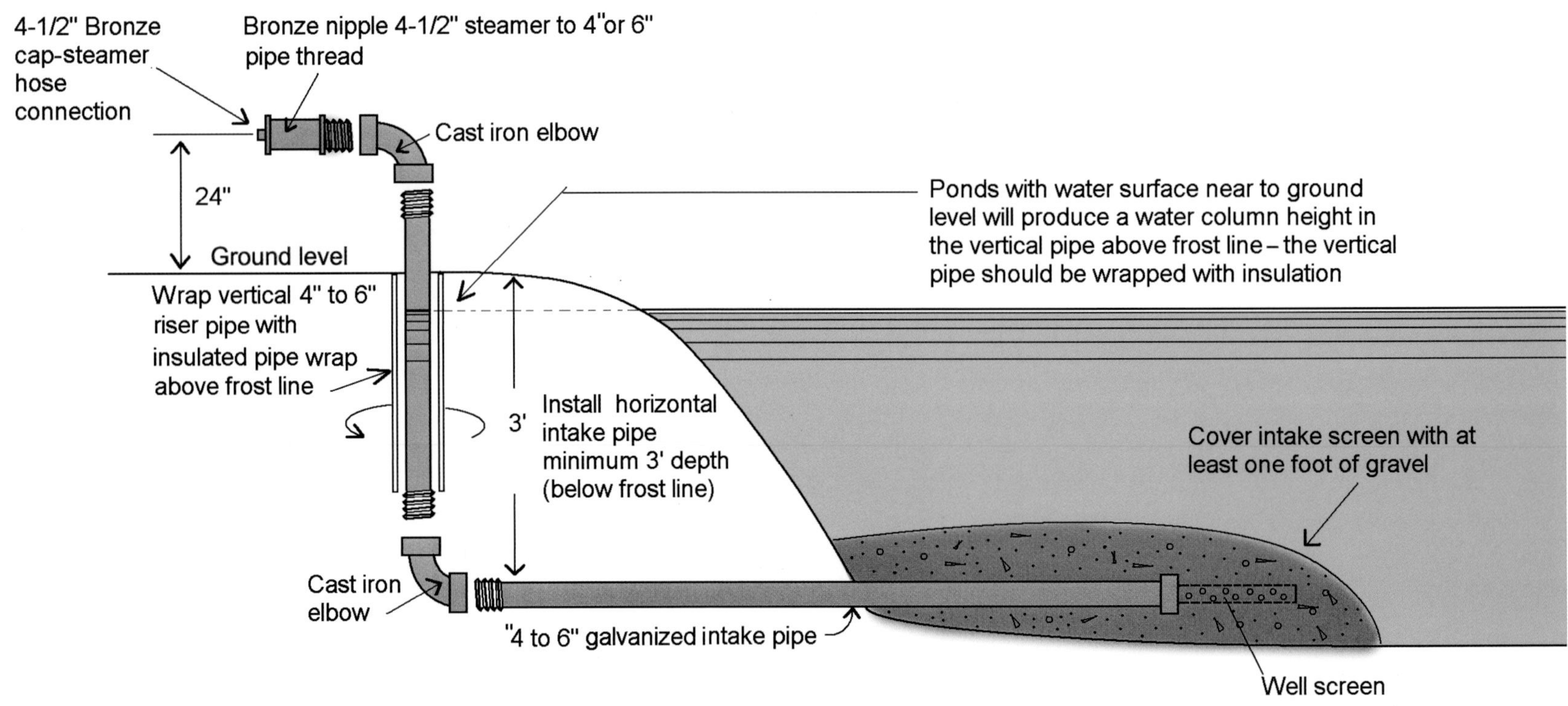

Figure 1.3 Diagram of a dry hydrant for fire-pond use. The inlet should be back-flushed periodically by reversing the flow from suction to mild pressure by pumping water directly out of the pond and back through the steamer-hose connection. [Adapted from Soil Conservation Service, US Department of Agriculture]

The importance of properly estimating water requirements can be illustrated by growers who take water continuously from a nearby stream or river. In some locales, growers irrigating large crop acreages next to low-flow rivers have dried up sources completely, particularly when, disregarding the effect of a severe drought, they have constantly pumped acre-feet of water during daylight hours when evaporation rate is highest. The source river bed becomes dry and cracked and loses all aquatic life. When these farmers construct large dug-out ponds adjacent to their croplands, water is collected from spring run-off and flooding. Stored separately and monitored, with occasional input from the river, these ponds signal a low-water warning before the river is pumped empty. Any government authority controlling water-taking would have an indication of future disaster through the draw-down of these ponds, and could move to avert major losses through direct pumping from the river.

Fire Protection

In some remote rural areas, a good water supply is needed for fire protection. If your pond is not too distant from your home and other out-buildings, a gasoline pump with a flexible fabric hose will suffice in warmer seasons. Make sure it is long (with enough sections) to reach all sides of your buildings. In winter, a dry hydrant is required since not only the surface of the pond, but also any permanent intake pipes left in the pond will be frozen. Suction capability of the pump must be high because of the height of the vertical standpipe extending below the frost line. Attempting to prime such an arrangement during the course of a fire is out of the question. Make sure you match the pump's suction capability with lift required. In the case of an excessive vertical standpipe height due to a deep shoreline, a foot valve can be installed in the horizontal section close to the inlet screen. This will retain water in the system providing there are no air leaks from pump to screen. Although water-storage requirements for fire protection alone are not great, the consumption rate per unit time is high.

Make sure you test your ability to unroll and lay out hose sections over the distance required if you plan on fighting a fire yourself. In my own situation, protection of my pine plantation was my prime concern, and the distance from pond to forest was excessive. Eight 50 ft. hose sections (121.92 m) were needed, and coupling them together, starting the pump, and running back to the nozzle required 20 minutes to accomplish. By that time, a fire in the pines would be raging through the understory of 3,000 trees and, with any wind at all, likely crowning. Self-extinguishing such a fire would be impossible.

A typical fire hose composed of polyester yarn with rubber lining 4 in. (10.16 cm) in diameter connects in 50 ft. (15.24 m) sections which can be managed one at a time. The weight limitation (62 lbs. per 50-ft roll/28.12 kg per section) negates carrying more than one coil of hose at a time, connecting it, and running back to get another. The operation really requires two people to be efficient.

A typical centrifugal fire pump operating at 83 psi, utilizing a 3 in. (76.2 mm) diameter hose, will deliver a stream of water at 265 gpm with a nozzle pressure of 50 psi. Sustained pumping for five hours will consume a foot of water per quarter acre of pond (i.e., a quarter-acre foot of water). On the other hand, if you are within reach of a municipal or town fire-fighting service, make sure to provide enough water-storage capacity for four streams of water. In this case, an acre-foot of water will be sufficient for most fire-fighting needs. Consult with your local agricultural official, your fire department, and a fire-pump dealer to help you in the design and capacity requirements of your pond for both irrigation and fire protection.

Chapter Two

Planning the Pond

Site Selection and Suitability

A successful pond is not simply a hole dug out in a wet area and filled with water. The resulting body, if permanent, will become a complex biological and zoological system that ultimately forms part of the surrounding watershed. Ponds are normally supplied with water from surface streams, sub-surface springs, or general run-off sources, in that order of priority, for continuity of supply. Drainage areas feeding the proposed pond can possess a highly variable degree of run-off. Soil types and land-management practices will affect run-off and influence water-storage potential. Usually, surface run-off— containing silt and excessive nutrients—is the poorest source of water for constructed ponds because water quality is often unreliable. When considering a dug pond, or an *offline pond*, your chosen site should be above a floodplain with some nearby indication of the existing water table (wet ground, sloughs, etc.). When considering a by-pass-type pond, or an *online pond*, seek good indication of a suitable stream flow. Nearby forest cover along with additional trees and shrubs planted adjacent to the pond site will reduce silt, helping to filter run-off. Surface water flowing through agricultural lands, golf courses, and other heavily fertilized areas will carry dissolved fertilizer into any proposed pond.

Be careful not to dig a pond in a wetland because you will be destroying a threatened part of our natural heritage. Any wetland marsh is subject to periodic flooding, particularly when located near a river or lake where water levels may be highly variable. The marsh may dry out completely in late summer. A swamp or wooded marsh is also unsuitable for a dug pond as excessive leaf fall adds to bottom sediments. Eventually, a pond in such a location will progress toward eutrofication and return to a swamp environment. Peat bogs and fens also should be avoided as these landscapes act as sponges, soaking up rainwater and

A successful pond is a complex biological and zoological system that ultimately forms part of the surrounding watershed.

snowmelt to release water slowly in drier seasons. These natural mechanisms filter water very efficiently, reducing downstream silting, and should never be converted to ponds. Constructed ponds in certain watersheds on small streams can damage stream ecology by raising water temperatures downstream, and affecting the sustainability of fish populations.

Good site conditions coupled with proper design and construction provide a successful, manageable pond. If fish are a consideration, the pond should be at least 8 ft. (2.5 m) deep with banks at a three-to-one slope. It is also advisable to create a pond one acre (0.4 ha) or larger in size for suitable habitat, oxygen content, and spawning opportunities. Locations to avoid include those where run-off from barns or sewage systems could enter or influence the pond through groundwater. Potential indicators for a good offline pond site include down-slope wet corners of fields and areas supporting tell-tale cattail growth, as long as these are not extensive enough to indicate an existing marsh ecosystem. To avoid major aquatic weed infestation, your pond should have a minimum depth of 3 ft. (1 m) to discourage the growth of most submergent and emergent weeds. If you have chosen to build a by-pass pond, water flowing into the pond should be free of pollution and sediment. Remember that in a grove of trees or abutting a forest wall, autumn leaf litter will gradually accumulate on your pond's surface, and trapped within the pond, will sink to the bottom contributing to organic muck on the bottom. This was the No. 1 culprit in building up the "ooze" layer in my pond. Make sure you leave adequate space around your pond perimeter for landscaping and wildlife planting. Depending on your pond's function, site furnishings (such as a shed to house a water supply system, an aerator, or tool storage) should be considered at the site-selection stage, because more space for these may ultimately be required.

Pumps and aerators most likely require access to electrical hook-ups, and a light fixture comes in handy inside a tool-storage shed. Distance to electrical mains should be considered carefully for potential overload. Select appropriate gauge wire for the run. More elaborate landscape ponds require more infrastructure (gazebos, picnic shelters, or perhaps a sauna facility) as outdoor extensions to the rural home. All of these require suitable space.

Access

Access to the pond for future maintenance, enlarging, etc., must be planned at the earliest stage of design. Failure to do so, and failure to design a route for heavy-equipment access to the banks of your pond will likely result in future restrictions on maintenance. Drag-line dredges are heavy machines and can carry up to 60 ft. (18.3 m) booms (some units have telescoping booms). The majority of older units move on steel tracks, which will chew up an asphalt road or sink deeply into boggy marshland. Many contractors have steel mats, which they lay down in wet or soggy ground for their machines, or they supply used auto tires for the machine to run over on normal residential, asphalted roads. It is much better to provide for and maintain a crude road on stable ground for this purpose. Usually, pond owners landscape the area accessing the pond with a nice layer of managed turf, but a drag line will chew this up beyond imagination, destroying years of growth, and possibly, plantings. Plan for access carefully. It is essential. Keep right-of-way relatively clear of vegetation, as once overgrown, it requires much effort to clear, and may even contravene municipal tree by-laws which would prohibit such activity or require a variance.

Topographic and Soil-Type Requirements

A suitable pond location should have level topography which will allow for economical construction. It should have soils with sufficient clay mixture to contain water. For economic reasons, the site should allow for the largest volume of water with the least amount of excavation or landfill (in the case of a dammed pond). A level site will reduce the cost and effort of soil removal and disposal of excavated materials.

A pond's bottom and dam structure must be composed of a soil mix which will minimize seepage. Clay soils are always the best for lining a pond, minimizing leakage. Most sites with gravel or sand, being naturally porous, will lose water through seepage. On the other hand, swampy soils become difficult to drain and require costly maintenance, often disrupting the original swampland in the process. Limestone and shale bedrock sites, exhibiting fractures and stratification, will leak naturally. If a dam or simple impoundment is required, its maximum height should be no more than 20–25ft. (6–7.6 m). Any earth structure higher than this will be expensive to build and will exhibit thermal stratification due to its depth, unless there is a good turnover with fresh water flowing in and out. Installation of a bottom-draw structure, which aids in the reduction of thermal stratification, will also be expensive. Dams or impoundments must be high enough, however, to accumulate a depth of 6 ft. (1.8 m) of water and to maintain that level on a constant basis.

Ponds are frequently located in valleys or depression sites which have the capability to store water during heavy rainfall or spring run-off, but these sites often cannot sustain the accumulation, and eventually dry up during hot weather months, often shrinking to boggy, smelly areas with low water levels, clogged with weeds.

Water-Supply Requirements

A water supply sufficient to fill your pond rapidly is important to maintain a relatively constant annual water level. Water supply that overflows, flushing nutrients out of the pond, is not as desirable as it might seem, because fish tend to escape. Earlier, impounded

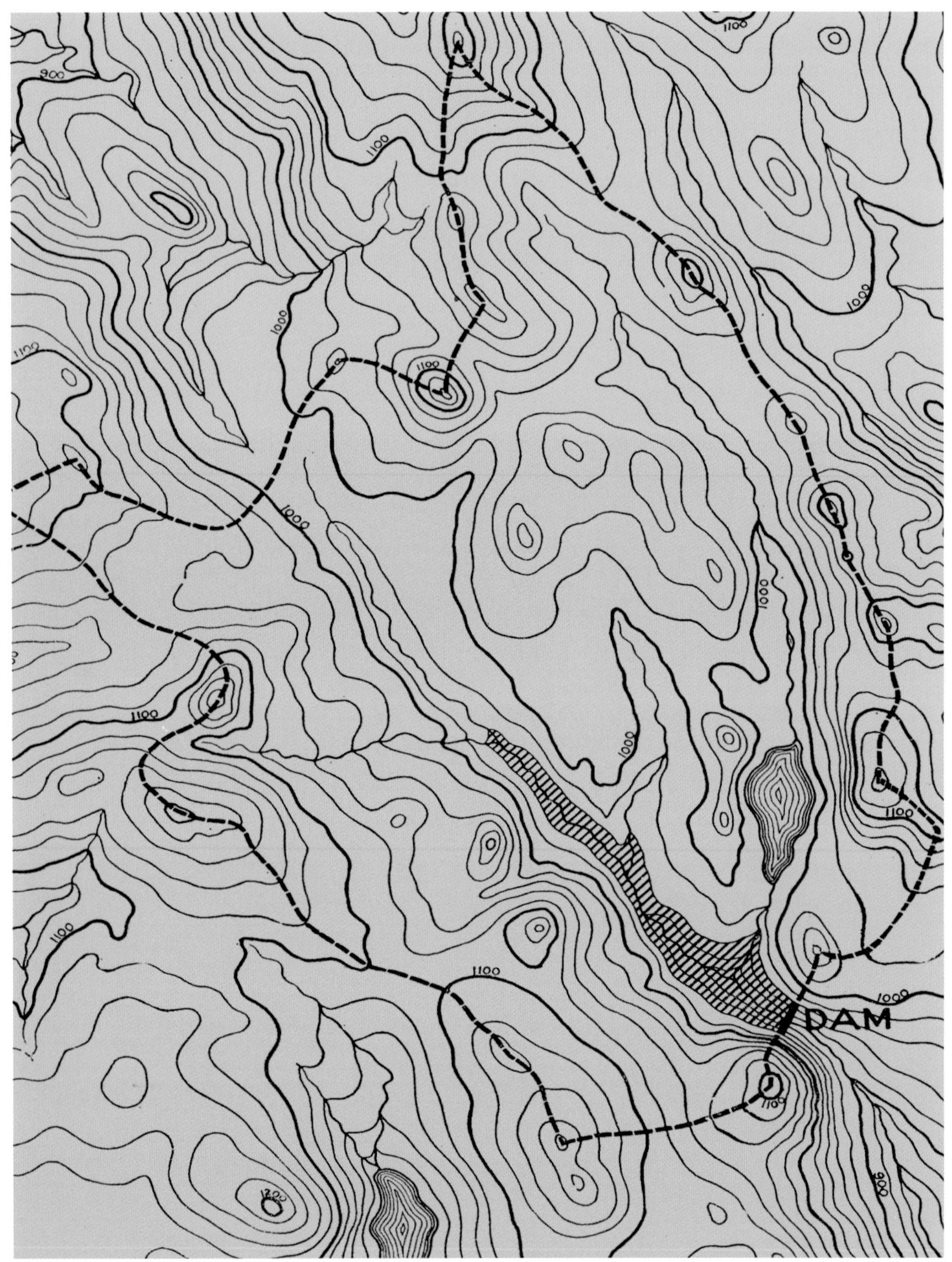

Figure 2.1 Plan showing the limits of a watershed (heavy dashed line) and the optimum location for a dam [Courtesy of Breed and Hosmer; Elementary Surveying*]*

small streams were often satisfactory sources, but today, due to flooding, silt load, and the blocking of fish migration, they are generally no longer permitted by most stream regulatory agencies. In addition, the tendency of impounded small streams to increase temperatures downstream offsets their advantages.

Construction of a by-pass pond or online pond adjacent to the stream with inlets and outlets (screened or closed as necessary) leading to the stream body is a wiser solution which provides some measure of control over silting and flooding while maintaining fish migration in the stream proper. This alternative still causes an undesirable warm-water increase to the stream or creek body, but can be controlled by closing the outlet and inlet pipes and re-opening the inlet pipe only when necessary to maintain levels. The pond then becomes essentially a dug-out pond within the flood plain.

Surface run-off resulting from rainwater flow or seepage is the most common water source for ponds, and larger catchment areas are required for areas with less rainfall intensity or with rapid soil infiltration. Characteristics determining the adequacy of any drainage area vary according to topography, soil infiltration, vegetative cover, and existing surface storage. Storm characteristics must also be considered, relative to the amount, intensity, and duration of rainfall, which affects water yield. Tables are available for all of these parameters and adjustments must be made for local conditions (rainfall intensity and run-off

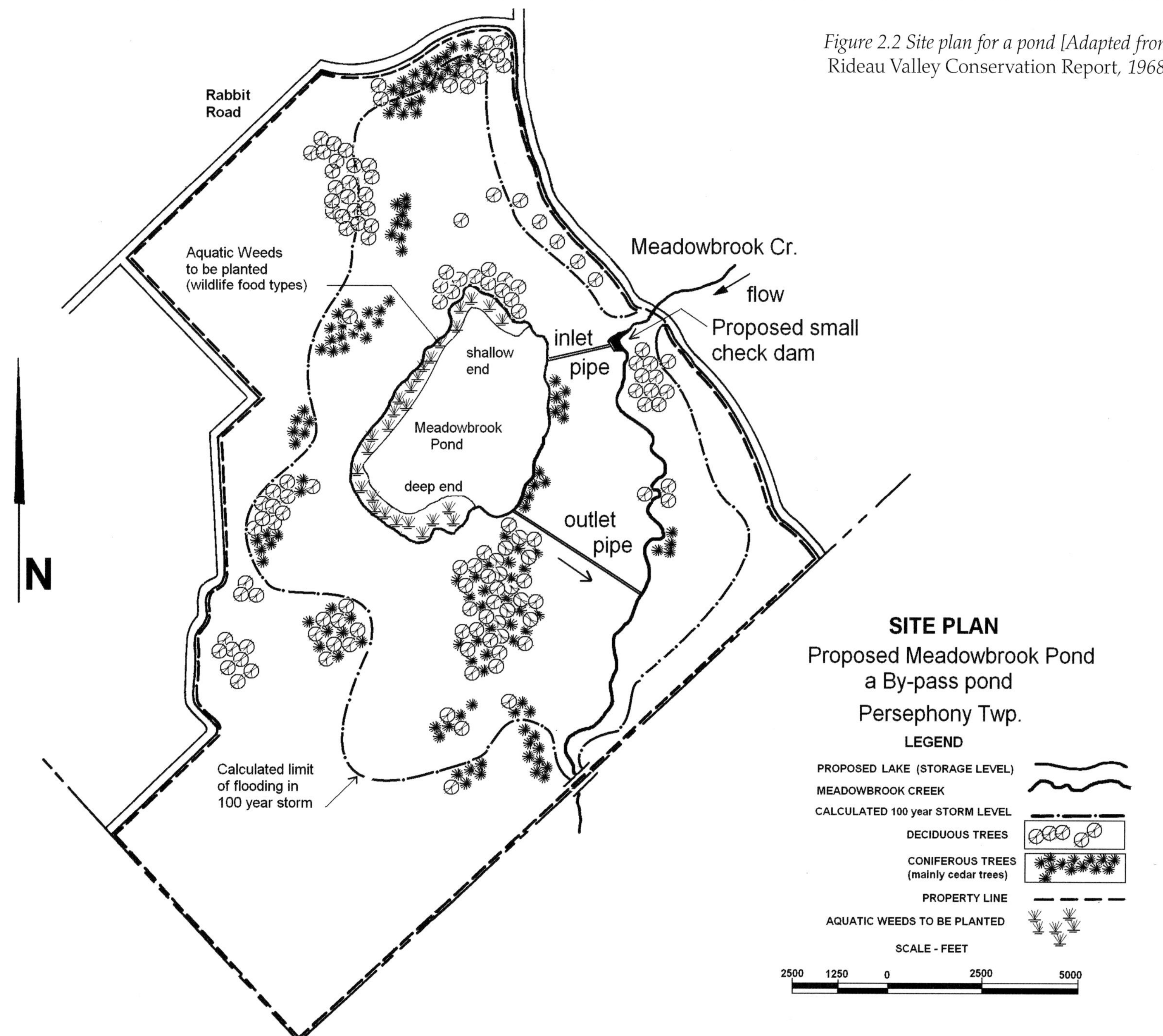

Figure 2.2 Site plan for a pond [Adapted from Rideau Valley Conservation Report, *1968]*

Pond Storage Capacity
Approximate size & capacity based on rectangular excavated ponds

Top Dimensions (meters)	Depth (meters)	Capacity (cubic meters)
30 x 18	3 3.5	750 760
36 x 18	3 3.5	969 1019
45 x 18	3 3.5	1292 1383
36 x 24	3 4	1420 1524
42 x 24	3 4	1792 1952
49 x 24	3 4	2148 2370
42 x 30	3 4	2357 2607
55 x 30	3 3.5 5	3203 3526 3895
60 x 30	3 3.5 5	3740 4127 4527
45 x 45	3 3.5 5	4113 4468 4960
55 x 45	3 3.5 5	5187 5792 6565
60 x 45	3 3.5 5	5915 6629 7521
60 x 60	3 3.5 5	8235 9236 10692

To convert meters to feet multiply by 3.281
To convert cu. meters. to cubic yards multiply by 1.308
To convert cubic meters to Imperial gallons multiply by 219.79
To convert cubic meters to litres multiply by 1000

Figure 2.3 Pond storage capacity table [translated to metric measure from Farm Ponds in Ontario, *Ministry of Agriculture and Food, Ontario].*

curves). (See Ponds for Water Supply and Recreation Agricultural Handbook #397, The Soil Conservation Service, U.S. Department of Agriculture.)

Sandy soil types in the drainage area will drastically reduce the effective pond supply. Springs, wells, and groundwater are the best sources if a landowner is lucky enough to have these. Aquatic life is usually best sustained in groundwater, which often contains just enough of the required nutrients. Some well waters contain excessive amounts of carbon dioxide or nitrogen and must be oxygenated through aeration before using. Many groundwater sources contain an overabundance of harmful minerals dangerous to fish and aquatic animals. It pays to have your water sources analyzed before pond construction to promote a healthy aquatic environment.

Estimating Storage Capacity

In order to guarantee that the proposed pond will have sufficient capacity for storage events (heavy rainfall, storms), seek a professional's calculation. Your local conservation authority may offer this service, or you may require the services of an engineer, landscape architect, or hydrogeologist. The calculation should determine peak discharge (Q) in cubic feet per second (or cubic metres per second) for the watershed containing the pond site. Basically, an air photo and topographic map are combined to define the overall watershed limit, the contours establishing the average slope and the overland flow distance that water takes to travel from the height of land to the proposed pond site. A final check of field conditions should be undertaken to discover any new uncharted avenues for loss of run-off, and also to determine the vegetation type, along with management practices in the watershed. These parameters are used to determine the run-off coefficient (i). Once the watershed boundary is ascertained, the area (A) of the watershed can be calculated.

The rainfall-intensity parameter (C) in this calculation is the most difficult to obtain, being found from intensity/duration/frequency curves produced for your geographical region. The storm frequency is usually taken as a hundred-year "design" storm event by most watershed authorities (eg. "the largest storm that will occur in one hundred years.") The Rational Equation, or Manning's formula, can be used to determine peak discharge (Q) over a specific duration storm: $Q = CiA$.

Several more complex formulas refine the run-off coefficient (i) and the rainfall intensity factor (C). The calculations are best researched by a professional to suit your site conditions precluding the design of dam structures or emergency spillways for larger pond and lake designs.

Important Physical and Chemical Properties of Pond Water

The physical and chemical properties of water are essential factors to consider in pond management. Some important properties include temperature, pH (specifically alkalinity), dissolved oxygen, turbidity, the concentration of phosphorus, and, to a lesser extent, nitrogen.

Temperature relates inversely to the amount of dissolved oxygen (DO) in water. Pond fish require about 5 ppm (parts per million) DO, and almost all other organisms (excluding anaerobic bacteria) require dissolved oxygen.

Any pond is affected largely by what goes on in the drainage basin that supplies it. Sediments from erosion in the drainage basin settle to the bottom of the pond, while organic matter enters in a dissolved form that supplies nutrients to aquatic plants. Dead aquatic plants, along with dead animals, end up as nutrients for further plant growth, while those not decomposed settle to the bottom, forming the organic mud or ooze. Very little of the mineral and organic substances that enter the pond leave it, even in out-flowing water. The linked food relationships between organisms form a food web which stabilizes the pond's biological and zoological community. Enrichment from leaves, fertilizers, or human and livestock wastes can destroy the pond's suitability for fish and increase the development of algae and other aquatic plants.

The amount of phosphorus usually resulting from these sources increases the total production of pond life, which does not always benefit fish production. Acidity-alkalinity property (or pH) enters into the equation here, insofar as alkalinity of the water

A woodland marsh, most valuable left alone as habitat for waterfowl and wildlife.

(usually the amount of calcium carbonate present) is a controlling factor. When the water is of low alkalinity, the presence of small amounts of phosphorus results in the production of algae that water fleas and other fish-food organisms eat. However, as more phosphorus is added to low-alkalinity water, a point is reached where the beneficial algae cease to increase. Continued addition produces blue-green algae, a class not palatable to algae-eaters. The blue-green variety flourishes but when phosphorus reaches critical levels, the algae dies, consuming an excessive amount of dissolved oxygen.

In more alkaline waters, greater phosphorus loading is well tolerated, producing algae classes that promote fish production. In general, the more alkaline a pond is, the greater its potential for producing fish. The optimum conditions also depend on temperature and the degree of buffering from dissolved minerals that protect the water against extreme acidity. Alkalinity also reduces the threat of poisoning of fish as a result of certain dissolved metals, and is ideal at a concentration of 150 to 250 ppm. Alkalinity of 40 ppm is a critical point below which fish production declines.

Nitrogen compounds found in rainwater as the product of electrical discharges, industrial smoke, etc., are utilized by nitrogen-fixing organisms such as bacteria and blue-green algae.

Turbidity, or the amount of suspended material in water, can be extensive enough to reduce photo-synthetic activity at a shallow depth, affecting the growth of algae. Streams and ponds, particularly on-stream types, and by-pass ponds can be clouded by sediment from flooding and bank erosion. While several fish species (trout, smallmouth bass) require clear water, others, like walleye, can tolerate turbid waters. Excess turbidity can reduce the ability of fish to feed and breathe. The source of sedimentation must be controlled, as fine materials in suspension, such as clay, are difficult to precipitate or remove. Silt-laden water covers and destroys fish eggs, suffocates bottom-dwelling animals, clogs fish gills, and reduces the ability of fish to detect and catch prey. Buffer strips of vegetation can help protect watercourses and ponds from silt-loading from surrounding land uses.

In many locations, some of these criteria cannot be met even with considerable management. A pond could have somewhat less than optimum conditions, and still produce a worthwhile fish habitat or a scenic enhancement to a property.

Chapter Three
Regulations, Permits, Approvals, and Liabilities

Initial Pond Construction, Alterations, Filling, and Dredging

In Ontario, the Ministry of Natural Resources (MNR) no longer issues work permits for all projects around water. In Canada, under the Federal Fisheries Act, it is the responsibility of the person constructing a pond to ensure that fish habitat is not altered, disrupted, or destroyed. Fact sheets are available to assist the owner or contractor with ideas about design and the use of various materials to reduce the impact on fish habitats and water quality.

The following procedures require permits:

- Construction of crib docks and boathouses in larger ponds and lakes, which require a work permit from the Ministry of Natural Resources (MNR). (Generally this applies to cribs exceeding 160 ft^2 or 15 m^2, including the area covered by ice "glancers" and boulders)
- Dredging or filling lakes or ponds
- Removal or displacement of rocks and boulders within lakes or ponds

Activities that do not require Ministry of Natural Resources permits include:

- Building docks—floating, or on posts, or cantilevered over the water surface
- Removal of old docks and boathouses
- Minor repairs to existing structures

Any minor permit does not relieve the owner/contractor from the requirements or permits needed from other federal, provincial, or municipal legislation (such as conservation authorities). All work done should not interfere with or disrupt adjoining properties.

Shoreline-related projects requiring an MNR work permit may also require permission from the Department of Fisheries and Oceans: the Fisheries and Oceans review is required before any MNR work permit will be issued.

Be aware when you dig, permits are required for most alterations to water bodies in general—destruction or alterations of habitats is an offence falling within the Lakes and Rivers Improvement Act (or similar acts in other countries).

Other potential approvals to keep in mind are:

- Conservation authorities, municipalities, the Canadian Coast Guard, the Ministry of the Environment, the Department of Fisheries and Oceans, the Trent-Severn Waterway Authority, and other similar authorities may require approvals. Permits for works within a water body include those for building dams, diversions, channelization, and ponds, all of which likely fall within the Lakes and Rivers Improvement Act.
- Municipalities may require a building permit to be issued for boathouses or large sheds/gazebos, etc., placed around the pond. If the construction might interfere with adjacent water uses (water supply, recreation, or support of aquatic life), the Ministry of the Environment must be consulted. Minor activities such as a small boathouses, docks, or shoreline stabilization projects may not require approval. It is best to check.
- In Ontario, Parks Canada and the Trent-Severn Waterway Authority also require written permission before commencement of any proposal to dredge, fill, or carry out any work that may alter the beds of rivers, lakes, or shorelines, or may affect water quality. This applies to all interconnecting waterways within the Trent-Severn Waterway.

Various Acts in Ontario may also limit the scope of work or necessitate approval:

- The Lakes and Rivers Improvement Act provides that holding back or diverting water must receive approval of the Ministry of Natural Resources.
- The Public Lands Act provides that no person shall deposit material on public land or water without approval.
- The Beach Protection Act provides that no sand, gravel, stone, or other substrate be removed from any bed, banks, shoreline, or waters of any lake, river, or stream without a license from the MNR.
- The Fisheries Act provides that no person shall carry out work that results in harmful alteration, disruption, or destruction of fish habitat without authorization.
- A permit is required from your local conservation authority for construction on and fill placed in a flood plain, or for the alteration of a watercourse.
- The Ministry of Transportation and Communications (MTO) in Ontario requires approval for works within 5 mi. (8 km) of a provincial highway.
- Several regional municipalities and local municipalities in Ontario require permits for thinning operations and removing trees. Tree by-laws generally apply to forested parcels above a specific acreage. (Minimum acreages are specified with stem diameters and numbers of trees per acre/hectare to determine exemption or application of the by-law on your property.)

Permit to Take Water

In Ontario, a permit for water-taking is required by

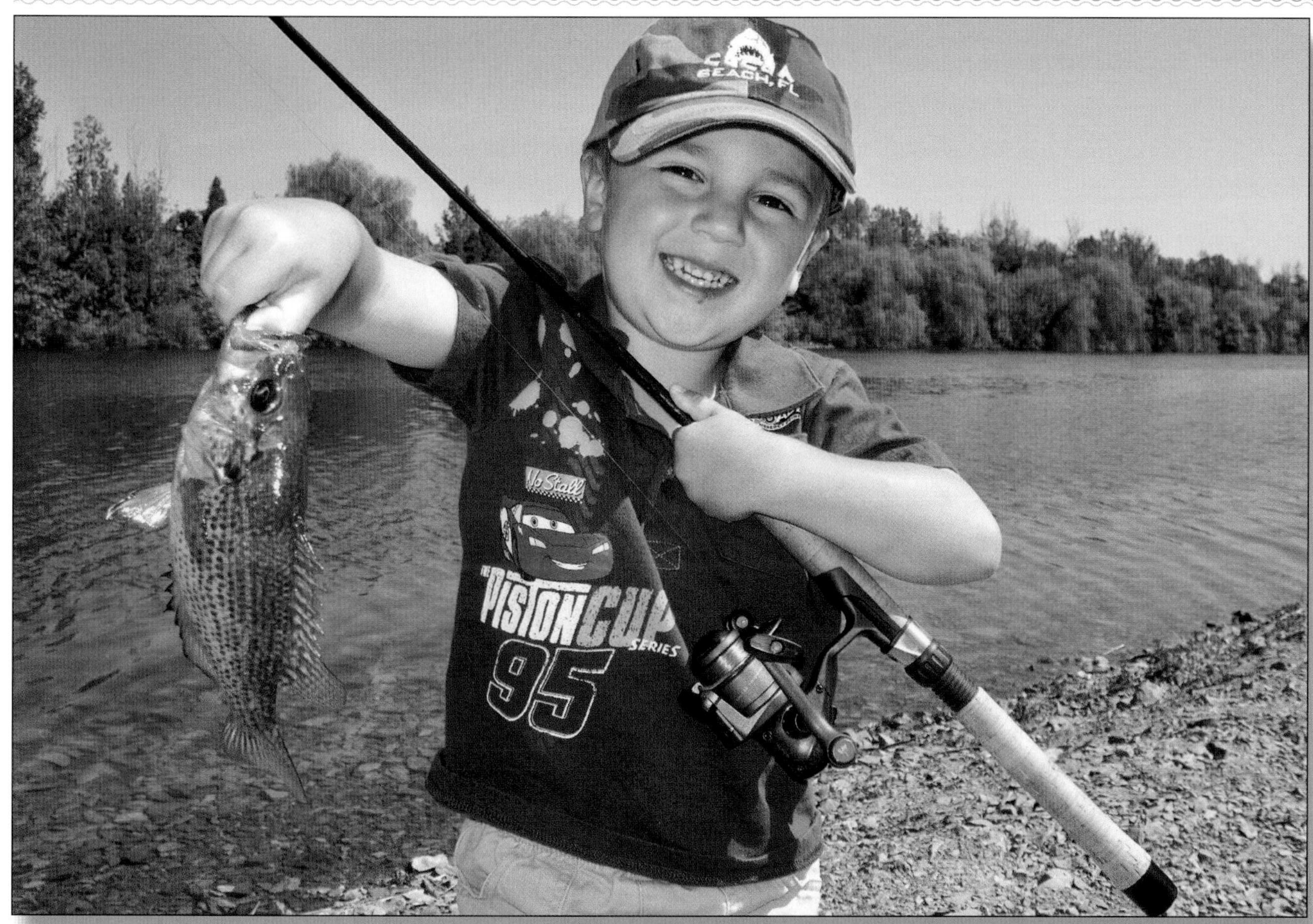

the Ministry of the Environment if you are taking water into storage (a dam, a pond, etc.) in-stream or off-stream, or for irrigation at a rate of more than 13,208.6 US gal. (50,000 L) per day.

Violations of some of these acts result in very costly fines (up to a million dollars in the case of the federal Fisheries Act), risk of imprisonment, and a requirement to return the site to its original state. In the United States, each state has its own laws and regulations governing ponds, lakes, and watercourses in general. Ohio, for instance, has several laws applying to impounding water:

- Aquaculture permits are issued by the Ohio Department of Natural Resources, Division of Wildlife, for persons producing aquatic organisms for sale as food.
- Dams are controlled under Ohio's Dam Safety Laws if they are over 10 ft. (3 m) in height and create a storage capacity of more than 50 acre-feet of water.

A boy holds up his first catch. [Photo by Ron Arnold]

- Various laws govern the management and taking of wildlife—since wildlife is attracted to a pond or lake, management is required to control nuisance species.
- Water-rights legislation in Ohio is complex, and decisions are based on civil case law.

For any individual American state, it is wise to contact your county's office of the U.S. Soil Conservation Service for help in choosing the site and designing your pond. Ducks Unlimited might also be able to give you very valuable assistance or even a subsidy for partial construction costs. Before undertaking any construction or management activity, contact your nearest office of the Department of Natural Resources for instructions on how to proceed within the law, and what permits or approvals you will need. This action may also result in tips, brochures, or workbooks from state officials on the best way to accomplish your design objectives.

Pond Safety and Liability

Site selection can also involve the aspect of liability, since the failure of a structure through excessive storm water overtopping the banks, or a burst dam, could result in flooding an adjacent parcel and properties downstream. Research any utility services on your property, both underground and overhead, which might preclude the installation of a pond or be affected by an excavation. It is imperative to build an emergency spillway on any pond, either in the form of a pipe system below the top of the bank, or as a constructed, reinforced dip in the pond bank. Spillway choice is directed by the inflow rate, size, and pond depth, but usually a reinforced dip in the pond bank is the most trustworthy avenue when erosion control materials are used to finish the spillway surface.

Several small-diameter pipes, no larger than the single pipe shown in the photo on the right can serve as emergency spillways for a small pond, but a reinforced dip in the dam where it meets the bank is more suitable for a larger impounded pond.

In most cases, the pond owner is liable for costs in injury suits, and it is wise to check with your home and property insurance company for details on coverage and costs. Pond owners should avoid the following:

- Interfering or influencing a neighbor's property adversely, or affecting the right to use it
- Diverting watercourses and drainage patterns
- Unreasonable use of water (water-taking)
- Creating excessive silting downstream or in-pond discharge during construction or future work, which might affect drinking water supplies, recreation, or even aesthetics
- Creating habitat for offensive species (i.e., muskrats, beaver, and raccoons, or mosquito-breeding sites) that could be traced to your management techniques should these species invade adjacent properties

Safety Issues

Every effort the pond-owner makes to secure reasonable life-saving techniques and safety precautions will pay big dividends should a legal problem arise. The following measures are suggested:

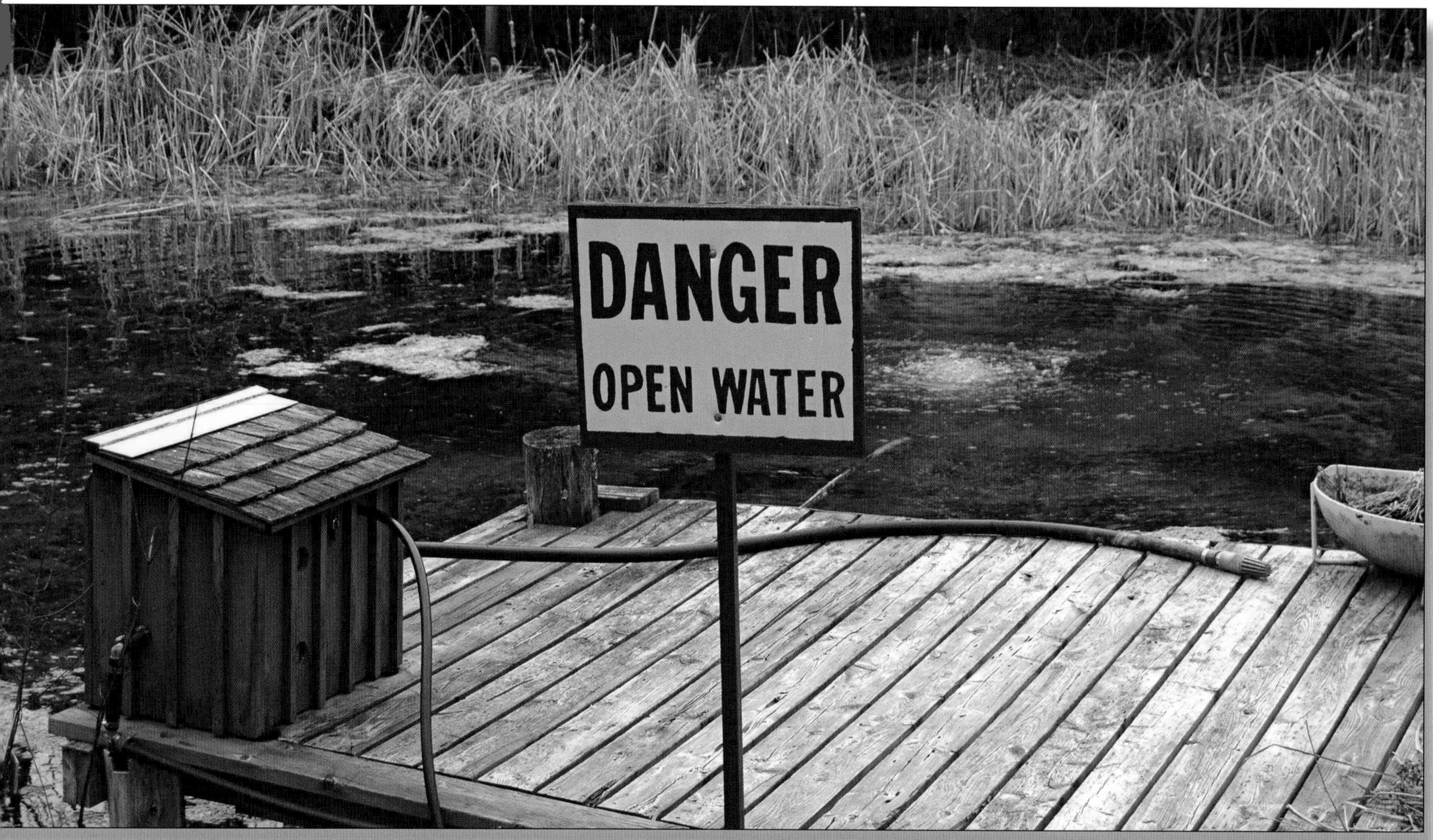

Putting up danger signs around the pond during winter freeze-up will help reduce your chances of being charged with negligence should an accident occur. This is particularly important if you install an aerator, bubbler, or other device to maintain open water or to enrich the water with oxygen.

- Provide a suitable life-ring, rope, and safety pole with a hook on a highly visible, easily accessible safety station.
- If you have installed an aerator or bubbler in your pond with the result that, during winter months, open water is present, several large signs should be erected stating the dangers thereof. These should be positioned at normal access points or at all corners of the compass around the pond or lake.
- Erecting no-trespassing signs around the pond may protect you from liability in some states, counties, and municipalities.
- It may also be wise to include an emergency number on your posted signs to call for assistance.
- Secure all dam structure gates, spillways, valves, etc., that control water flow in or out of a pond or

over a dam with a chain and lock.

- Enclose any pumping station or aerator pump within a small shed or waterproof box and lock the door or lid to prevent possible electrocution to trespassers who may tamper with it.
- Dry-dock and lock all boats or canoes to avoid their use on water while you are absent.

Permits Required for Pond/Lake Construction in the United States

If you are planning to construct a pond or lake in the USA, there are State laws that govern dredging, filling, dam construction and flood plain modification. For example in Michigan, the Inland Lakes and Streams Act requires permits for:

- Dredging or filling to create a lake or pond
- Damming a permanent stream (no matter how small the dam is)
- The dam construction itself when the structure impounds more than 5 ac. (2.02 ha) or has a head of 5 ft (1.5m) or more
- Placing fill or structures in the flood plain of any river or stream (the Water Resources Act, Flood Plain Modification Section). The same act also stipulates that engineering drawings are required

(Also see Chapter Eleven under "Regulations and Permits Required for Applying Herbicides or Pesticides")

Chapter Four

Natural Pond Succession

Watershed and Pond Management

A pond is largely influenced by run-off from adjacent lands and organic accumulation from leaf litter and other sources. If the soil (or rock) in the drainage basin surrounding the water body is rich in nutrients, plant growth is expected to become prolific. As a result, small animals and fish will thrive and, in turn, support a healthy population of larger predatory fish. Lakes and ponds in southern Ontario are located on softer, more nutrient-rich limestone rocks than the granitic rocks of northern Ontario, which have a poor supply of nutrients and are extremely hard, resisting erosion. Nutrients from soil erosion and run-off from adjacent lands wash down into the pond or lake. Nitrogen arrives as ammonia or as nitrates from its primary source in the atmosphere, and phosphorus, almost always present in native soils, can become excessive near septic-tank beds, sewage-treatment plants and sod producers, and due to poor farming practices.

Phytoplankton, which comprise the microscopic plant life in any pond, utilize minerals in solution from soil and organic litter as nutrients. Aided by sunlight and carbon dioxide gas from the atmosphere, phytoplankton combine soil and organic matter to create new plant growth. Zooplankton—the microscopic animal life in the pond—feed on phytoplankton and, in turn, provide food for larger pond creatures such as insects, crustaceans, and small fish, which form the diet for larger fish. Dead animals, along with wastes, decompose partially through the action of scavenger animals, microorganisms, and chemicals. These partially decomposed materials eventually rest on the pond bottom, creating an organic sludge containing nutrients for continual plant growth.

From the time a pond is dug, a natural succession takes place. This begins with the growth of shoreline

It is a soothing employment on a fine summer day to sit in the warmth of the sun overlooking the pond.

NATURAL POND SUCCESSION

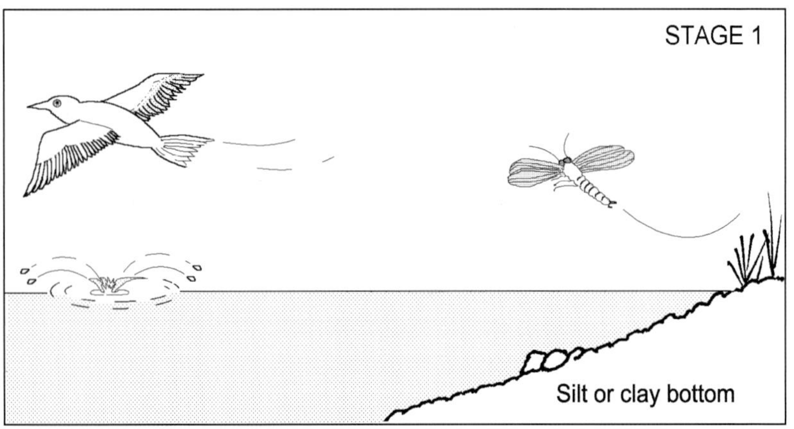

- Following initial construction, the pond water clears gradually while birds and other wildlife import seeds to the pond.
- Seeds initiate new aquatic plant growth around the edge of the pond.

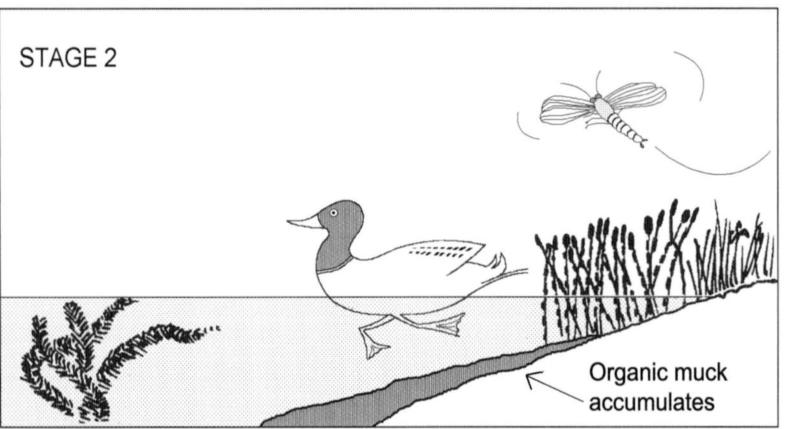

- As more wildlife inhabits the pond, organic wastes accumulate on the pond bottom.
- Submergent aquatic vegetation appears, growing up from the pond bottom. Typical species are common waterweed, coontail, chara, and horsetail.

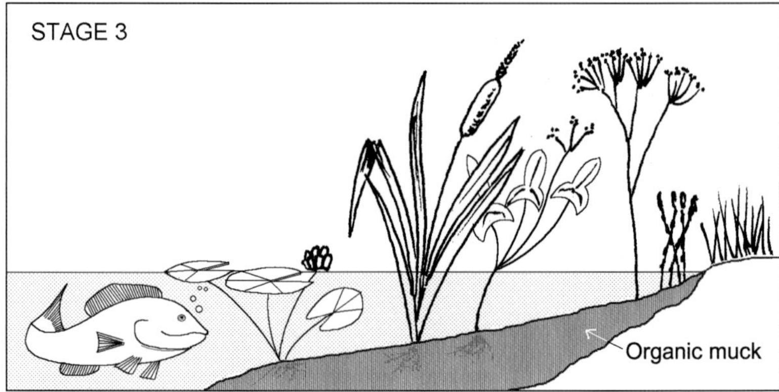

- Emergent aquatic plants invade the shallow edges of the pond.
- As plants mature and die they decompose and increase the organic layer accumulating on the pond bottom.

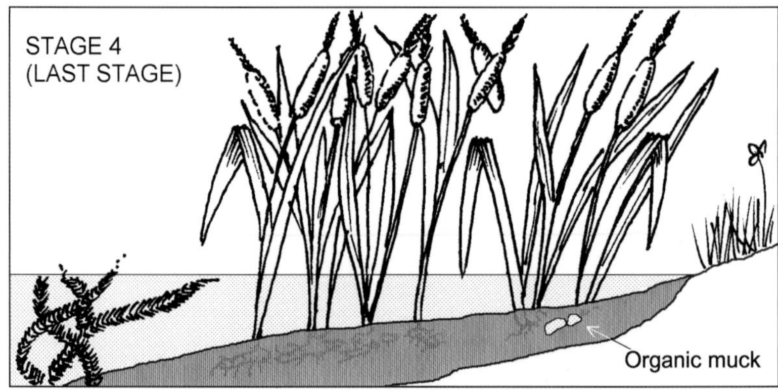

- Increasing organic waste promotes a massive growth in vegetation, and plants begin to fill the open water area of the pond.
- The pond will gradually become a marsh.

Figure 4.1 The stages of pond succession.

plants and emergent aquatic vegetation within the pond. These plants decay, along with phytoplankton and zooplankton, causing sediment to accumulate at the bottom of the pond. Increased plant production from higher nutrient levels results in more dead plants falling down through the water column to the bottom. This cycle results in more decay which, in turn, places a greater demand on the already reduced oxygen of the cold lower regions of the pond or lake, ultimately stressing the pond and creating a mucky *benthic* zone. As the pond matures, it will slowly become a wetland or marsh unless aggressive management efforts are made to interrupt the nutrient cycle.

At this point the pond owner must question his/her original objectives. "Was the primary objective to create a swimming pond, a fish pond, or simply a wildlife habitat? Should action be taken to intervene and slow down the process?" To alter the progression from "swimming hole" to "swamp," for instance, proper watershed and pond management must be undertaken.

Thermal Stratification, Bottom Sediments, and Oxygen Depletion

If you have owned a pond for several years, you will be familiar with some of the unpleasant aspects of management: algae growth, aquatic weeds that flourish around the perimeter, surface scum, and bad odors. These problems are normally the result of such factors as lack of initial pond depth, silt running into the pond, excess infiltration of nutrients (phosphates and nitrates), and lack of circulation, which limits the opportunity for oxygen to spread throughout the pond. Often, simple natural succession plays a major role in the transition of a pond from a clear pool to an unsightly mass of weeds and surface scum. This progression occurs in ponds that are dug in a wetland or swampy area. Before examining the factors producing these problems, the special situation created within swamp-derived ponds must be addressed.

Following a pond's completion, shallow-water areas

A pond margin rapidly filling in with pioneer vascular plants (pioneer stage).

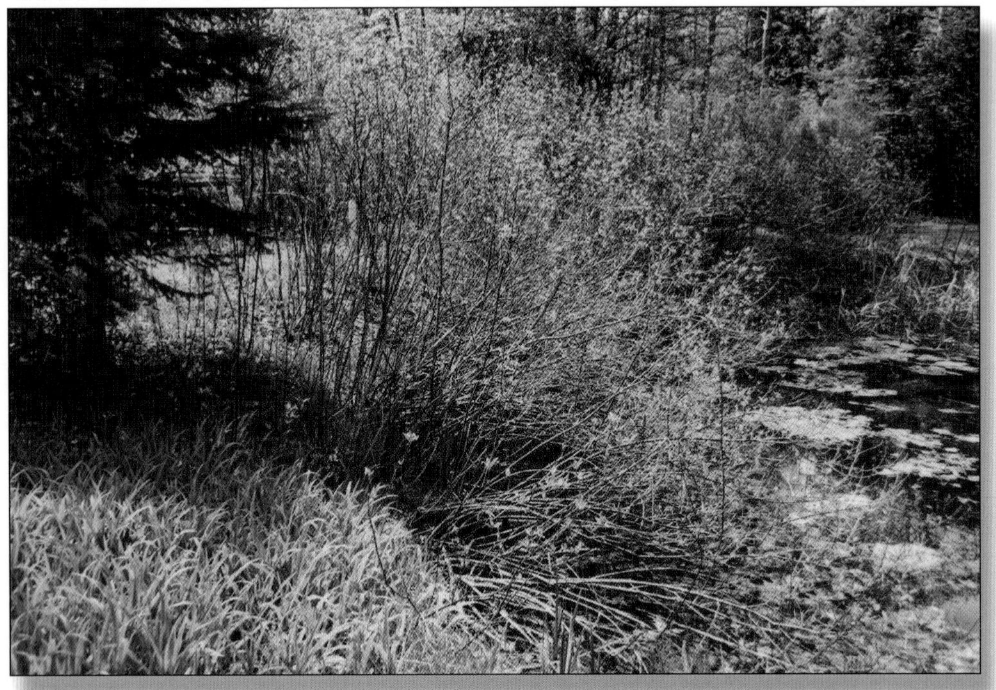

A pond perimeter being converted to a shrub environment—red osier dogwood predominating (mesophytic stage).

encourage the growth of phytoplankton and invertebrates to replace lost habitats present in the original marsh site. This is the onset of natural succession, which responds to environmental changes that reduce water depth and saturation of the soil, thereby improving aeration. Pioneer vascular plants and emergent aquatics such as horsetail, cattail, marsh marigold, and iris growing in shallow water where there is adequate light penetration hold sediment and build up organic matter.

Gradually, the shallow margins of the pond accumulate enough sediment to shift the plant habitat from aquatic weeds toward shrub growth. This process, which takes considerable time, initially encourages shrubs such as pussy willow and red osier dogwood, but will eventually support lowland pioneer vegetation such as poplar, alder, birch, and willow species on drier segments of the bank. This zone might occasionally be flooded, but the water table is quick to fall. When left unmanaged, such an environment will proceed toward mesophytism, creating a habitat in which trees and shrubs become dominant species, while the site acts as a giant natural filter. If at any time this process is to be halted and the original pond situation restored, the owner must consider re-dredging the pond. Therefore, the access path to the pond must be kept plant-free for heavy equipment to reach it. Such is the danger of building a pond in a swamp environment; you will forever be fighting Mother Nature to maintain an artificial situation on an original wetland ecosystem.

Dug-Out Ponds

Four main factors—depth, nutrient levels, oxygen content, and circulation—are critical management criteria for the more common dug-out pond. Shallow ponds (those less than 8 ft. or 2.5 m in depth) present more pond-bottom area (the benthic zone) to sunlight. If the benthic zone of your pond is exposed to sunlight all day, you can expect weeds to flourish. In deeper dredged ponds, enough sunlight rarely reaches the bottom benthic zone to accelerate weed growth; thus most plant growth will confine itself to the perimeter of the pond (the littoral zone). It is wise to keep pond shores stabilized to prevent

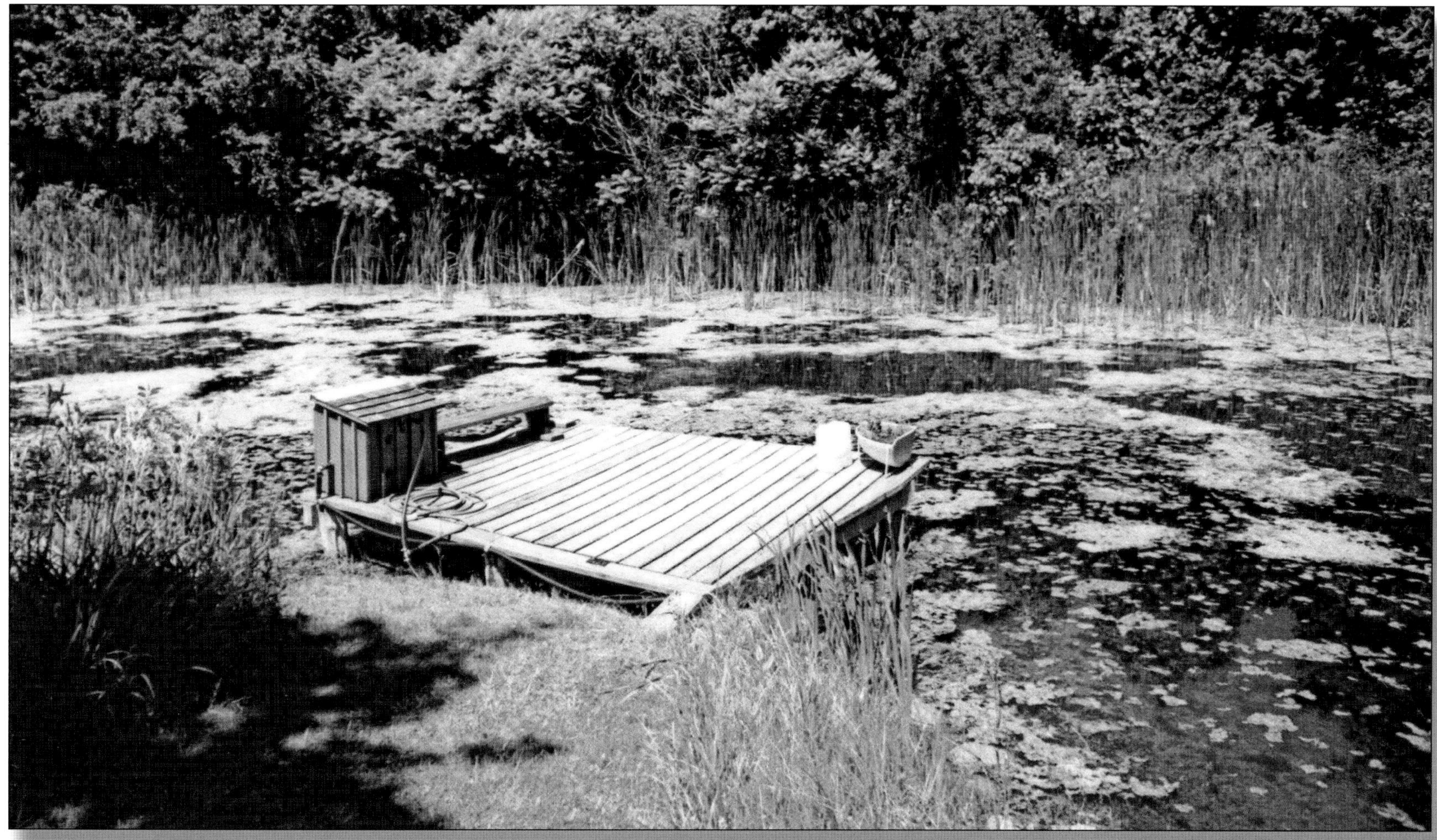

silt from running into your pond. Underwater ledges often slump into the pond from soft fill around the banks, promoting excessive aquatic plant growth, particularly if peat or a rich loam was used to form the banks when the pond was constructed. Make sure your contractor uses a clay-based soil mix for the total pond perimeter. In the case of an impounded pond, the entire dam, particularly the core, must be formed from a soil with a high percentage of clay.

Nutrient load in ponds is a major contributor to aquatic plant and algae growth. The appearance of algae mats early in spring—often in conjunction with cloudy water and an odor problem—is an indication of high nutrients. Phosphates and nitrates are the most common causes; they may filter in from a nearby golf course, a nearby tile bed or from the landowner's fertilized lawn. It pays to examine your immediate watershed if you suspect an overabundance of nutrient. Ask

Our own pond undergoing excessive algae growth before aeration.

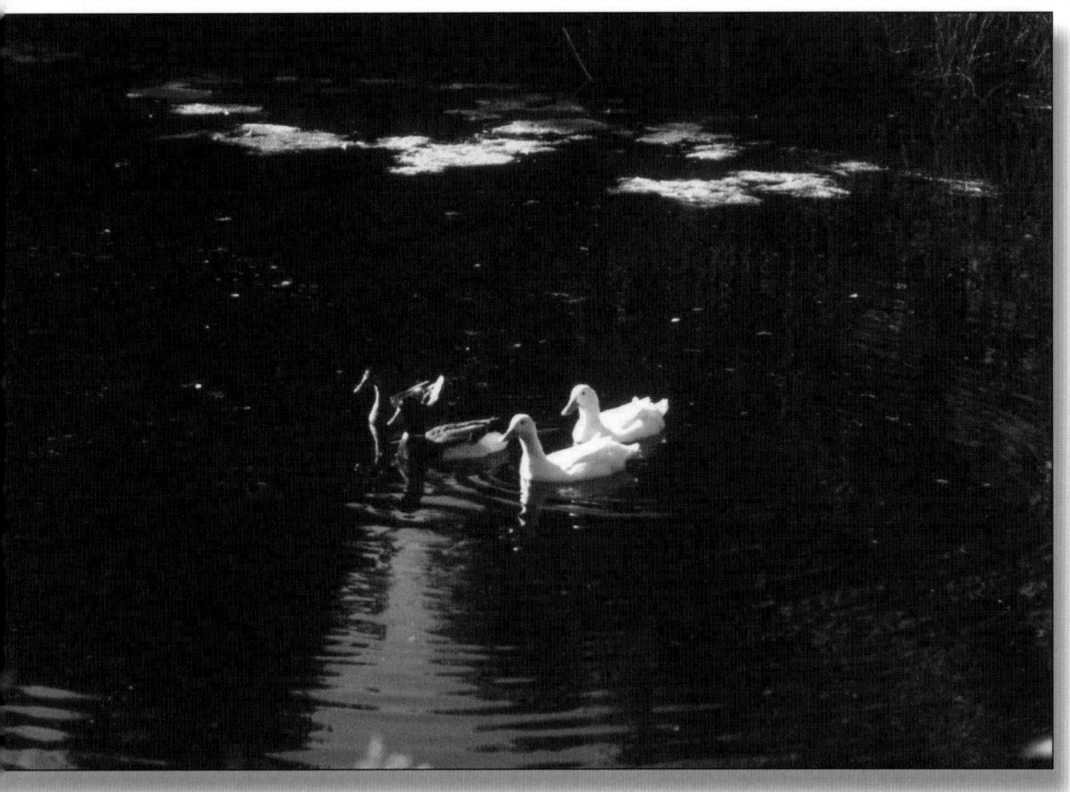

These domestic ducks at first converted the pond surface into a clean sheet of water, but it quickly reverted to its murky, weedy state. Introducing the ducks to the pond was an experiment, but the water volume wasn't sufficient for their waste products, and their proximity to a forest made them easy prey for a red fox who took up residence nearby.

yourself how the pond is fed: do spring freshets circulate through land that is fertilized? Is your property surrounded by agricultural land, and where does that land drain to? How close is your septic-tile field to the pond? (The accepted minimum is 300 ft. or 91.5 m.)

Pond temperatures have a lot to do with excessive weed growth. Shallow water is warmer than deep water, and deeper ponds accumulate warm water on the surface but cooler water at the bottom. Warm water retains less oxygen than cold (as much as 50 percent less), but aquatic plants grow a lot faster in warmer water. Billions of microscopic algae and larger plants grow and flourish in such shallow waters. They constitute food for a multitude of animals, which are in turn eaten by birds and other animals. Bacteria and fungi are also present, breaking down dead plant and animal tissue. In most streams, rivers, and lakes, the natural flow of water carries these nutrients away, but in ponds the nutrients generally accumulate and remain as bottom sediments—decayed material, shell fragments, and other biological leftovers of the benthic zone. Owners interested in maintaining a wildlife pond will benefit from stabilization of this benthic zone. The denizens of a pond bottom—including snails and mayfly larvae—thrive on decaying material. These animals are, in turn, a major food source for ducks and other animals. This, the pond's natural cleaning process, is called organic digestion, and carries on quite well on its own. Added phosphates, nitrates, and other organic materials that filter in from man-made sources overload the system to create undesirable conditions. Be aware that a large duck population in your small pond will contribute to excess organic waste, and the benefits ducks bring by eating plants can be easily outweighed by their waste deposition.

Thermal Stratification

Aerobic bacteria require oxygen to live, multiply, and break down material. With adequate oxygen, aerobic bacteria will multiply and effectively aid the organic digestion process, improving fish life and preventing odor problems. Wind and wave action upon surface waters (the epilimnion) encourages oxygen in the air to be dissolved and distributed throughout the upper layers of the pond. Microscopic phytoplankton and zooplankton in this layer feed upon each other and are, in turn, eaten by small fish and other animals. As surface temperatures increase on a sunny day, thermal layers begin to form and, with a temperature difference of only a few degrees Celsius between the top and bottom layers, the natural mixing of pond water stops. Organisms in the lower layers consume whatever oxygen is left in the water; this oxygen cannot be replenished without circulation. These organisms, including fish, thus start to show stress and soon begin to perish.

On the surface, conditions become ideal for algae blooms. Rising temperatures, the subsequent layering, and increased nutrient loading can lead quickly to toxin-producing blue-green algae. Phytoplankton and zooplankton are the first to show stress and will disappear, along with the organisms that feed on them. Foul odors and unpleasant scum are typical results. The effects of thermal stratification are evident in many lakes, ponds, and even reservoirs. Using treated waste water as a source for the pond or lake invites vulnerability, with thermal stratification occurring more rapidly and with greater intensity thanks to a higher amount of suspended nutrients upon which algae and bacteria feed and multiply.

Mechanics of Thermal Stratification

Water between the surface and pond bottom is naturally separated into four layers. (See Figure 4.2, p. 44.) The warmer upper layer, called the epilimnion, contains the highest levels of dissolved oxygen. Immediately below the epilimnion is the thermocline or metalimnion, where the most rapid drop in temperature and oxygenation occurs. Under the metalimnion is the hypolimnion, where anaerobic organisms such as bacteria and certain blue-green algae reside as the only living organisms. Little oxygen exists here, but some methane gas is present. Methane is especially sensitive to traces of oxygen.

The bottom layer, the benthic layer or benthal (sometimes called ooze) is largely devoid of oxygen, and is composed of septic sludge and decomposing

Extreme algae proliferation and stagnation in a shallow bay of Lake Simcoe.

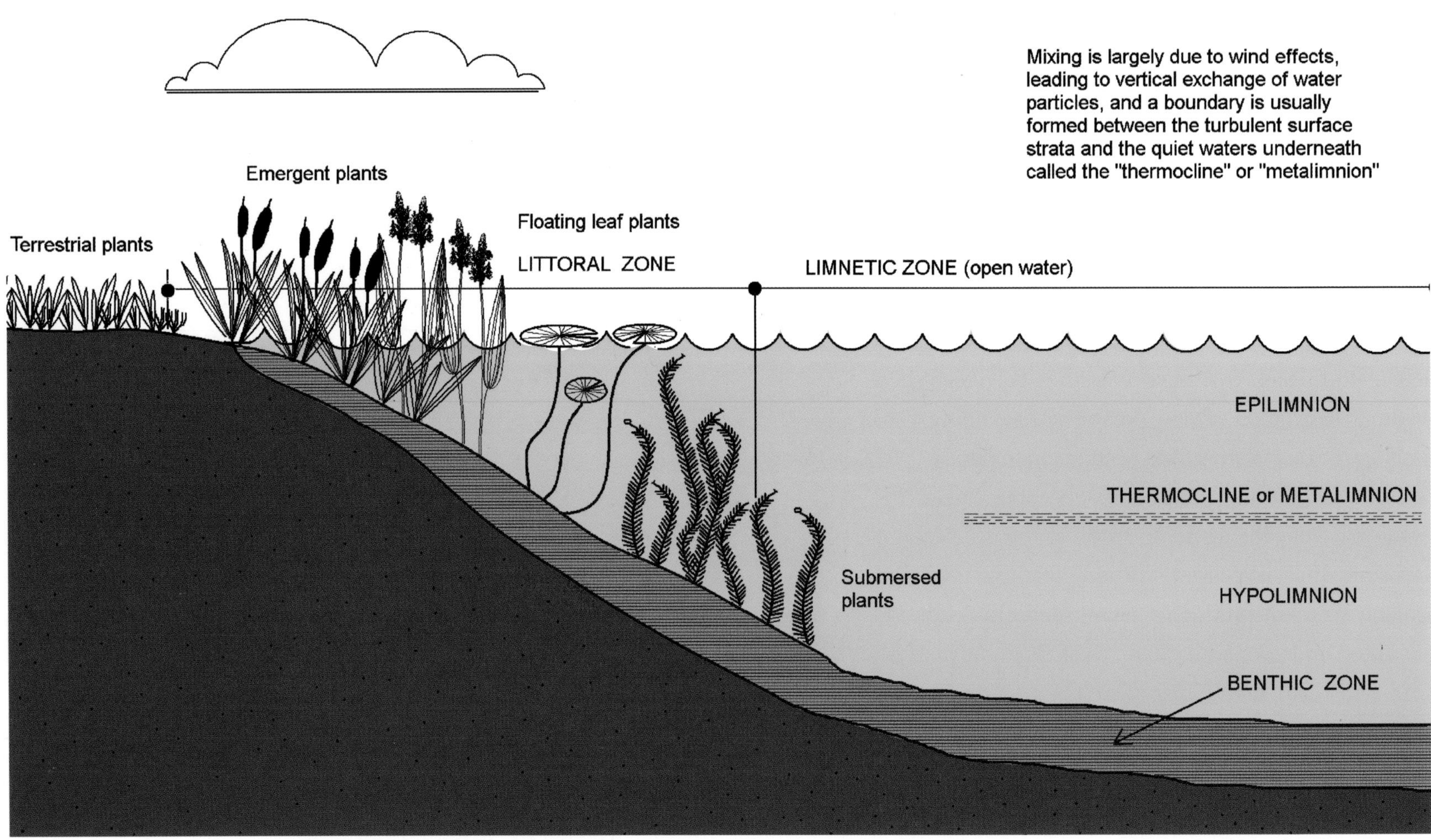

Figure 4.2 Cross-section of a pond showing layering in the water column.

plants and animals. The decomposition of organic matter in the benthic layer often produces methane gas, which, upon saturation, forms bubbles that rise to the surface. These are particularly noticeable when the barometer is falling, or when the bottom layers are poked with a stick. Any pond might develop a layer of black ooze that can be a repository for heavy metals and other toxic chemicals. Soluble products of organisms broken down in the benthal layer are given off to the water in the strata adjacent to the bottom and are often carried up again as nutrients in the process of eddy diffusion (the vertical interchange of water particles due to wind). This process is especially effective in spring when the temperature difference between surface and bottom water is not great.

Spring and Fall Turnover

In winter, most lakes or ponds are sealed by a layer of ice and snow. Water just below the ice is close to freezing, but the remainder of the water column is at around 4 °C (39.2 °F)—the temperature at which water is heaviest. When ice melts in spring, increased solar irradiation continues to warm the cold water at the surface until it reaches this temperature. Under normal circumstances, surface water will warm up at a greater rate than the underlying layers, but spring breezes mix the warmer water into the cold. When this occurs, the entire lake or pond is roughly at the same temperature, mixing the water and all its plant and animal life. This mixing is termed the spring turnover and can last for several days as the temperature of the whole body of water increases, reaching equilibrium.

Often, a pond or lake is divided into two layers, a condition precipitated by its upper surface heating up too fast during calm, hot days in spring with no wind effect. The surface then becomes increasingly light and resists mixing with the heavier, colder water down below. At this point, even a strong wind might not be able to mix the layers. Below the maximum mixing depth (13 ft. or 4 m), the temperature falls rapidly and the water is uniformly cold right to the pond or lake bottom. This condition results in a division of the water column into two distinct layers, with only a narrow transition layer between them. The water body will retain this condition with no mixing for the rest of the

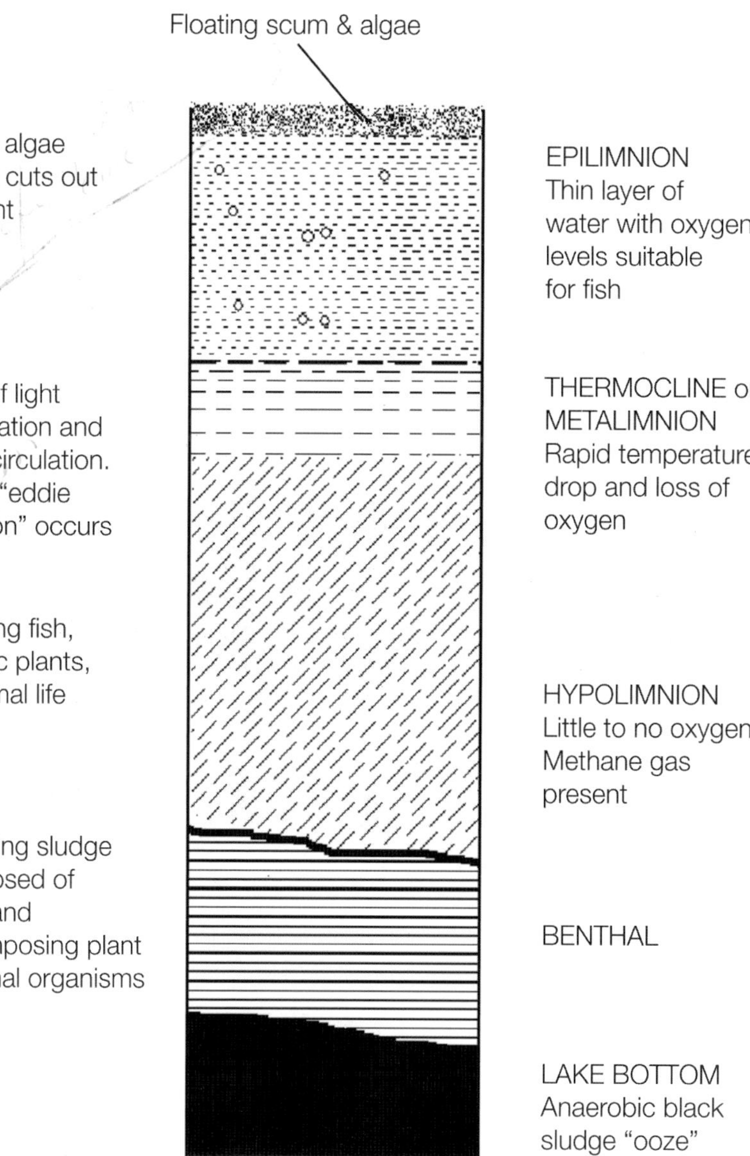

Figure 4.3 Water column showing thermal stratification leading to eutrophic conditions in a pond or lake.

Horsetail (Equisetum) *can become invasive in a pond environment.*

summer, with the upper layer getting warmer and the lower layer remaining just as cold as it was in spring. This changes in late September or October when the upper layer cools down and becomes heavier, and complete mixing takes place again.

A serious phenomenon can occur at low bottom temperatures when the breakdown of organisms proceeds more slowly than the deposition of organic material. The gradual accumulation from deposition, along with the contribution of products from the breakdown to the water column can convert a pond or lake to a eutrophic state—a state in which high nutrient content subjects the water body to excessive algae blooms, resulting in water that is low in oxygen and of poor quality. Surface algae can reduce the amount of sunlight penetrating the pond's surface, affecting phytoplankton and other plants dependent upon photosynthesis. Algae mats can also reduce wind and wave action, thereby inhibiting oxygen from being distributed throughout the water column. This reduction eliminates eddy diffusion (which helps spread oxygen throughout the top layers) and the mixing effect that the wind might offer to produce spring turnover. Algae consume more oxygen at night than they give off during the day (through photosynthesis). As the oxygen level is depleted in the lower water strata, a deadly cycle is created whereby decomposing plants and animals become food for algae.

In our own pond, this transition began shortly after construction with the emergence of horsetail (*Equisetum*), initially along the pond's edges, then in the water to a depth of no more than a foot. Early the next year, we noticed a "rug" of chara (stonewort) beginning to cover the pond bottom in its deepest sections, along with an occasional cattail emerging around edges on the far side. The cattail had, apparently, taken hold in a shallow area where our contractor had left an underwater ledge, or perhaps where a slump had occurred from the loose, peat-rich bank fill. In later years, when chara had filled the entire pond, this shallow area proved to be problematic as the cattail proliferated, forming a thick marsh habitat.

Removing the ledge by excavation would have displaced the shorebirds nesting in the cattail, destroying the now-established wildlife habitat. By this time, the smallmouth bass I had transplanted into the pond were consuming frogs, smaller fish, and various crustaceans. They enjoyed the protection of the chara, wiggling their way down into it whenever I approached. The pond was alive with dragonflies, frogs, nesting birds, bitterns, a lone snapping turtle, and an occasional great blue heron. To alter its state at this point by dredging a large part of it seemed cruel, as it would adversely affect an ecosystem that had taken years to develop. This was a major turning point in our perspective of use. Our pond was evolving into a wildlife pond, and unless we took drastic physical action to alter it, we could never again look back upon it as a swimming pond.

To offset the ugly mats of chara floating on the surface, I planted seeds of yellow iris (*Iris pseudacorus*) around the pond. I had obtained these from seed pods growing in nearby garden ponds; I broke the pods apart and pushed the seeds down into the muck of the bottom just at water's edge. Over successive years, this small effort amounted to a blaze of yellow ringing the pond every June. If only for the few weeks it bloomed each year, the thick mass of iris seemed to push back the cattail advance. Once the flowering was over, iris stems merged with those of the cattail and the image of the pond was once again that of a developing swamp.

Yellow iris around the shoreline of our pond.

Every fall, throughout the first ten years or so, leaf litter from the nearby forest margin fell on the surface of our pond, blowing around in the light autumn breeze. Waterlogged and decaying, the leaf debris settled to the bottom by Christmas to form a putrid, black "ooze." Building up gradually, this bottom sediment would release bubbles of methane gas if disturbed with a stick, indicating its eutrophic state. At about this time, the fish began to disappear, although frogs, dragonflies, bitterns, and shorebirds remained.

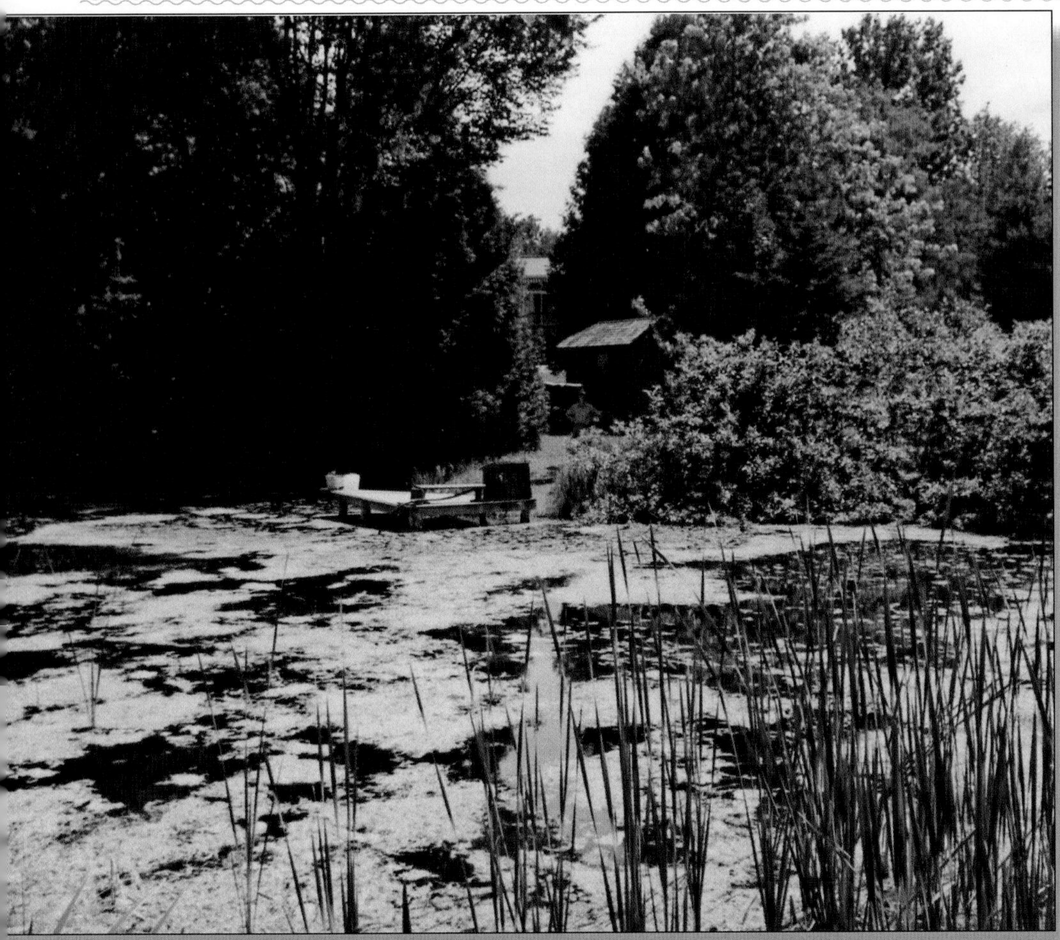

Chara mats on the surface of our pond in midsummer.

In addition, during summer, the methane bubbles accumulating under the thick mats of chara floating on the surface contributed to the buoyancy of the mats. Often, during the hottest of summer days, the water temperature would provoke heating of the gas which, released from the ooze, would attach itself to the underside of the chara leaves. This mechanism buoyed them to the surface. The continuous up and down movement of chara exemplified the pond's crude digestive system; the water body was turning into a smelly cesspool.

Attempting to eliminate methane production and improve water quality, I built a "bubbler system" from a war-surplus compressor, reversing the intake and pressure ports to aerate the pond. Linked to a timer, the air pump cycled on and off four times per day, producing a column of bubbles which emerged as "froth" on the surface. I used a simple plastic lawn sprinkler, weighed down at the bottom with a cement block, to produce a fine stream of bubbles. At start-up, a distinct odor of methane could be detected, though this faded after several minutes. Although the air pump did not eliminate the ooze layer, it relieved bottom sediments of trapped methane gas in the vicinity of the bubbler, mixing it with the upper horizon of pond water and releasing it into the atmosphere. After several years of employing this method, I began to wonder if this process was entirely beneficial, since it was apparent I was gradually losing fish. It occurred to me that spreading methane gas upward through the mid-to-surface water column might be chasing the fish out of their only habitable zone. The air-pump system parted the chara weed mass only directly above the bubbler unit on the bottom, exposing a clear, round, open-water area. Although this technique did not alter the production of chara, it provided a small aesthetic relief from an otherwise continuous surface mat.

Following this technique, I took aggressive action

and began raking up the heavy mats of chara onto a raft that I had built for the purpose. The task was arduous and futile; the wet chara, weighing in at hundreds of pounds, loaded up the raft quickly, producing a dangerous platform to stand upon. When the raft surface was filled, I poled the tilted raft to shore to pitch the chara into a wheelbarrow and dispose of it onshore. Work progressed slowly, and it soon became apparent that I could spend weeks at the task, which was inefficient to begin with. Often, after hours of labor, the extent of chara was not appreciably reduced, and I was exhausted. Annoyed at the lack of efficiency, I became overzealous with the quantity I accumulated on the raft, taking on much more than the raft could handle. It was a delicate balance between just enough to keep the raft level and the next load that would tilt the raft precariously, tossing both the load and myself into the churned-up, murky water. It became apparent that dredging the ooze out along with the chara would be the only practical solution. Natural succession was proceeding at an alarming rate; the pond was becoming an efficient, uncontrollable biomass production unit. A more practical solution would have been the installation of a wave-maker, such as the Algae Mill, or a similar wave-production unit powerful enough to circulate the entire pond volume. Had this been utilized at the first indication of chara production, the digestion of the ooze accumulating on the bottom would have been more successful, and the spread of chara would have been halted. Unfortunately, the electrical service line that I had installed underground (and under the access road) running 200 ft. (61 m) to the pond was not heavy enough to carry the load of a half-horsepower pump or higher. This restriction prevented the use of proper aeration equipment; it illustrates the importance of pre-planning all your requirements for pond construction and maintenance.

Chara within the depths of the pond growing right up to the surface.

Chapter Five

The Pond Ecosystem

Creatures of the Pond

Small plants and animals are key players in the ecology of a freshwater pond. Fish and other animals inhabiting lakes or ponds depend upon green plants which thrive in the water. There are many strange species of plant-consumers, and it is difficult to cover them all in one book. The range of animals, both visible and microscopic, is enormous. Large animals, such as snails, creep onto stems and leaves of water plants in shallow areas, while smaller species, like Mayfly larvae and a host of other insects, find habitat in the shallow bottom areas about the water fringe where they can find an abundance of algal scum to feed on. Bottom-dwelling species in deeper water sustain themselves by consuming dead plants and animals that sink to the bottom. Small midges that hover over the water's sunlit surface are the adult phase of a species that inhabit the ooze at the pond bottom for most of their life.

Many microscopic animals feed on surface algae in the upper layers of open water. Of these, the most bizarre might be the rotifers, or "wheel-shaped" species, which have mouth parts fringed with hairs. These hairs move constantly, beating in a circular manner, guiding food into the animal's mouth.

Other underwater animals like the water flea and the copepods (both crustaceans), feed by filtering algae out of large amounts of water relative to their size. In some cases, these animals feed by simply catching other microscopic animals or plants. Vegetarian animals (zooplankton) feed on tiny plants (phytoplankton), converting them into animal matter. This, in turn, provides food for larger animals such as insects, crustaceans, and small fish. Microscopic zooplankton, as prey, provide direct nourishment for larger animals in the pond, and ultimately, they are responsible for providing essential food for even larger fish in the pond food chain. Both as scavengers and as prey, these species recycle dead organisms back into living tissue, and are an essential part of the

A frog peeks out of the water in search of insects.

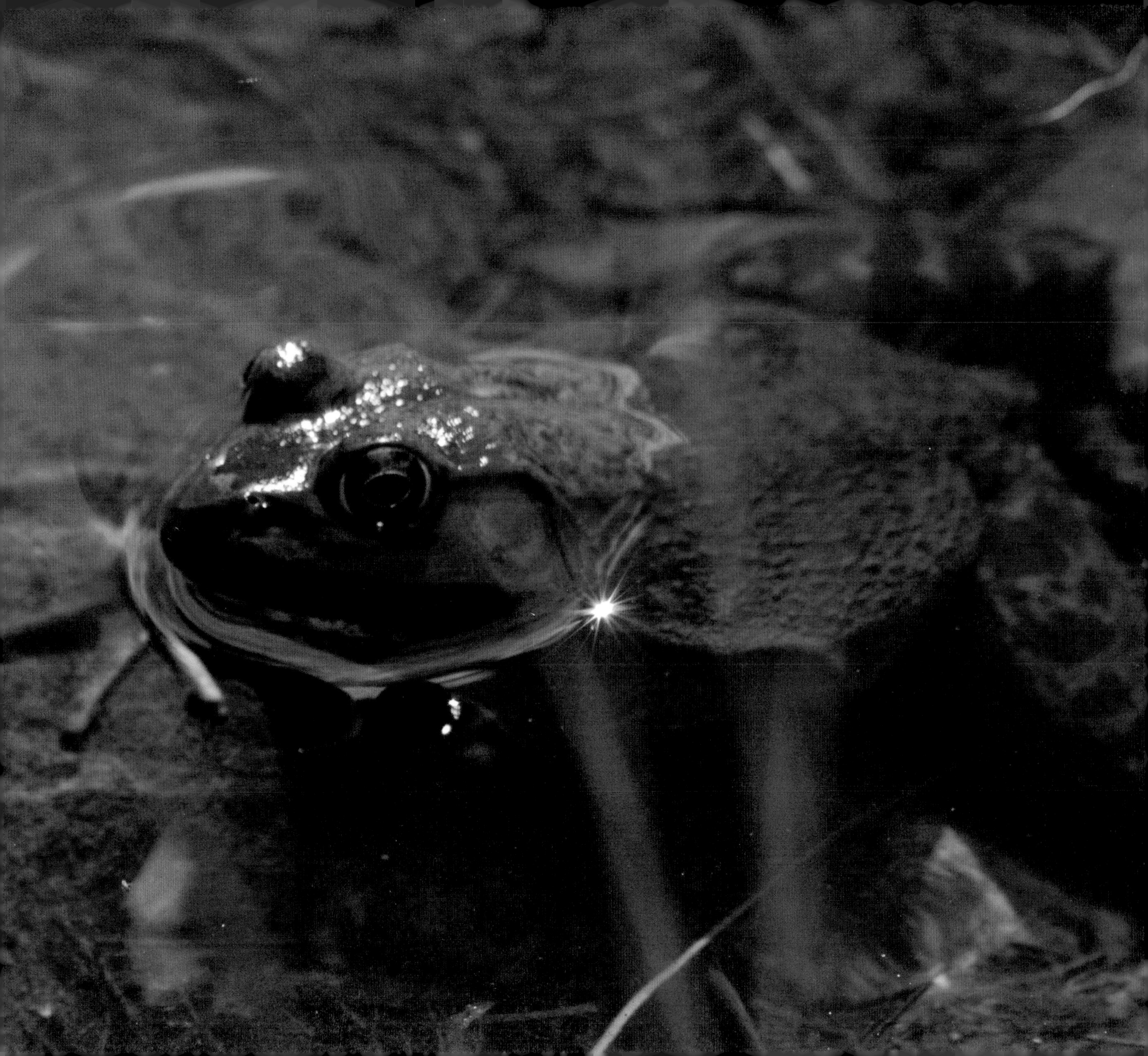

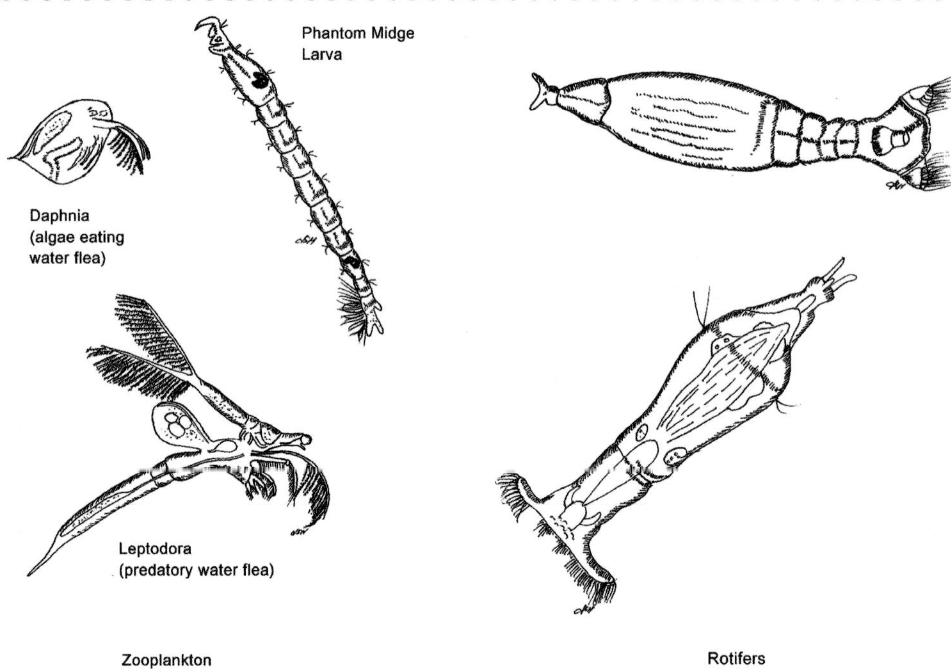

Figure 5.1 Selected zooplankton [adapted from Peck Lake Trail: Ecology of an Algonquin Lake*].*

food web. Zooplankton, along with microorganisms and chemicals, are the "catalysts" for partial decomposition of dead plants, animals, and wastes that lie on the pond bottom forming the organic muck. This material, along with redissolved minerals, provides nutrients for plant growth and plays an active part in the life cycle of a pond.

A field guide will help you identify the following larger pond inhabitants and discover more about their life cycles and required habitats. These capsule descriptions should serve as an introduction.

Predaceous Diving Beetles (Family Dytiscidae)

The diving beetle is a large, black beetle over 1.5 in. (40mm) long. It has a yellow border around the thorax and wing cases. In certain lighting conditions, the black portions of the beetle are iridescent and appear green. These beetles have long, flattened hind legs, fringed with thick hairs, for water propul-

A black predaceous diving beetle—*Dystiscus marginalis.*

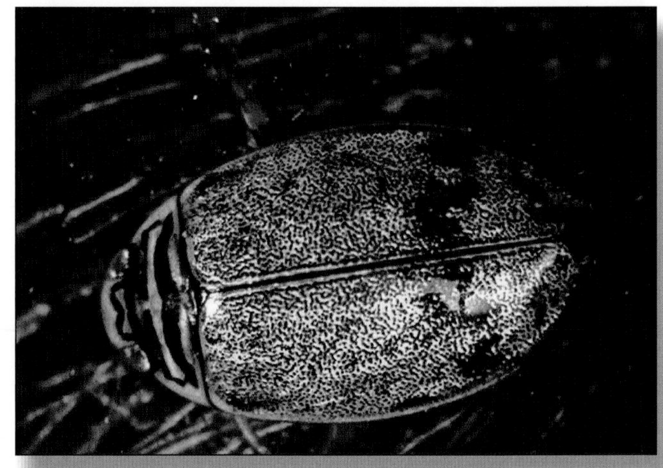

A colored predaceous diving beetle—*Dystiscus thermonectus* [Photo by B. M. Drees].

sion. The female is larger than the male and lays her eggs in small slits she cuts in the stems of water plants; one egg is laid in each slit. Larvae pupate in chambers near the water's edge, becoming adults before winter. They emerge white in color and soon harden, developing normal black coloration. Both adult and larvae are ravenous predators; often called water tigers, they prey upon larger animals in the pond, such as tadpoles and small fish fry. The larvae usually tackle larger pond creatures and use their hollow jaws to suck juices from their prey. Diving beetles prefer still-water ponds with plenty of aquatic vegetation. Another species, *Thermonectus* sp., which ranges in length from 0.625 in. to almost 2 in. (2.5 mm–50 mm), might be colored black or brown with distinctive spots, lines, or mottling on the wing covers.

Water Scavenger Beetles (Family Hydrophilidae)

These beetles are very similar to the predaceous diving beetle, and are often confused with it. Most species of these beetles—both as adults and larvae—are aquatic, and are principally scavengers, feeding on a variety of aquatic animals. The body is generally black to brown, elliptical, and dorsally convex, with short antennae clubbed on the tip. Bodies might sometimes be patterned: they are up to 1.5 in. (40 mm) long. The hind legs are flattened, and usually bear a fringe of hairs.

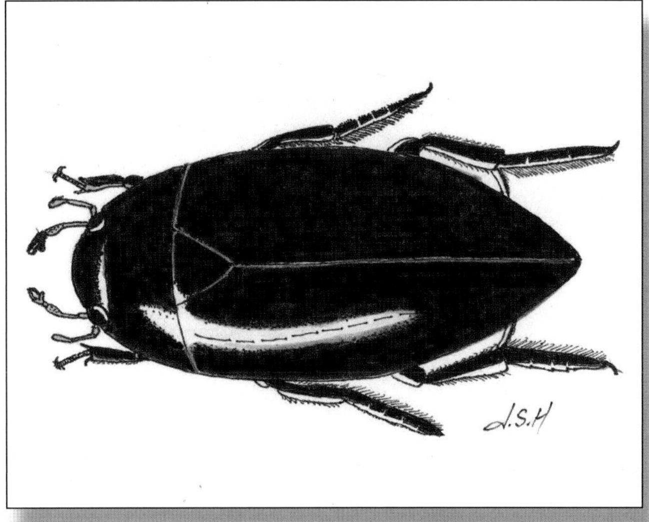

A water scavenger beetle.

Backswimmers (Family Notonectidae)

These boat-shaped bugs, each about half an inch long, swim upside-down in a series of jerky movements, propelled by their long hind legs. The backswimmer has natural camouflage that conceals it from enemies and potential prey: because it swims belly-up, its black-and-white mottling, when seen from below, blends in with ripples of light and shadow on the pond's surface, while the mud-brown underbody, seen from above, blends in with bottom sediments. These bugs are often seen on the surface of the pond, their bodies suspended vertically in a head-down manner, as they either search for prey or replenish their oxygen supply. Rows of hair fringes at the tip of their abdomen break through the water surface to obtain a fresh supply of oxygen, which the insect stores beneath its wings and in the

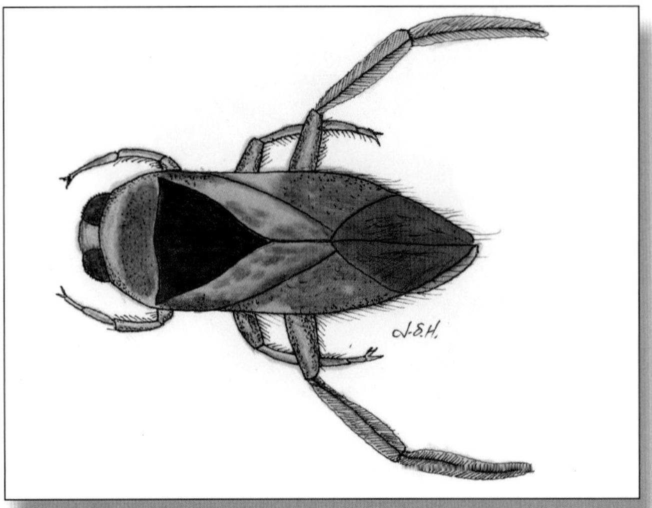

A backswimmer

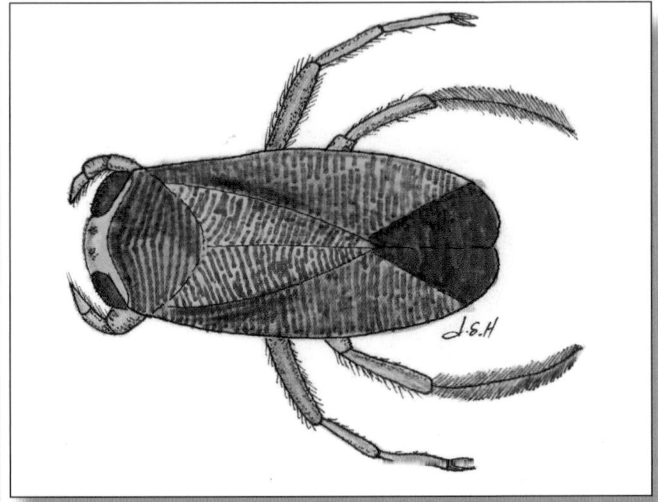

A water boatman

troughs between its hair fringes. Backswimmers are carnivorous, feeding on tadpoles, small fish, and crustaceans. Spotting their prey from the surface, they dive down, seize their victim with their forelegs, then insert their beak-like mouth to pump an enzyme into their quarry (dissolving its insides) which aids in the digestion of body contents.

Do not handle a backswimmer with bare hands, as it will inflict a burning sting with its pointed beak.

Water Boatmen (Family Corixidae)

A relative of the backswimmer, the water boatman has a greyish, elongated body up to half an inch (3–12 mm) long. The boatman lacks the sucking-style beak of the backswimmer. It does have specialized front legs with which it rakes and sifts the pond's bottom material. These insects have broad heads with large eyes and caliper-like front legs, which anchor their otherwise buoyant bodies. The boatman rows forward in breast-stroke fashion, aided by its oar-like hind legs which are fringed with fine hairs. It frequently carries an air bubble on its body or under its wings, and draws from this supply during long periods underwater. Clinging to vegetation, the males "chirp" to attract females. Most water boatmen eat algae and minute aquatic organisms, while some are predaceous, feeding on mosquito larvae and aquatic pests. They are surprisingly strong fliers, often stimulated to fly great distances in search of more favorable environments. After mating in the spring, females attach a large number of eggs to submerged vegetation, where many are consumed by fish and water birds. The adults themselves are important prey for larger pond animals.

This photograph of a giant water bug shows the extent of its front legs, which it uses for grasping prey.

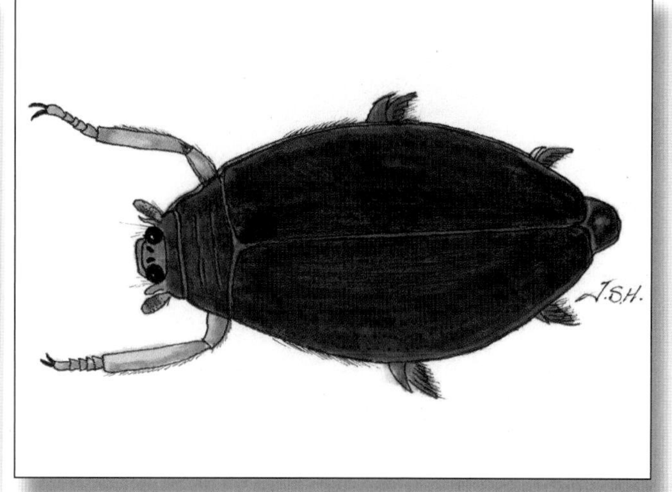

A whirligig bug

Giant Water Bugs (Family Belostomatidae)

The family Belostomatidae contains the largest bugs in the order. This water bug is about 1–2 in. (20–50 mm) long, with front legs perfect for grasping prey. Its hind legs are somewhat flattened, oar-like, and adapted for swimming. These bugs are usually seen suspended in a quiet pond or lake, the tip of their abdomens just piercing the water surface, and their brown-black, flattened, oval bodies hanging below. They are fairly common in ponds, where they feed on insects, salamanders, tadpoles, small fish, and small vertebrates. Giant water bugs can inflict a painful bite to humans. The female lays her eggs on the male's back, and he carries them around until they hatch. The larger giant water bugs, most of which belong to the genus *Lethocerus*, lay their eggs on aquatic vegetation. Some giant water bugs leave the water to fly about, often attracted by lights. When disturbed, some species play dead, while others emit an odorous fluid from the anus. Sometimes these bugs make a soft, chirping sound when annoyed.

Whirligigs (Family Gyrinidae)

Whirligig beetles are normally seen twirling on pond surfaces. The name derives from their habit of swimming rapidly in circles on the water's surface when alarmed. These bugs have peculiar, divided eyes, which can see both below and above the water. They are also unusual in that they gather in groups, which is thought to result from a number of factors including hunger, sex, water temperature, parasites, and stress.

Whirligigs carry a bubble of air trapped underneath their abdomens—this allows them to dive underwater and swim for a long time. They are at home

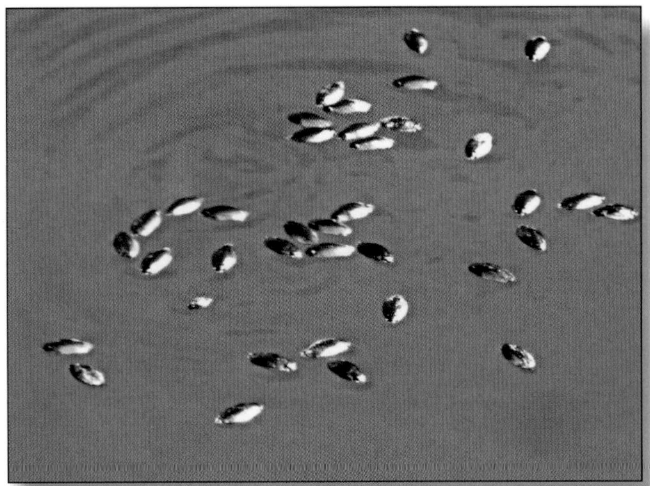

A group of whirligig bugs swimming in circles on a pond [Photo by George Peacock].

A green darner dragonfly. This specimen had collided with another dragonfly and fallen into the water, and was rescued on a rake handle. Left to dry out on the pump house roof, it offered a good photo opportunity.

both above and below the water surface. Their bite might cause humans a local allergic reaction. Both adults and larvae are predaceous.

Dragonflies and Damselflies (Order Odonata)

Dragonflies and damselflies play a significant role in the general ecology of the pond. Dragonflies are easily recognized by their two pairs of delicate, membranous wings, which "clatter" over the pond surface as they forage for food. The dragonfly can be distinguished from the damselfly by wing position: the damselfly holds its wings close to its abdomen while the dragonfly holds its wings at a near ninety-degree angle to the abdomen. The dragonfly is also generally a stronger flier. Dragonflies can also be distinguished from damselflies by prominent compound eyes which touch on top of their heads; damselfly eyes are well-separated. These are among the most beautiful and spectacular insects flying about the pond; they are also among the most ancient of living creatures.

As invertebrates, their lifespan involves a series of molts, during which the larvae consume fish spawn, tadpoles, smaller insects, and thousands of mosquito larvae while they themselves serve as food for fish and frogs. Emerging from the larval stage, the dragonfly leaves its aquatic environment to start a new life, flying off into the surrounding countryside. Adults do not make their way back to water until ready to mate. This dispersal of young adults has been a factor in their survival—it allows them to find aquatic alternatives, should their birthplace environment dry up. Suitable sites for dragonflies are unfortunately

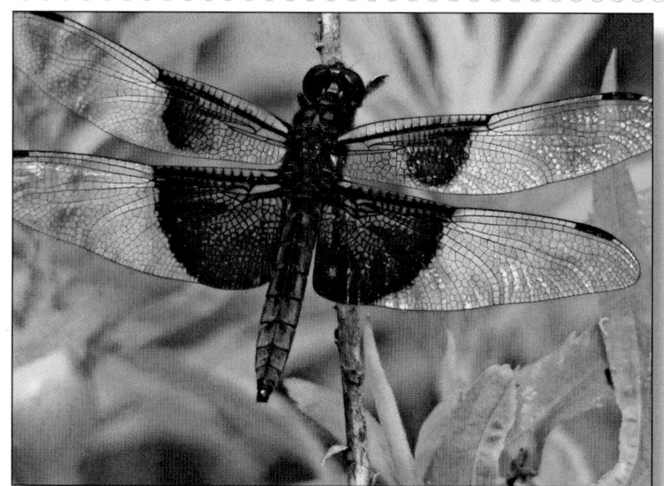

A common skimmer dragonfly [Photo by Ivan Foster, Pefferlaw].

disappearing as marshlands and ponds are drained or polluted. Ponds created for wildlife should not be allowed to become overgrown with cattail or too shaded by overhanging trees if the pond owner wants to attract dragonflies and damselflies.

Crayfish (Family Astacoidea)

Crayfish, sometimes called crawdads, are relatives of the lobster. They are scavengers, feeding largely upon snails, algae, insect larvae, worms, tadpoles, and some aquatic vegetation. Dead fish and fish eggs are also favorite snacks. Adults are most active at dusk, emerging to forage for food until daybreak. Young crayfish are usually found exploring the pond bottom while older crayfish spend their daylight hours hiding under a rock, in aquatic vegetation, or in marginal pond debris. Generally, they exhibit a slow walk, but

A damselfly [Photo by Gene Hanson].

A Common Crayfish [Courtesy of Calvin Knaggs]

if alarmed, will move swiftly, swimming backward with rapid flips of their segmented tail.

Crayfish live short lives, usually less than two years. They breathe through feather-like gills and live in bodies of water that do not freeze to the bottom—brooks and streams with running fresh water which provide shelter from predators. Most crayfish species cannot tolerate polluted water—a possible warning flag for your pond system. If none are present although the habitat seems appropriate, your pond might just have inhospitable bottom characteristics or unsuitable water qualities.

Fertilization and egg laying occurs in spring; the female secretes a jelly-like fluid which glues the eggs to swimmerets under her abdomen, where they are aerated as the swimmerets move. The egg mass resembles a bunch of blackberries; once hatched, the young stay attached to the mother for about ten days, making occasional sorties on their own before finally leaving.

Crayfish themselves serve as important food for larger fish, turtles, and grackles. They are usually full-grown at a length of 3 in. (7.5 cm). Crayfish can be a nuisance to the prospective pond owner if their dens are found in the soil of a site to be excavated. In this case, the dam must be built over a core, which needs to be extended to the bottom of any crayfish den-holes found on the site. All holes must be filled in, compacted, and eliminated to guarantee that no water leakage will occur through them, under or around the proposed dam.

Leeches (Annelida; subclass Hirudinea)

Known for centuries—and with good reason—as bloodsuckers, many of these flattened aquatic worms feed on a variety of invertebrates such as amphibians, frog eggs, reptiles, waterfowl, fish, and mammals (including humans). Others are scavengers that carry out the essential role of aiding in the decomposition of dead organisms. All leeches have a rear sucker which connects to the host for feeding and releases an anesthetic to prevent the host from feeling the attachment being made. An anti-clogging enzyme (hirudin) is also released into the host's bloodstream. The leech will stay attached until it has had its fill, but due to the anticoagulant, the bite may bleed long after the leech is removed.

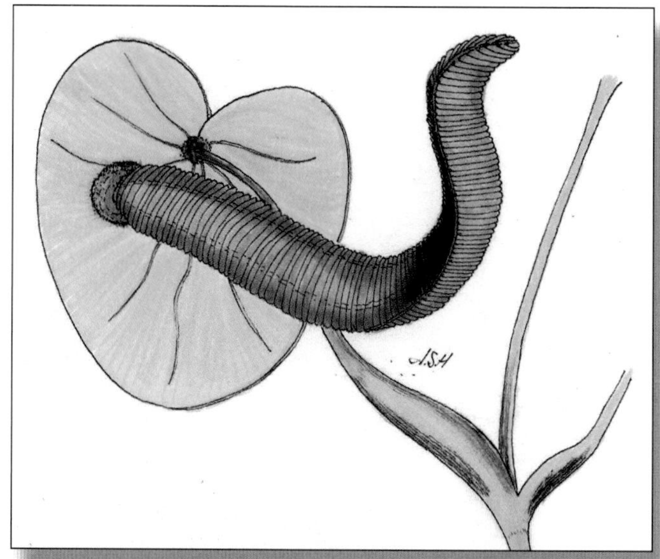

Leech attached to the underside of a yellow floating heart.

The blood-sucking (hematophagous) forms select one or two specific animal hosts such as frogs, turtles, or fish to feed upon. The snail leech (*Glossiphonia complanata*) has a multi-branched intestinal tract that allows it to feed on pond snails. The medicinal leech (*Macrobdella decora*) regularly feeds on human blood when it can get it. This is a colorful leech. Its green back is spotted in red and black, while its belly is a bright orange. The medicinal leech's appetite is not restricted to humans.

There are freshwater, terrestrial, and marine leeches. Like earthworms, they are hermaphroditic (i.e., having both male and female reproductive organs). Some species will nurture their young and provide food, transportation, and protection. Important to pond owners, leeches serve as food for fish, aquatic insects, crayfish, and also to some specialized leeches.

Bullfrog [Photo by William Heyd]

Frogs

Frogs create a chorus of trills, ribbits, croaks, and chirps as dusk falls on a rural pond, particularly a naturalized pond. What would lily pads be without frogs upon them? Amphibians, which evolved before the reign of the dinosaurs and have thrived for about 300 million years, are now facing an extinction crisis. Studies reveal that nearly 32 percent of the world's amphibian species are threatened, and at least 43 percent have declining populations.

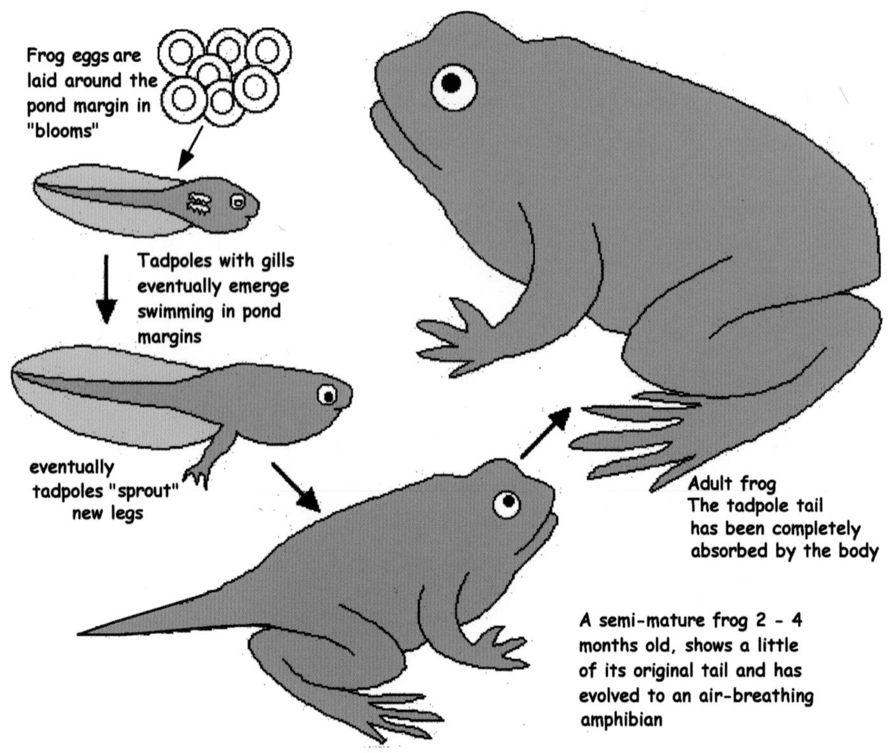

Figure 5.2 Diagram of a frog metamorphosis [Courtesy of Toronto Zoo's Adopt-a-Pond Wetland Conservation Program].

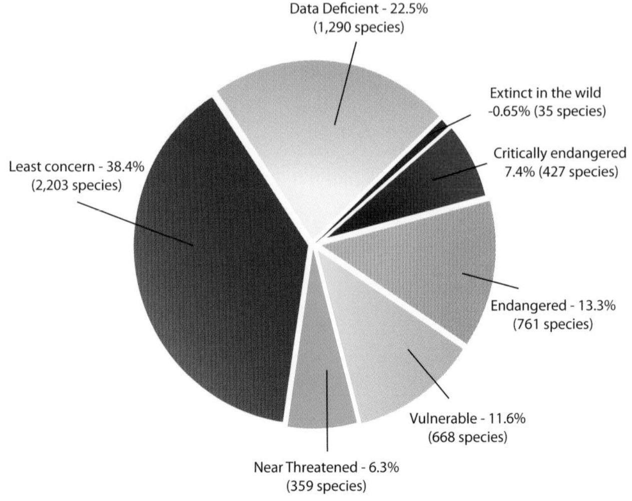

Figure 5.3 Pie chart showing the declining state of the world's amphibian species.

Frogs are especially vulnerable to extinction because they depend on both land and water. Deterioration of either land- or water-habitat bases influences them adversely, as their thin skins are permeable to air and water, along with toxins, infections, and pollutants. Research suggests the present decline in frog population is due to a parasitic fungus, amphibian chytrid, which was accidentally spread by African clawed frogs used worldwide for laboratory studies and pregnancy tests prior to the 1950s.

When the fungus finds a suitable site, it can kill its host amphibian within three months. At present, scientists have no remedy for eradicating the fungus in the wild. Zoos and conservationists throughout the world marked 2008 as the Year of the Frog to raise awareness and funding.

Unfortunately, even if a protected reserve of chytrid-free frogs is created, introducing the amphibians back into a contaminated habitat could result in failure. The length of time the parasite lasts after the original population disappears is unknown.

Other causes of frog decline include:

- excessive capture
- habitat destruction (filling and development of marshes and wetlands)
- chemical and bacteriological pollution
- toxicity resulting from waste dumps
- epidemic diseases
- ultraviolet radiation due to loss of ozone-layer protection

A leopard frog; Forks of the Credit Provincial Park, Ontario.

A green frog; Peck Lake, Algonquin Park, Ontario.

A green tree frog; Pefferlaw, Ontario [Photo by Ivan Foster].

Wood Frog [Photo by George Peacock].

Spring Peeper [Courtesy of Calvin Knaggs].

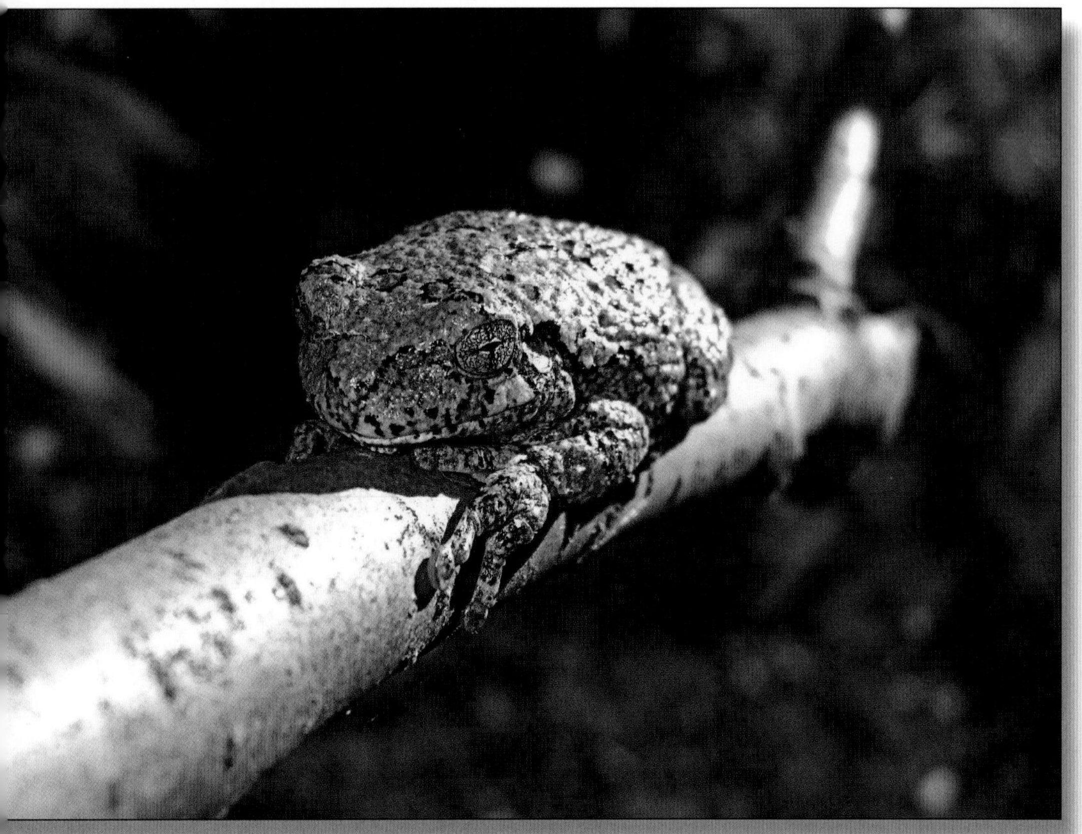

A gray tree frog [Photo by George Peacock, Keswick, Ontario].

Frogs, therefore, need tender loving care and provision of a suitable habitat. This should be a major aim of any rural pond owner—providing a suitable niche for these necessary creatures. Part of that obligation includes the supply of a suitable tree canopy to shade areas of the pond, and the provision of water lilies and suitable aquatic plants. It is fascinating to watch the life cycle of frogs progress from mating, through egg-laying, to tadpole production, and finally metamorphose from tadpole into meat-eating frog. It is in the tadpole stage that frogs are most susceptible to disease, to parasitic attacks, and to being eaten by fish, birds, and other frogs. Adult frogs benefit pond owners, as they eat a variety of insects while themselves serving as food for other pond creatures (herons, fish, turtles, snakes, etc.).

Some frogs that might be found in a variety of pond environments are:

- Leopard frog (*Rana pipiens*)
- Green frog (*Rana clamitans melanota*)
- Green tree frog (*Hyla cinerea*)
- Copes gray tree frog (*Hyla chrysoscelis*)
- American bullfrog (*Rana catesbeiana*)
- Wood frog (*Rana sylvatica*)
- Northern spring peeper (*Pseudacris crucifer*)

Painted Turtles (*Chrysemys picta*)

Eastern, western, southern, and midland painted turtles, *Chrysemys picta*, are common from southern Canada into the United States. These turtles are related to other water turtles such as sliders and cooters, and live in ponds, lakes, marshes, and slow-moving rivers with soft, muddy bottoms. Their life span in the natural environment is commonly five to ten years, but in captivity, they can live for as long as twenty years. The maximum size of the carapace (top shell) in the female, which is slightly larger than the male, is about 10 in. (25 cm). The plastron (undershell) has a magnificent design that looks hand-painted. It is usually solid yellow, or mostly yellow with a distinct pattern in the center, but might also be a complex pattern of yellow and red. Around the underside of the shell, where the skin, head, and limbs are exposed, there are yellow and red striations and spots of color. The skin tone generally varies from olive-green to solid black.

Behavior

Painted turtles can often be seen basking in the sun on floating logs or rocks at the waterside during warmer months—May to October. Some individuals bask simply by floating on the surface of the water. They expose themselves to the sun because they cannot generate enough heat to regulate body temperature. Basking usually lasts for about two hours but not much longer, as overheating can kill a painted turtle in a short time. Younger painted turtles prefer a carnivorous diet of larvae, beetles, crickets, worms, and maggots. As they grow older, they consume more plant material. Most turtles will begin to eat once the water temperature reaches 60 °F (15.5 °C).

Reproduction

Mating occurs in spring when water temperature is still low, but might also occur in the fall, before hibernation. Normal breeding season lasts from late spring to early summer. Males begin to breed between the ages of three and five; females take a little longer, from six to ten years, and are larger at maturity. Painted turtles nest on land, preferring soft, sandy soil with exposure to the warm sun. The female digs a shallow nest with access to water with her hind feet. Once the eggs are laid, the female covers the hole with sand and leaves the nest unattended. Hatchlings emerge within seventy-two to eighty days, digging their way out of the nest, immediately independent. Many animals—including muskrats, mink, raccoons, snapping turtles, snakes, bullfrogs, larger fish, herons, skunks, foxes, and fish crows—prey upon newly hatched painted turtles. Adults are preyed upon by alligators, raccoons, bald eagles, osprey, and red-shouldered hawks.

Global warming is allowing earlier nesting, but the species is very adaptable. To hibernate, the turtle buries itself deep into the mud at the bottom

A painted turtle on a log in Lake of Two Rivers, Algonquin Park, Ontario.

A mature snapping turtle, Forks of the Credit Provincial Park, Ontario.

of streams and ponds. This insulates the animal, preventing it from freezing during winter. Painted turtles can survive without oxygen at 36 °F (3 °C) for five months, longer than any other air-breathing invertebrate. Northern turtles may remain dormant for up to six months. They are an excellent addition to your pond or small lake.

Common Snapping Turtles (*Chelydra serpentina*)

There are two species of snapping turtle: alligator, *Macroclemys temminckii*, and common, *Chelydra serpentina*.

The much larger and slower alligator snapping turtle is a denizen of the more southern United States.

The common snapping turtle has a much wider range, extending as far south as Ecuador. Its Latin name, *Chelydra serpentina*, translates as "serpent turtle"—deriving from the creature's long neck, fast strike capability, and aggressive characteristics. These animals should be treated with respect, as, on land, they will snap and strike at anything in self-defense. The snapper's head is large, with two barbels on the chin. The extended head can strike straight forward, out to the sides, or backward, across their carapace toward the rear of the shell. When threatened, they rise up, hiss and emit a musky odor. In the backward extended position, the head turns upside down, often reaching as far as two-thirds of the way back to the rear of the shell.

Although the common snapping turtle has the largest range of any turtle in North America, it lives longest in the northern portions of the range, where the life span is often thirty to forty years. It is not uncommon to find a 40–60 lb. specimen, but the average mature snapper weighs around 20 lb. (9.07 kg).

The carapace is oval, widening toward the strongly serrated rear, and varies in color from tan to brown, olive, and almost black. The carapace has three broken ridges (or keels) of coarse scales running the length of the shell, with a border row giving way to the heavily notched, rear portion. The carapace is covered with scutes (trapezoidal shaped plates) that form a horny external armour all the way to a long tail, itself covered in sharp ridges. The skin is brown to dark brown with many tubercles on the neck, legs, and tail. The much smaller undershell is cross-shaped, and, like the skin underneath, is yellow relative to the carapace. The moderately long tail is covered with three rows of plate-like tubercles that diminish in size toward the end, reminiscent of the Stegosaurus.

Habitat and Food

Snapping turtles have a preference for bodies of water with muddy bottoms, where they can hibernate or conceal themselves. Generally cold tolerant, they do like to bask in the warm sun in the spring, usually on pond banks, perhaps while in search of good egg-laying locations. They spend most of their time on the lake or pond bottom, waiting in ambush for prey (other turtles, frogs, fish, crabs, snails, water fowl, small reptiles, and animals). They will eat almost anything, dead or alive, that they can catch. Snappers consume prey whole or tear larger animals to pieces with their strong claws; they will drag live prey into the water to drown it first. I have seen them eating carrion, and in this respect, they are useful scavengers. Their attack is lightning quick, with a quick thrust and extension of the neck.

As kids, when we lived on the banks of Grenadier Pond in Toronto, we often encountered specimens weighing up to 30 lb., and used to tantalize them. Provoked into grabbing the blade of a hockey stick with their strong jaws, these animals could be dragged hundreds of feet before releasing their grip. It was a test of courage to try and pick one up by the carapace without having our fingers ripped by their powerful claws or being bitten as the turtle extended its powerful head backward. We were fascinated by their courage and tenacity and respected them, as well as our fingers—and never failed to release them back into their favorite muddy habitat.

A hatchling snapping turtle, Forks of the Credit Provincial Park, Ontario.

Reproduction

Snappers reach sexual maturity when their carapace is about 8 in. (20 cm) long. They will mate from May to November, with females in southern ranges starting earlier. Nests are chosen within easy reach of water, but some individuals travel great distances to lay their eggs. The soft ground of a road shoulder is a favorite nest site, many a female meets its end on a highway. If traffic is not too busy, escorting the

female off the road (carefully!) can be quite easily achieved with the aid of a stick. Twenty to forty eggs are a typical clutch, with more in northern ranges to ensure survival. Incubation periods vary from fifty-five days to as much as a hundred and twenty-five days. The warmer the temperature, the faster the eggs hatch. Temperature determines sex, but this is not a linear relationship—range is extremely critical, and temperatures between high and low will produce both sexes. Snapping turtles are a reminder of the prehistoric past, fascinating in their appearance and habits. Handle them with great care and respect.

A snail on a plant stem [Photo by George Peacock].

Snails (Mollusca; class Gastropoda)

Snails are found in jungles, ditches, in the ocean, and even in the Arctic. They may live in fresh water or salt water, but many live on land. Adult snails have coiled shells. Creatures otherwise snail-like but lacking a shell are called slugs. Land snails are, in fact, in a minority, as marine snails comprise the vast majority of specimens. Those found in fresh water are mainly herbivorous, although a few land species are predatory carnivores.

Some snails respire through a lung (Pulmonata group), while those with gills form another group (Paraphyletic). Both species have evolved and diversified over time: many species with gills are found on land, and many with a lung can be found in fresh water or at sea.

Snails are equipped with thousands of structures—which are really tiny teeth, located on a ribbon-like tongue that works like a file—to rip food into digestible bits. Most snails must have moisture to thrive, and during the day they live in damp, shady locations, often hibernating. They seal the "doorways" to their shells until the outside air is damp again.

Freshwater snails live among other water plants in rivers or ponds. They are also found under logs and stones, and at the margins of ponds and rivers or in damp woods surrounding them.

The Importance of Aquatic Plants

Emergent aquatic plants help to stabilize and protect shorelines and pond margins. Both floating and submerged types provide shelter and food for various fish species. Some submerged plant varieties also offer food for waterfowl and habitat for the insects upon which waterfowl feed. They provide spawning habitat for fish, larvae, snails, and invertebrates. Lakes and ponds benefit from the oxygen plants produce, and from their capability to absorb nutrients such as phosphorus and nitrogen. Shorelines with loose peat or mud soils require vegetation to hold sediments, prevent erosion and avert turbidity within the waters of the pond. Emergent varieties can help dampen wave action on these shorelines, reducing sediment release and turbidity in the water.

The selection of native plants to supply food and cover for wildlife ponds can be quite unlike those suitable for recreation or swimming ponds. Swimmers can tolerate only floating types planted in containers and controlled emergent plants around the perimeter. Wildlife ponds benefit from the very species that would be banned in swimming ponds. Pond perimeters, in general, need to be protected after construction with selected marginal vegetation to maintain water clarity. Utilizing plant species with both deep and shallow roots will reduce erosion and prevent sediments from entering the pond or lake. Avoid introducing species—particularly, invasive varieties—which proliferate quickly and clog waterways.

Divisions of Aquatic Plants

Plants growing on/in ponds or lakes can be divided into two general groups: algae and rooted leafy plants.

Algae

Free-floating varieties including planktonic algae and duckweed, which can occur anywhere in a lake or pond. Algae are single-celled plants or colonies of cells lacking true roots, leaves, or flowers. There are three types of algae:

- Planktonic algae (generally microscopic)
- Chara-type algae
- Filamentous algae

Planktonic algae drift free in the water and are generally microscopic. Prolific growth creates blooms and the pond or lake water becomes turbid or murky. Blooms may range in color from green to blue-green or—rarely—red. Filamentous algae are thread-like or fine and net-like. They often grow, moss-like, on rocks. They may also form surface scum or a slimy mat on the pond or lake bottom. Chara-type algae are represented by two species—*chara* (muskgrass) and *nitella* (brittlewort). Chara grows upward from the pond bed without true roots. When crushed between the fingers, both feel gritty and produce a musk-like odor. Often, they have a white or brownish crust of lime on the leaves. Chara becomes a real problem if over-fertilized.

Vascular Aquatic Plants (rooted plants)

Vascular aquatic plants (called macrophytes) are rooted leafy plants which occur in the littoral zone, down to a depth of approximately 15 ft. (4 m). These are divided into three classes:

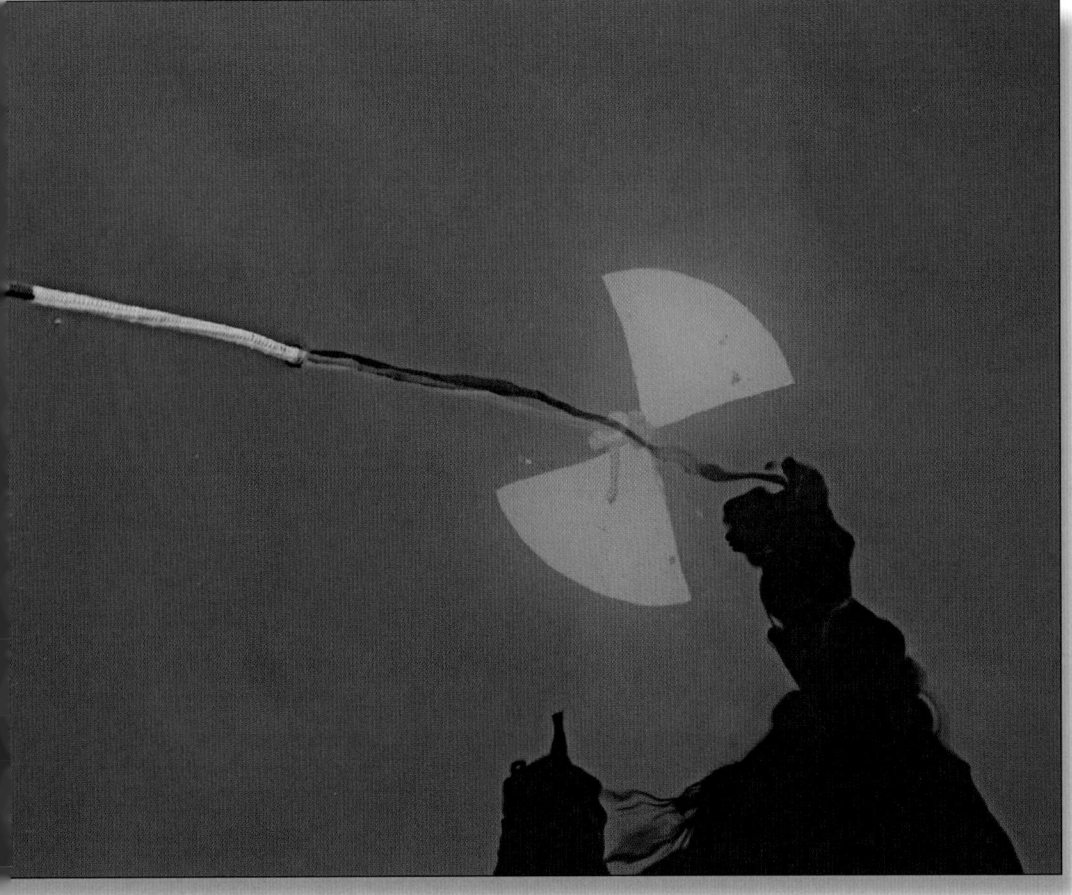

Using a Secchi disk to determine water clarity [Photo courtesy Gabby Liddle]

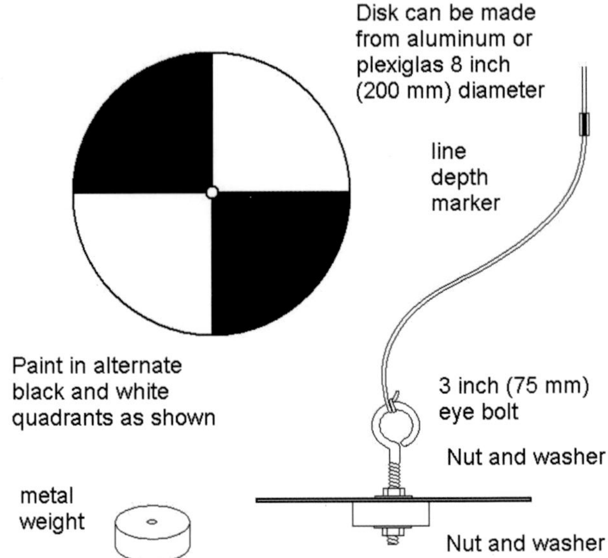

Figure 5.4 Constructing a Secchi disk.

- Submergent
- Emergent
- Floating leaf

The distribution of aquatic plants is determined by light availability, which is controlled by water clarity. This can be measured by a Secchi disk, which is lowered into the water to a depth where it cannot be seen. The greater the depth at which the Secchi disk remains visible, the clearer the water. As a guideline, the greatest depth for plant survival is twice the Secchi depth taken in midsummer. Examining soil composition in your selected site will allow you to determine how well aquatic vegetation will prosper. This can be achieved by digging a simple test pit with a backhoe and examining the soil profile. Aquatic plants are more likely to favor muddy or soft, sedimentary materials and are less likely to thrive in substrates of sand or gravel. Newly constructed ponds or lakes, particularly impounded ones (i.e., with dams), have soil compacted by heavy machinery, making it too hard for normal growth. Water chemistry also influences the selection of species. Aquatic plants vary in tolerance to pH; some prefer acidic environments, while others prefer alkaline conditions.

Selected Aquatic Plants for Ponds and Lakes

Planktonic Algae

Generally microscopic, these species are categorized by waterworks personnel in water-treatment plants as taste-and-odor algae, filter-clogging algae, etc. Because they require microscopic aid for identification, I am not covering their varieties here. Excellent manuals for microscopic identification purposes are published by waterworks associations.

Chara-type Algae (two species illustrated)

Muskgrass (*Chara sp.*)

Description

- Called muskgrass or skunkweed because of its foul, musty, garlic-like odor
- Often confused with submergent aquatic plants
- Has a "grainy" or "crunchy" texture
- Grows in cylindrical, whorled branches

Habitat

- Found in springs and alkaline ponds
- Grows well in hard water up to 10 ft. (3 m) deep if the water is clear

Wildlife benefit

- Spores and tubers eaten by diving ducks
- Presence retards mosquito-larvae development

Limitations

- Neutral-to-acidic or muddy waters unsuitable for chara
- Can be invasive if phosphate levels are high, spreading throughout the water column

Propagation

- By spores

Nitella, brittlewort (*Nitella gracilis*)

Description

- Bright-green algae often mistaken for aquatic plants
- Like chara, grows in whorls of forked branches at regularly spaced intervals along the stem
- Branches are not rough like chara but have a smooth texture
- Has microscopic spore-producing organs
- Lacks roots, but may attach to the pond bottom by holdfasts

Habitat

- Found in shallow to deep waters of soft-water or acid lakes and bogs
- Frequently forms a thick carpet or grows in clumps along the bottom
- Easily confused with chara, water-nymph, and coontail

Wildlife benefit

- Provides cover for fish
- Is food for fish and wildfowl
- Stabilizes sediment
- Removes nutrients directly from the water

Propagation

- Spreads by spores transported by wildlife and forms new plants from vegetative fragments

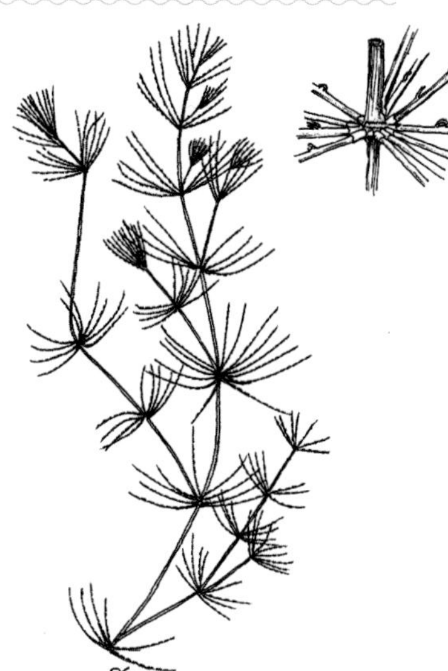

Figure 5.5 Muskgrass (Chara globularis)

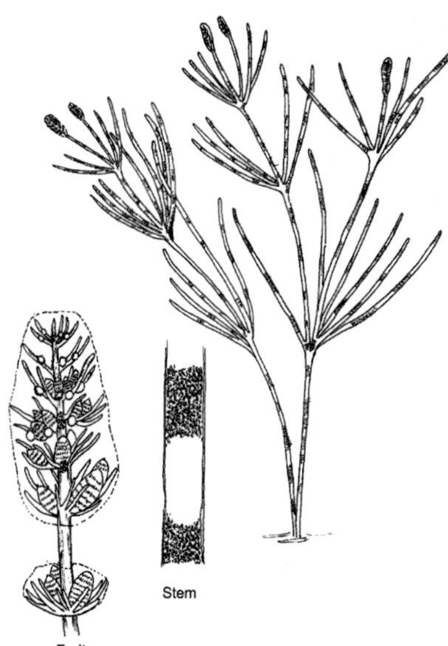

Figure 5.6 Nitella, brittlewort (Nitella gracilis)

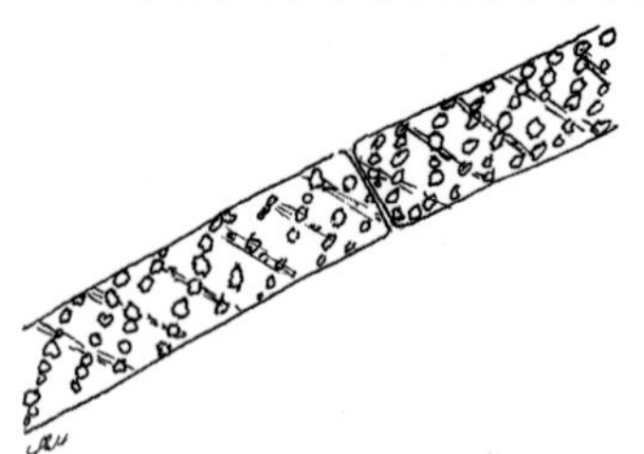

Figure 5.7 Spirogyra (Spyrogyra communis)

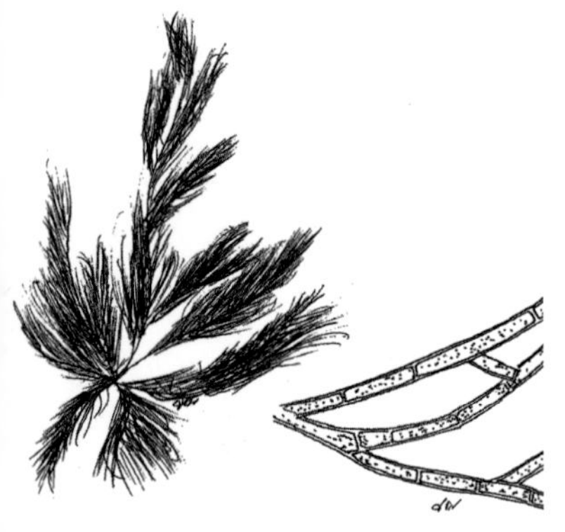

Figure 5.8 Cladophora (Cladophora crispata)

Filamentous algae

Spirogyra

Description

- Filamentous green algae named for helical or spiral arrangement of chloroplasts within its cell
- Unbranched, with its cylindrical cells connected end-to-end in long filaments
- Chloroplasts are embedded in the peripheral cytoplasm

Habitat

- Common in clean eutrophic water, developing slimy green masses
- Grows underwater in spring, but as sunlight and warmth increase, produces large amounts of oxygen that adhere as bubbles between the tangled filaments
- Filamentous strands come to the surface, where they are apparent as slimy green masses

Limitations

- Species can be a major influence causing minor alterations to benthic conditions
- Linked with increase in phosphate loading (like cladophora)

Propagation

- Fragmentation and mitosis form new filaments

Cladophora

Description

- Filamentous microscopic green algae with branching hair-like threads
- Does not undergo conjugation

Habitat

- Lives in pond and lake shoreline areas that are overfertilized
- Farm ponds not protected from fertilizer and silage drainage soon become clogged with cladophora
- Evident in most sewage outfalls and in water-quality ponds

Wildlife benefit

- Produces food and shelter for invertebrates and small fish

Limitations

- Produces a taste and odor problem in drinking water.
- Detached mats accumulate, fouling beaches and causing major alteration to benthic conditions—linked with increased phosphorus
- Will attach to zebra mussels, once they clarify the water

Propagation

- Fragmentation and mitosis

Submergent Aquatic Plants

Submergent plant species that grow underwater, with flowers and fruit that may rise above the surface.

Coontail (*Ceratophyllum demersum L.*)

Description

- Leaflets forked once or more
- Leaflets have toothed edges

- Has whorls of leaves at joints of stems
- Leaves are more densely crowded near tips of stems

Habitat

- Prefers alkaline or neutral ponds and sluggish rivers
- Spreads extensively and may crowd out other species
- Grows in shallow water
- Tolerates considerable shading
- Not successful in moving water
- Does not withstand draw-down operations in a pond or lake

Wildlife benefit

- Slightly attractive to ducks for food (seeds and leaves)

Limitations

- Can become a nuisance in smaller ponds with nutrient inflow

Propagation

- By seed and by growing tips which break off in the fall and drop to the pond or lake bottom

Water Nymph, Slender Naiad (*Najas flexilis*)

Description

- Completely submerged annual aquatic plant
- Has opposite leaves, finely toothed, often whorled and clustered near the tips of stems
- Leaves are up to 1.18 in. (3 cm) long and 0.08 in. (2 mm) wide, with broader bases clasping the stem
- Flowers are tiny and inconspicuous, hidden by leaf bases

Habitat

- Ponds, lakes and sluggish streams to depths of 12 ft. (4 m)
- Slender naiad tolerates brackish conditions

Wildlife benefit

- Entire plant is eaten by waterfowl: water nymph is considered to be one of their most important food sources
- Provides shelter for small fish and insects

Limitations

- None

Propagation

- Seeds, plants, and fragments
- Water-nymph pollen is transported by water currents
- Each oval fruit contains one seed about 0.12 in. (3 mm) long located in the leaf bases, and present in summer

Common Waterweed (*Elodea canadensis*)

Description

- Leaves are whorled with stiff segments
- Segments are crowded in the growing tips to give the appearance of a coontail
- No roots

Habitat

- Prefers alkaline or neutral ponds and sluggish rivers

Figure 5.9 Coontail (Ceratophyllum demersum)

Figure 5.10 Slender naiad, water nymph (Najas flexilis)

Figure 5.11 Common waterweed (Elodea canadensis)

Figure 5.12 Sago pondweed (Potamogeton pectinatus)

- Spreads extensively, crowding other species
- Grows in water up to 5 ft. (1.5 m) deep

Wildlife benefit

- Slight, as duck food
- Seeds and leaves occasionally eaten by ducks

Limitations

- Not successful in moving waters
- Drainage of pond or lake basin results in plant death, but new plants arise from seed the following year
- Can become a nuisance and is difficult to eradicate

Propagation

- By seed and growing tips which break off in the fall and rest on the bottom (growth resumes in spring)

Sago Pondweed (*Potamogeton pectinatus*)

Description

- Thread-like branching leaves
- Leaf tips have long tapering points
- Beaked seeds are borne on spikes
- Tubers grow on horizontal stems rising from base of stem

Habitat

- Grows well in neutral or alkaline lakes and slow sluggish streams or marshes
- Prefers rich, sandy bottoms in water up to 6 ft. (1.8 m) deep (varies with the turbidity of the water)

Wildlife benefit

- Most valuable duck food; both tubers and seeds are eaten
- Provides food and cover for fish

Limitations

- Plants will not grow in deep water if it is murky (turbid)

Propagation

- By rootstock and seed

Northern Water Milfoil (*Myriophyllum sibericum*)

Description

- Feather-like, olive-green leaves arranged in whorls of three to four
- Usually seven to ten leaflet pairs per leaf
- Stem is whitish-green in color
- Leaflet pairs at the base of the leaf are longer than those at the tip, giving the leaf a "Christmas-tree" shape
- Easily confused with Eurasian milfoil
- Has fewer and more widely spread leaflets than Eurasian milfoil
- Fruit nut-like, about 0.18 in. (3 mm) in diameter, separating into four chambers; one seed per chamber

Habitat

- Lakes, ponds, and rivers
- Tolerant of nutrient-rich, alkaline, and brackish waters

Wildlife benefit

- Provides cover for fish and invertebrates
- Supports insects and other small animals
- Waterfowl occasionally eat the fruit and foliage

Limitations

- Difficult to distinguish from the Eurasian milfoil, which is invasive

Propagation

- By seed from fruit

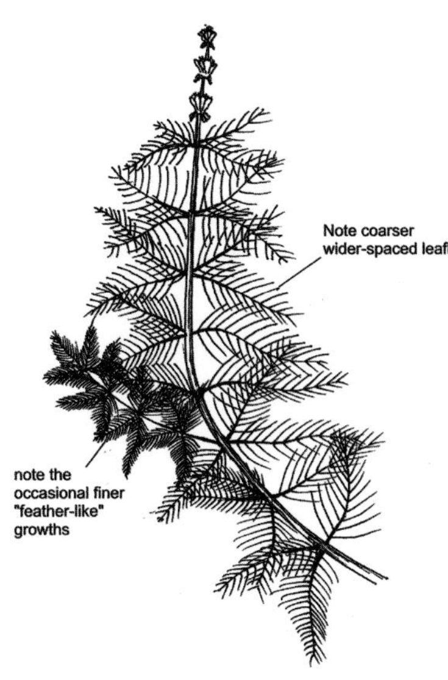

Figure 5.13 Northern water milfoil (Myriophyllum sibiricum)

Bladderwort (*Utricularia vulgaris*)

Description

- No true leaves; species have highly branched, finely divided, underwater leaf-like stems with small seed-like bladders
- Bladders are underwater traps which capture small invertebrates or tiny fish that trigger the trap door
- Appears dense and bushy underwater
- Sometimes anchored at base by root-like structures
- Flower is yellow, snapdragon-like and occurs above water on stout stalks with a spur projecting below the lip of the flower
- Flowers often have purple-brown stripes

Habitat

- Floats freely in shallow water or loosely attached to bottom sediment
- Stem is up to 6.5 ft. (2 m) long and can be afloat, submersed, or partly creeping on pond bottom

Wildlife benefits

- Provides food and cover for fish and food for muskrats and waterfowl
- Habitat for aquatic invertebrates

Limitations

- Some species (particularly swollen badderwort) can become invasive

Propagation

- By fragments and seeds; the common (vulgaris) can form bright-green winter buds up to 2 in. (5 cm) in diameter

Figure 5.14 Common bladderwort (Utricularia vulgaris)

Eel Grass, Tape Grass, Wild Celery (*Vallisneria americana*)

Description

- Submersed plant that forms tall underwater meadows
- Blooms all year and occurs almost always in wetlands
- One-inch (25 mm) wide leaves arise in clusters from the roots and can be several feet long
- Leaves have rounded tips and definite raised veins
- Single white female flowers grow to the water surface on very long stalks

Habitat

- Prefers clear waters of shallow lakes and sluggish streams
- Prefers a muddy bottom but will grow on sandy bottoms

Wildlife benefit

- Consumed by various animals, including the canvasback duck

Eel grass growing in a shallow-water pond margin.

Figure 5.15 Eel grass, tape grass, wild celery (Vallisneria americana)

- Animals can eat the entire plant, both leaves and tubers
- Aquatic life is abundant around this species

Limitations

- Severe wave action can damage slender stems and beds in general
- Ripping action of outboard motors pulls up leaves and leafstalks

Propagation

- By rootstock, seed, and tubers

Emergent Aquatic Plants

Plants that grow in or near water, with a major segment of the plant above water.

Pickerel Weed (*Pontederia cordata*)

Description

- Thick, shiny, broadly triangular leaves rise from the crown of the rootstalk
- Fruit contains one seed in a watery fluid
- Very ornamental, with blue flowers on a spike

Habitat

- Inhabits small shallow ponds, margins of streams and rivers
- Thrives in fresh or brackish water
- Tolerates mild pollution
- Prefers mucks to clays

Wildlife benefit

- Slight use as duck food
- Good habitat for pond and animal life

Limitations

- Severe wave action limits rooting of plant (by rhizomes)
- Transpires large quantities of water (undesirable for dug-out ponds which draw down by evapotranspiration)

Propagation

- By rhizomes and, in a lesser way, by seed

Cattail (*Typha latifolia*)

Description

- Perennial plant with the familiar brown cylindrical seedhead at top of stem
- Leaves are long, stiff, and upright

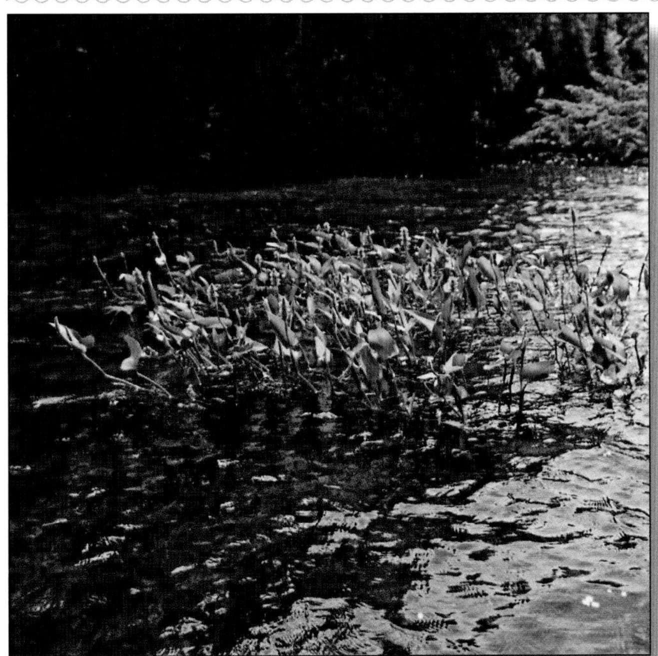

A pickerel weed cluster in Lake of Two Rivers, Algonquin Park, Ontario.

Habitat

- Grows on stream and lake margins, in pockets in fields and marshes
- Usually the most dominant plant on site
- Extremely aggressive, allowing little or no competition
- Must be controlled to stop widespread occupation of lakes and ponds, although a certain amount is very beneficial

Wildlife benefit

- Roots are winter food for muskrats and material for muskrat houses
- Plants offer excellent cover for nesting waterfowl
- Very little value as duck food

Limitations

- Prolonged flooding will kill the plants
- Successive mowing over a year will kill a stand
- Burning a stand will not eradicate it as roots are extensive and underground

Propagation

- By creeping rootstock and wind-borne seed from cylindrical seedheads

Common Spike Rush (*Eleocharis palustris*)

Description

- In general, small to medium-size perennial plants often confused with species of grasses, small rushes, or sedges
- Stems are unbranched, and have small fruiting spikes at the tips of the stem
- Rhizomes are long
- Soft, internally spongy leaves, often splitting

Habitat

- Can grow in shallow water or moist soils, densely vegetated marshes and even meadows

Wildlife benefit

- Submerged portions provide habitat for many micro and macro invertebrates, which in turn are used as food by fish and other wildlife species (amphibians, reptiles, ducks, etc.)
- After the plants die, their decomposition by bacteria and fungi provides food for many aquatic invertebrates

Figure 5.16 Pickerel weed (Pontederia cordata)

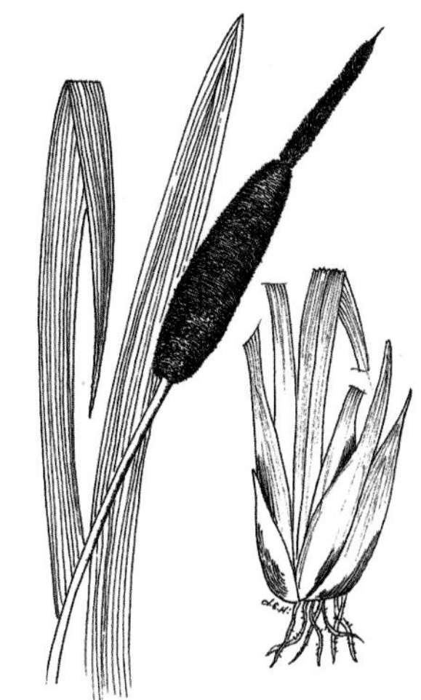

Figure 5.17 Cattail (Typhus latifolia)

Cattail around the margin of a pond.

- Ducks, geese, and muskrats all eat portions of spike rushes, from seeds to rhizomes and tubers

Limitations

- Very difficult to identify without detailed botanical keys

Propagation

- By seed from fruiting spikes

Figure 5.18 Common spike rush (Eleocharis palustris)

Hard-stem Bulrush (*Scirpus acutus*. Currently accepted species name is *Schoenoplectus acutus*)

Description

- Perennial heavily rhizomatous wetland plant
- Leaves are few and short, found at or near the base, commonly with a well-developed sheath
- Terminal panicle is made up of fifty or more spikelets, which may be on a short pedicel, or be sessile
- Fruits are less than 0.33 in. (2.5 mm) long, dark brown lenticular achenes

Habitat

- Found in marshes and along lake, reservoir, and pond shorelines
- Found in areas of standing water from 4 in. (100 mm) to 10 ft. (3 m)
- Grows on saline, alkaline and brackish sites
- Will grow more than 1.5 ft. (45 cm) in one growing season
- Grows on soils ranging from peat to alkaline and silts to sands
- Resistant to wave action and water-level alteration
- Develops thick beds, offering a nurse crop for a succession of other plants, ultimately forming a marsh

Wildlife benefit

- Excellent seed source for waterfowl
- Good cover for nesting and for young ducks
- Rootstalks and young shoots eaten by muskrat and beaver
- Muskrats use stems for house-building

Limitations

- Plants are slow to spread
- Fluctuating water level will speed spread

Propagation

- By rootstock mainly and some by seed

Figure 5.19 Hardstem bulrush (Scirpus acutus, Schoenoplectus acutus)

Hard-stem bulrush growing in the margins of a kettle lake [Photo courtesy of Forks of the Credit Provincial Park, Ontario].

Arrowhead, Duck Potato (*Sagittaria latifolia*)

Description

- Produces thin white tubers covered with a purplish skin
- Produces a rosette of leaves and an inflorescence on a long rigid stalk
- Inflorescence is composed of large flowers whorled in threes
- Three round white petals with three very short curved dark-green sepals make up each flower
- Leaves are wedge-shaped, very thin, like those of *Sagittaria cuneata*
- Spongy, yet solid, leaves have parallel veins meeting at middle and extremities

Habitat

- Perennial plant, grows in colonies covering large areas
- Often forms long bands following curves of rivers, ponds, and lakes
- Strong roots enable survival through variations in water level, slow currents and waves

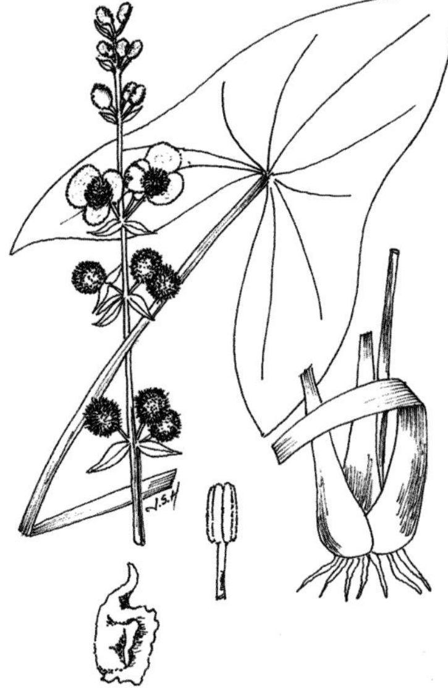

Figure 5.20 Duck potato, arrowhead (Sagittaria latifolia)

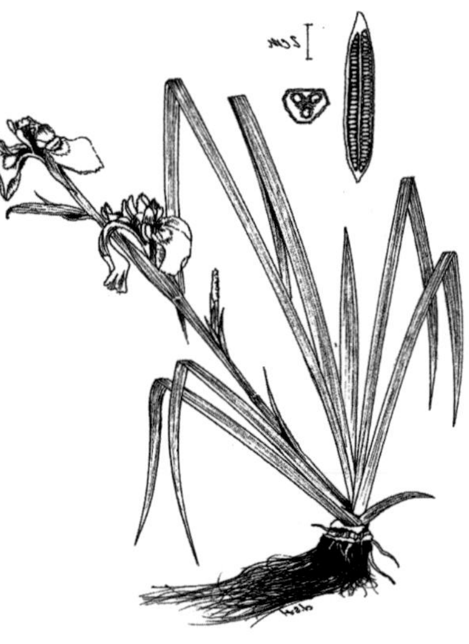

Figure 5.21 Yellow flag (Iris pseudacorus)

Figure 5.22 Wild iris, blue flag (Iris versicolor)

- Has an affinity for hard water and high phosphate levels

Wildlife benefit

- Despite its name, duck potato, ducks rarely consume the tubers, which are too deep to be accessible, but do favor the seeds.
- Beavers, porcupines, and muskrats eat the whole plant including tubers

Limitations

- Forms dense colonies on very wet soils
- Considered invasive in Australia
- Vulnerable to aphid and spider mite attacks

Propagation

- By water-borne seeds and tubers

Yellow Flag, Fleur de Lis (*Iris pseudacorus*)

Description

- Also called yellow iris
- Perennial plant grows up to 5 ft. (1.5 m)
- Fruit is a capsule containing numerous brown seeds

Habitat

- Grows best in very wet locations
- Common in wetlands
- Tolerates low pH and anoxic soils
- Spreads quickly

Wildlife benefit

- Takes up heavy metals through its roots (water treatment ability)
- Creates feeding and breeding habitat

Limitations

- Spreads fast like cattail and grows under the same conditions
- Can create dense stands that outgrow and crowd out other plants
- Tough to remove and eradicate on a large scale (even plowing rhizomes under is ineffective)
- Has invasive potential

Propagation

- Spreads by both rhizomes and water-dispersed seed

Wild Iris, Blue Flag (*Iris versicolor*)

Description

- Perennial plant, grows from fleshy, stout subsurface rootstocks
- Leaves are erect, flat, and sword-like
- Flowers are large, conspicuous, bright blue with yellow markings

Habitat

- Wet meadows and shores of rivers and lakes
- Grows generally in clumps or single plants
- Requires direct sunlight when in the wild

Wildlife benefit

- Provides cover when growing in clumps
- Adds to appearance of ponds, marshes, and stream banks
- No evidence that seeds are eaten by wildlife

Limitations

- Spreads outwardly through rhizomes, producing a perimeter of plants around a barren center

Yellow flag encircling a pond.

- Thick stands are not possible without replanting the centers

Propagation

- By rootstock only

Horsetail (*Equisetum*)

Description

- A "living fossil," the only known genus of the entire class Equisetopsida which dominated the understory of late Paleozoic forests for 100 million years
- Resembles a horse's tail
- Stem is coated with abrasive silicates (silicon crystals) and has a gritty texture
- Perennial

Habitat

- Prefers wet sandy soils, though some are semi-aquatic and others are adapted to wet clay soils
- Stalks arise from rhizomes deep underground—almost impossible to dig out

Wildlife Benefit

- Submerged portions provide habitat for many micro and macro invertebrates, which are in turn used by fish and other wildlife species
- Has no direct benefit to animals

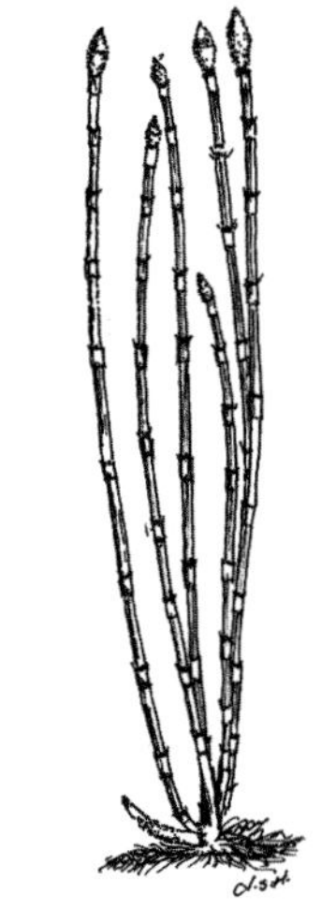

Figure 5.23 Horsetail (Equisetum *Sp.*)

Figure 5.24 Three-square rush, chairmaker's rush (Scirpus americanus)

Limitations

- Can be invasive, often lining the entire perimeter of a newly excavated pond
- Many species are unaffected by herbicides, although lime can be used to eradicate the plant, bringing the soil back to pH of 7.0 or 8.0
- Can be poisonous to grazing animals

Propagation

- By cone-shaped spore

Three-Square Rush, Chairmaker's Rush (*Scirpus americanus*)

Description

- A perennial with triangular stem and stiff sparse leaves at the base of the plant
- Single erect bract rises from the base of the flower spikelet

Habitat

- Shallow-water areas (up to one foot or 30 cm deep) of sandy lakes, wet sand bars and stream banks
- Requires sandy soil or light gravel (mucky marsh flats are not suitable)

Wildlife benefit

- Nutlets are eaten by waterfowl
- Muskrats will eat the stem and stalks
- Plants can form heavy stands of cover—habitat for ducks and small animals

Limitations

- Survival after transplanting is poor
- Requires special habitat conditions
- Has limited value as duck food

Propagation

- By rootstock
- Seed may be germinated in a box of sand

Arrow Arum (*Peltandra virginica*)

Description

- A perennial with large, light-green, arrow-shaped leaves
- About 10 in. (25 cm) wide and up to 30 in. (75 cm) long
- Leaves on thick stalks rising from mass of fibrous roots
- Seed envelope is often submerged

Habitat

- Inhabits lake and stream margins in shallow water
- Prefers muddy, silty soils

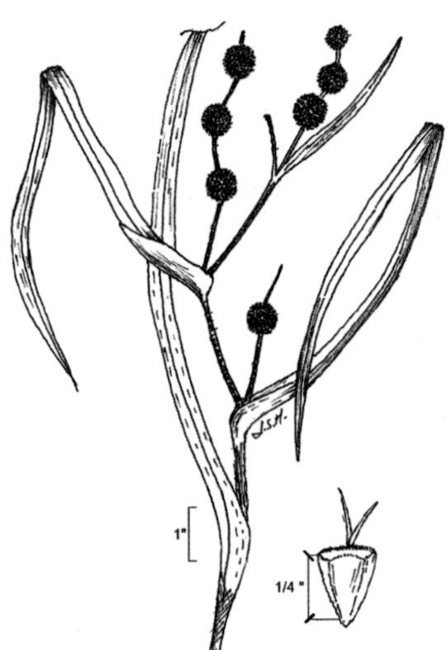

Figure 5.26 Giant burreed (Sparganium eurycarpum)

Figure 5.25 Arrow arum (Peltandra virginica)

- Grows well on stream deposits and flood plains

Wildlife benefit

- Harbors pond animal life and is important as duck food
- Seeds are generally too hard for food

Limitations

- Poor reproductive ability

Propagation

- Seeds are not distributed widely; reproduction largely by spreading roots

Giant Burreed (*Sparganium eurycarpum*)

Description

- A perennial that grows to about 5 ft. (1.5 m) in height
- Seedheads are globular burs with nut-like seeds
- Leaves are long, ribbon-like, and broadly triangular in cross-section

Habitat

- Shallow margins of lakes and ponds
- Prefers slightly alkaline water and soil

Wildlife benefit

- Nut-like seeds and tubers are eaten by ducks
- Leaves and seed are used by muskrats
- Leafy growth is used as cover by nesting birds and muskrats
- Its spreading root habit is a good buffer against wave action
- Very rigorous on river flats which are subject to flooding

Water shield in Lake of Two Rivers, Algonquin Park, Ontario.

Limitations

- Seldom forms thick beds due to marginal growth
- Competes with cattail (remove cattail for better success)

Propagation

- By seed and rootstock

Water Shield, Dollar Bonnet (*Brasenia schreberi*)

Description

- A perennial plant with small floating leaves, oval to elliptical
- Distinctive gelatinous slime on underside of leaves and coating stems
- Leaves green above with reddish-purple underside

Figure 5.27 Water shield (Brasenia schreberi)

- Stems attach at center of leaves
- Small flowers up to 0.74 in. (12 mm) rise above the surface and are dull red in color

Habitat

- Found in soft, acidic waters
- Forms large colonies

Wildlife value

- Submerged portions provide habitats for many micro and macro invertebrates
- Seeds are consumed by ducks and other waterfowl
- Roots and stems are eaten by muskrats
- Its gelatinous slime has anti-algal and anti-bacterial properties—used in homeopathic medicine

Propagation

- Developing flowers release pollen
- Plant exhibits wind pollination
- Spreads rapidly and is difficult to control

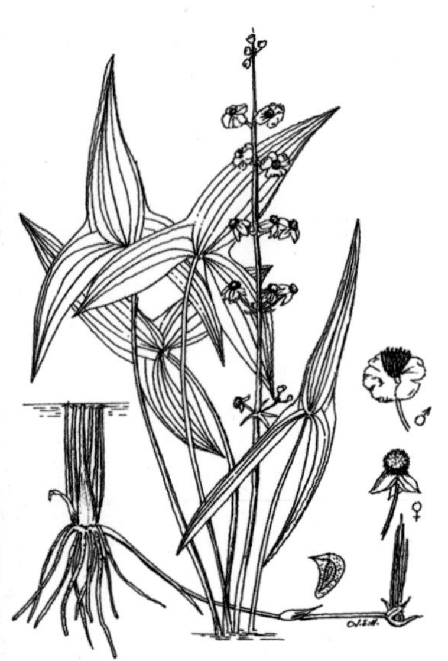

Figure 5.28 Northern arrowhead, wapato (Sagittaria cuneata)

Northern Arrowhead, Wapato (*Sagittaria cuneata*)

Description

- Confused with *Sagittaria latifolia* but has cuneate or wedge-shaped leaves
- Leaves shaped like an arrowhead
- Indian tribes used arrowhead for food in winter

Habitat

- Found chiefly in freshwater streams and swamps, marshes, ponds, and lakes
- Prefers shallow water, such as that at the mouth of small streams

Wildlife benefit

- Tuber floats to surface when ripe and is eaten by ducks
- Muskrats will eat the leaves, retarding plant growth

Limitations

- Spreads rapidly
- Wave action can damage roots
- Prolonged flooding within a few years duration will kill it

Propagation

- By tubers and seed

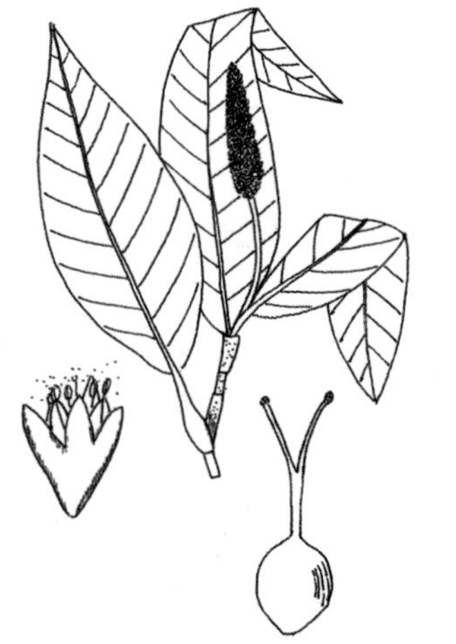

Figure 5.29 Marsh smartweed (Polygonum coccineum)

Marsh Smartweed (*Polygonum coccineum*)

Description

- Perennial, grows up to 3 ft. (1 m) high
- Exhibits two forms: terrestrial and aquatic
- Stems are unbranched and thicken to form nodes at leaf joints
- May exhibit a red-striped stem
- Leaves are alternate, oblong, tapering at both ends but pointed at tip, and show a smooth margin
- Leaves can be up to 6 ft. (2 m) long on swamp species
- Plant exhibits tall, slender, and erect flower clusters
- Spike-like flower clusters may be red, pink, or white in color

Habitat

- Prefers water up to 4 ft. (1.2 m) deep and muck soils of decaying plant material
- Slightly alkaline water is preferred
- Seed production requires cover of water during growing season

Wildlife benefit

- Seeds are important duck food
- Good habitat around roots for fish and waterfowl

Limitations

- Requires special soil element combination to maintain seed production
- Leaves eaten by larvae of cucumber beetle

Propagation

- Mainly by root division, some seed propagation

Yellow water-lily growing in a wetland near Cedar Key, Florida [Photo by Dorothy Saffarawich].

Floating Aquatic Plants

Plants with leaves that float on the surface. They may or may not root in the pond bottom.

Yellow Water-Lily, Cow Lily, Spatterdock (*Nuphar advena*)

Description

- Perennial plant grows in eutrophic freshwater beds, roots fixed into pond or lake bottom
- Scaly rhizomes grow up to 16 ft. (5 m) long
- Thick round stems up to 6.5 ft. (2 m) long support the floating leaves and flowers
- Rubbery leaves resemble arrowheads or hearts up to 18 in. (45 cm) long
- Large, glossy, wax-like, yellow—sometimes tinged with red or green—flower has eight to seventeen yellow sepals arranged in a cup shape with ten to twenty smaller yellow or green petals obscured by the stamens
- Flower has a distinctive knob-like stigma
- Ribbed fruit is an egg-shaped capsule with many seeds
- Seeds are released in a watery glob when fruit splits

Habitat

- Found in shallow lakes, ponds, and slow streams
- Rhizomes are buried deep in the pond bottom
- In fall, leaves and flowers turn brown quickly and die; rhizome lives on in the pond or lake bottom

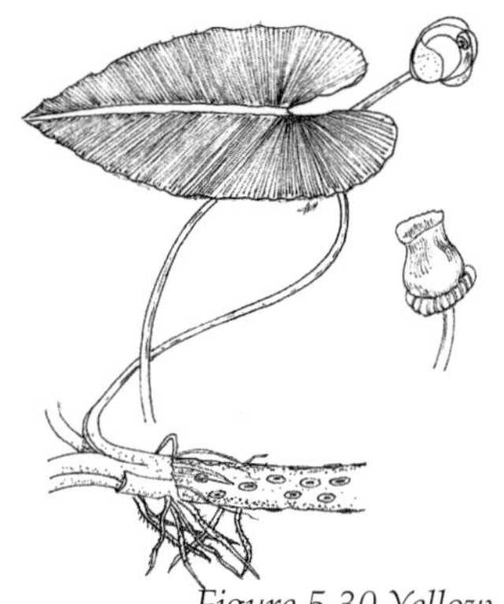

Figure 5.30 Yellow water-lily, spatterdock (Nuphar advena)

Floating leaf pondweed in a gentle flowing stream [Ragged Falls, Oxtongue River Provincial Park, northern edge of Haliburton County, Ontario].

Figure 5.31 Floating leaf pondweed (Potamogeton natans)

- When water levels drop leaves are above water, but when they rise again the leaves float on the water
- Edible roots and seeds can be popped like popcorn, but can be bitter

Wildlife benefit

- Beavers and common muskrats eat the rhizomes, and beavers also eat the leaves
- Waterfowl such as wood ducks, mallards, and Canada geese eat the seeds
- Frogs, salamanders, and aquatic insects attach egg masses to the leaves and stems
- Lily pads provide resting places for terrestrial insects such as dragonflies and bees
- Fish (largemouth bass, black crappie) use the lily pads for shelter as do painted turtles, snapping turtles and many others

Limitations

- Rhizomes can multiply quickly forming new rhizomes
- Yellow pond lilies can grow quickly to form huge colonies

Propagation

- By seeds and rhizomes

Floating Leaf Pondweed (*Potamogeton natans*)

Description

- Perennial plant with two types of leaves—floating leaves are oval and heart-shaped at the base, submerged leaves are ribbon-like and about fifty times as long as they are broad
- Flowers and seed are borne on spikes which rise out of the water

Habitat

- Ponds, marshes, and slow-moving streams
- Grows in water up to 5 ft. (1.5 m) deep
- Will continue to grow after pond draw-down
- Thrives on moderately firm, rich soils

Wildlife benefit

- Seeds and roots are a source of food for ducks
- Aquatic animals abound in the mats of floating leaves

Limitations

- Thick mats of floating leaves stop competition by

other submerged plants

- Plants require shelter from violent wave action

Propagation

- By seed and rootstock

Duckweed (*Lemna minor*)

Description

- A true floating plant
- Does not root, but gathers nutrients through "roots" beneath its fronds

Habitat

- Floats on the surface of ponds, marshes, and slow-moving rivers
- Creates rafts or mats of plants by late summer, usually from phosphate-enriched waters
- Thick mats prohibit growth of other submerged plants by obstructing sunlight

Wildlife benefit

- Good duck food
- Not recommended for farm ponds and small bodies of water due to rapid growth and potential for clogging the water surface

Limitations

- Not successful in open reaches of water where wind and wave can beach the plants
- Thick mats clog waterways, eventually decompose on bottom and contribute to an oxygen deficiency

Propagation

- By vegetative division

Duckweed forming a thick carpet on the Maskinonge River [Keswick, Town of Georgina, Ontario].

Water Smartweed (*Polygonum amphibium*)

Description

- A creeping perennial with elliptical or oval glossy leaves
- Dark-pink flowers and seeds are borne on short spikes
- Large sheaths at leaf bases hide most of the stem

Habitat

- In shallow water or soft mud at the edge of ponds
- Tolerant to changes in water level
- Is not subject to wave-action damage

Figure 5.32 Duckweed (Lemna minor)

Figure 5.33 *Water smartweed* (Polygonum amphibium)

- Found mostly in alkaline or mildly acidic pools, streams, and marshes

Wildlife benefit

- Seeds are eaten by waterfowl
- Small aquatic life collects under the leaves and around stems

Limitations

- Cucumber beetle lays eggs on the plant, and larvae chew leaves severely

Propagation

- Principally by root cuttings
- Seeds can be held over winter but must not dry over five months

White Water-Lily (*Nymphaea odorata*)

Description

- A perennial with round floating leaves (pads) and cream-white flowers

Habitat

- Shallow water of ponds, lakes and marshes
- Will grow in clear water up to 10 ft. (3 m) deep
- Established mat of water lilies allows no competition from other emergent aquatic plants except cattail and burreed
- Tolerant to wave action and change in water level

Wildlife benefit

- Seed is used slightly as duck food
- Floating leaves provide good fish habitat
- Floating leaves maintain cooler pond water underneath

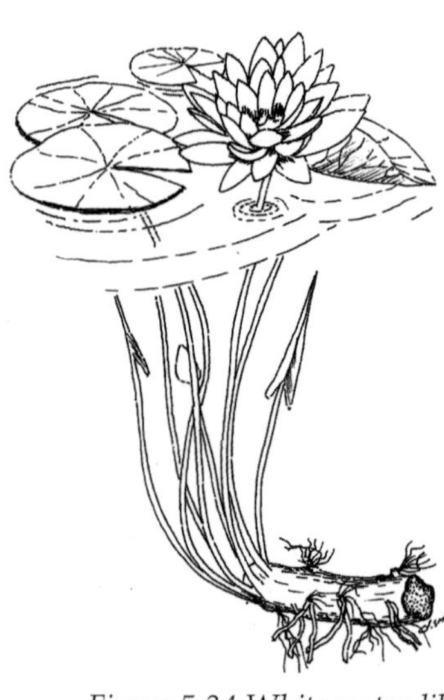

Figure 5.34 *White water-lily* (Nymphaea odorata)

Limitations

- Very hardy and competitive once established
- Difficult to eradicate

Propagation

- By extensive root systems and seed

Watermeal (*Wolffia* spp.)

Description

- A tiny, light-green, free-floating rootless plant less than 0.06 in. (1 mm) in diameter
- Smallest seed-bearing plant in the world

Habitat

- Tends to grow in dense colonies in quiet water, undisturbed by wave action
- Often associated with colonies of duckweed

Wildlife benefit

- Not known as important food for ducks but many will consume it and transport it to other water bodies

Limitations

- Very invasive plant, as dense colonies of watermeal can cover the surface of a pond or lake and cause oxygen depletion and fish kills
- Colonies, or rafts, will also block sunlight penetration to other aquatic plants
- Removed by raking or seining
- Small leaf is difficult to remove

Propagation

- An aggressive invader of ponds or lakes

White water-lily along a northern lake margin [Oxtongue Lake, Haliburton, Ontario].

Invasive Plant Species

Becoming aware of species that are invasive in a pond or lake and preventing their spread saves expensive and difficult removal efforts. Never introduce aquarium species into ponds, lakes, rivers or streams. When you are planting aquatic environments or even backshore areas, be certain the plants you use do not include exotic invasive species.

Purple Loosestrife (*Lythrum salicaria*)

Purple loosestrife was originally sold as a garden plant, but escaped and naturalized to marsh and wetland habitats. Its bright purple flowers spread out over large areas, producing a copious amount of seed. It quickly competes with native vegetation, overrunning it, clogging ditches, and destroying fish-migrating and -spawning routes. It can rapidly degrade wetlands and diminish their value for wildlife and fish habitat. More than 190,000 hectares of wetlands, marshes, and riparian meadows have been affected in North America. Loosestrife can also invade drier sites and encroach on agricultural crop and pasture land. Recently, biological control has

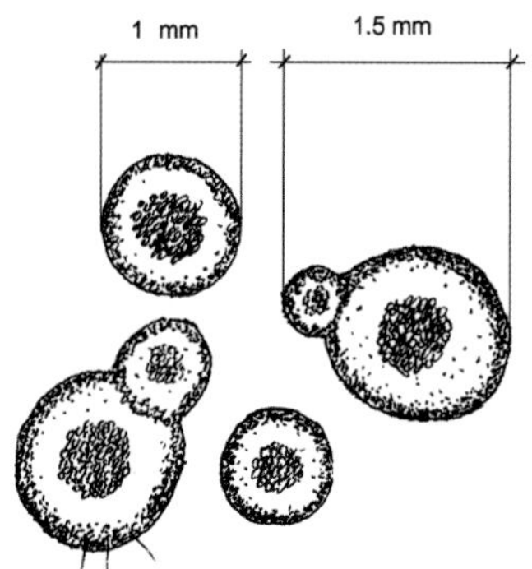

Figure 5.35 Watermeal (Wolffia *spp.*)

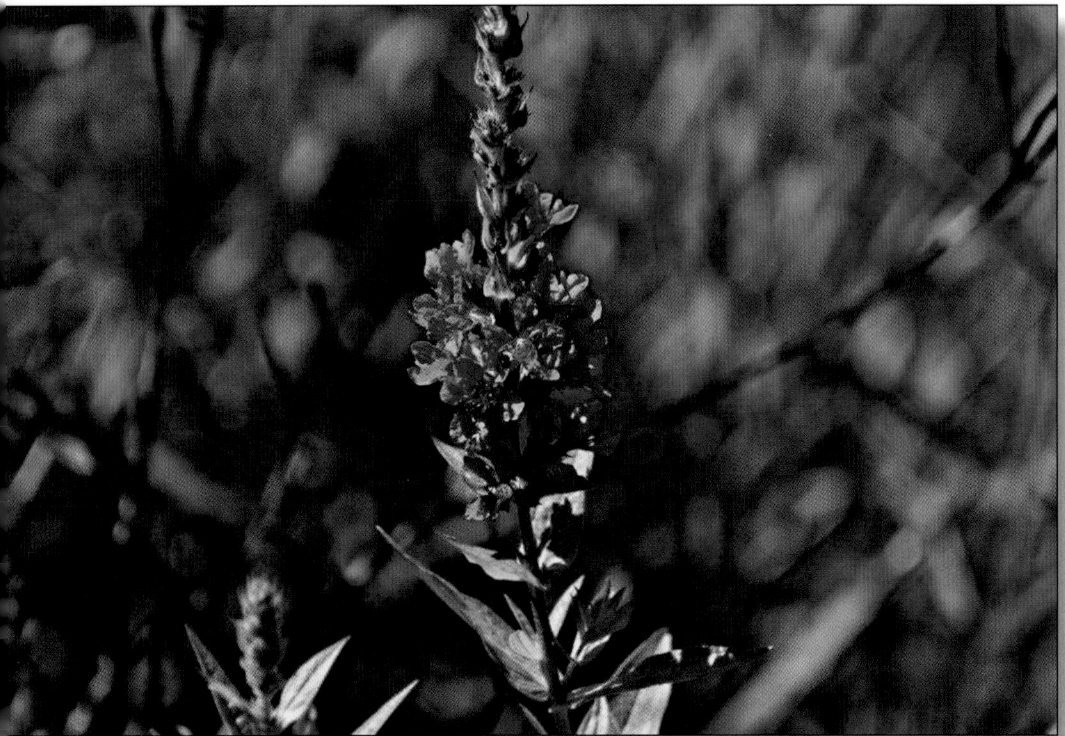

*Purple loosestrife (*Lythrum salicaria*) in flower [Photo by Ivan Foster, Pefferlaw, Ontario].*

SEVERAL OF THE MOST INVASIVE SPECIES

EMERGENT SPECIES

Purple loosestrife (*Lythrum salicaria*)
Flowering rush (*Butomus umbellatus*)
European Frog-bit (*Hydrocharis morsus-ranae*)
Yellow Floating Heart (*Nymphoides peltata*)

SUBMERGED SPECIES

Eurasian watermilfoil (*Myriophyllum spicatum*)
Curlyleaf pondweed (*Potamogeton crispus*)

involved utilizing the leaf-eating Galerucella beetle. It is now unlawful to sell the plant.

Exotic Flowering Rush (*Butomus umbellatus*)

Figure 5.36 Exotic flowering rush (Butomus umbellatus)

Exotic flowering rush grows as both a submersed species on the margins of lakes and ponds, and in low-moving water down to a depth of 10 ft. (3 m); it is an emergent plant of shoreline areas. Leaves are pointed, long, and triangular in cross-section, not toothed, but parallel-veined and twisted. Flowers occur in an umbel-like inflorescence from July until September. *Butomus umbellatus* is not a true rush but a perennial plant with rhizomes. Considered a serious invasive

Exotic flowering rush [Courtesy of Smithsonian Institute]

plant in the Great Lakes area of North America, it is deemed endangered in Israel due to diminishing habitat. It is difficult to control and spreads through open or lightly vegetated areas by seed and rhizome production. It is considered aggressive and capable of displacing native wetland plants.

Eurasian Watermilfoil (*Myriophyllum spicatum*)

Easily confused with native northern watermilfoil, Eurasian watermilfoil is a rooted plant with submersed leaves. It grows very fast, forming continuous mats on the water's surface and blocking light from reaching other submersed species. Eurasian watermilfoil can quickly cover the littoral areas of a lake or pond, and can restrict boating, swimming, and even fishing. Distinguishing characteristics between the native and the Eurasian species are the pairs of leaflets in each leaf and the plant's overall rigidity. The native northern variety has five to ten leaflet pairs, while the exotic Eurasian has twelve to twenty-one pairs. The Eurasian watermilfoil has delicate feather-like leaves arranged in whorls of three to five around the stems, which are up to 10 ft. (3 m) long and spaghetti-like. Leaves are usually limp when out of the water while those of the northern watermilfoil are considerably more rigid. Eurasian watermilfoil can grow from broken-off stems, thus increasing the rate at which the plant can spread. Flowers are produced in spikes up to 0.5 in. (12 cm) long at the leaf axils. Each tiny individual flower is inconspicuous and orange-red.

Exotic Curlyleaf Pondweed (*Potamogeton crispus*)

Well established for at least a century in North America, this is the first aquatic plant to appear in spring, its stems emerging from the water surface and flowering in June. It forms mats, which decompose and become a physical and visual nuisance in summer. The plant produces vegetative propagules which—like seeds—lie in pond or lake sediment. Curlyleaf pondweed is difficult to control or eradicate once established. It is often confused with Richardson's pondweed (*Potamogeton richardsonii*), which is not considered invasive.

Figure 5.37 Eurasian watermilfoil (Myriophyllum spicatum)

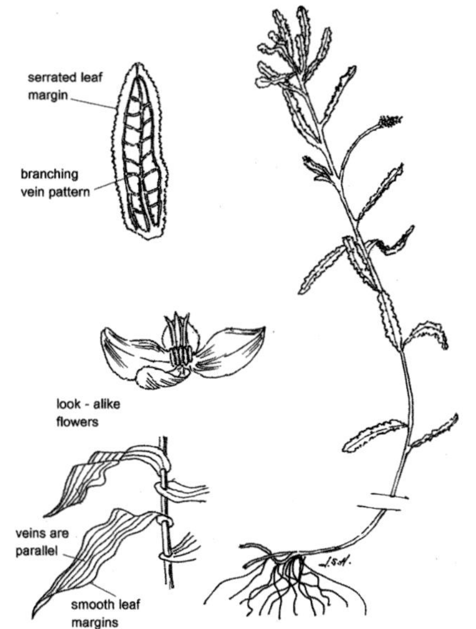

Figure 5.39 This diagram of exotic curlyleaf pondweed shows the difference between curlyleaf and Richardson's pondweed.

Figure 5.38 For comparison, Northern watermilfoil (Myriophyllum sibiricum)

Figure 5.40 European frog-bit (Hydrocharis morsus-ranae)

European Frog-Bit (*Hydrocharis morsus-ranae*)

A free-floating aquatic plant of open-water marshes and standing-water pools of swamps, the European frog-bit looks like a miniature water lily. It forms thick mats that inhibit light penetration and hinder the movement of fish, waterfowl, and boats. It tangles with its own colony and amongst other vegetation to form a dense, stabilized mass. Leaves of the plant are thick and heart-shaped, 1–2 in. (25–60 mm) wide, with smooth edging and spongy purplish undersides. The flowers are small and showy, with three white petals and yellow centers. Plants rejuvenate each spring, forming turions, or vegetative buds, which float to the surface, producing new plants in new locations.

Figure 5.41 Yellow floating heart (Nymphoides peltata)

Yellow Floating Heart (*Nymphoides peltata*)

A perennial water-lily-like plant that carpets the water with long-stalked heart-shaped leaves. Showy five-petaled yellow flowers occur on long stalks that rise above the water. Yellow floating heart, a native of Eurasia, was sold as an ornamental in nurseries and, of course, eventually escaped. It grows in dense patches, crowding out native species, and creating stagnant areas with low oxygen levels under the floating mats. The plants' masses make some difficulty for canoe-paddling, swimming, water-skiing, fishing, etc. The plant prefers slow-moving rivers, lakes, reservoirs, and ponds. It reproduces by water-dispersed seeds and by new stolons. Leaves broken off with part of the stem attached will also form a new plant. Yellow floating heart is widespread in eastern Washington, USA, along the Spokane River and elsewhere. Other similar-looking plants are spatterdock (yellow pond or cow-lily), which has yellow, ball-shaped flowers and large elephant-ear–shaped leaves, and watershield, which has small, floating leaves whose undersides are coated in a gelatinous slime. In addition, watershield has inconspicuous purple flowers.

Confirm the following characteristics for identification:

- Two to five bright yellow flowers on each stalk approximately one inch (25 mm) in diameter with a distinct fringe along the petal edges
- Petals arranged like spokes of a wheel
- Heart-shaped floating leaves with wavy margins and purplish undersides

CHAPTER SIX

POND DESIGN AND CONSTRUCTION

Depth, Shape, Surface Area, and Size Considerations

Your pond should have a minimum depth to meet proposed use requirements, and also to offset normal seepage and evaporation losses. Such losses vary across the continent amidst different climatic zones and soil types, as well as from year to year. Eastern Canada and the United States require a recommended minimum depth of 6–7 ft. (1.8–2.1 m). This holds true all the way south to the panhandle of Florida and west beyond the Mississippi Valley. In the Midwestern states and the Prairie Provinces, this requirement increases to 8–10 ft. (2.4–3 m), up to 14 ft. (4.3 m) in the arid western states. Deeper ponds are required where a year-round water supply is needed or where seepage losses exceed 3 in. (75 mm) per month. Fish ponds should have a depth of at least 12–15 ft. (3.7–4.6 m), at least in one part of the pond, to assure survival of the fish over winter, and to maintain a colder area in summer, particularly for trout species. Deep ponds over 15 ft. (4.6 m) may also be suitable for fish if a bottom draw-off spillway device allows de-oxygenated bottom water to be removed. Wildlife ponds need only be 4–5 ft. (1.2–1.5 m) deep with low, sloping banks to encourage vegetation and weed growth. Oxygenation in these ponds is not of great concern.

Building a pond is a major undertaking. Be aware that multi-purpose ponds rarely fulfill all their intended uses. Use often determines depth, bed and bank profiles, and what aquatic plant species should be planted. In the case of wildlife ponds, the bed or bottom of the pond or lake will provide a variety of microhabitats depending on the degree of irregular topography (flat bottoms producing little or no variety). Bank profile also determines rate of coloni-

An industrial backhoe begins construction of a dug-out type pond. Backhoes perform well on dry sites. However, in wet or mucky soils and peat, a dragline is more useful as it allows water to drain out of the bucket as it raises and swings a load.

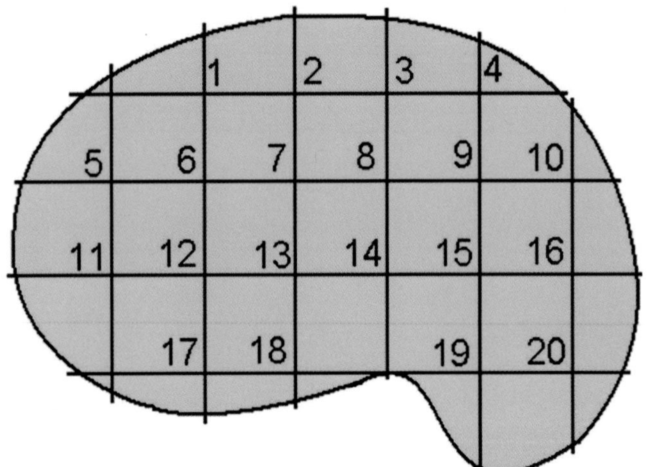

Figure 6.1 Pond depth from sounding along transects.

zation for the aquatic plants chosen. The nature of the edge (shape of the pond) is important for breeding water birds. A highly indented shoreline produces more nesting opportunities than a smooth, round shoreline. Likewise, fish ponds should have some indentations, even peninsulas, for fishing stations, while providing fish-nesting habitat.

Kidney-shaped ponds are normally the most successful, in particular when the longest reach of the pond is oriented in a north-south direction to minimize wave action and bank erosion. Owners find such ponds appealing.

Swimming ponds should be free of indentations or promontories which inhibit circulation and trap pockets of untreated water. Site restrictions—for instance, if the pond is located in a narrow valley or if trees on the site need to be preserved—may direct design toward a triangular, irregular, or even round shape. Square ponds are often the result of bulldozer excavation, seen in many farm-pond situations. These appear very unnatural and are difficult to manage, with corners that resist circulation, warm up excessively, and invite weed infestation.

Knowing how to manage your pond will require knowledge of its surface area and volume. Many algae-reduction techniques, chemical applications, and fish-stocking programs also require knowledge of pond volume and surface area. If you consult your local Fish and Wildlife Department or conservation authority, a field officer may be available to assist you with this calculation. However, you can achieve a very close approximation on your own using the formulas that follow.

Surface Area Calculation

Rectangular Ponds

If your pond is rectangular or square, the surface area is simply length x width. You can usually regard an irregularly shaped pond as a rectangle or square, computing the area from straight boundary lines that approximate the actual shorelines. If your units are in square feet, divide by 43,560 to arrive at acres. If you want your result in hectares, then use length x width in meters to obtain square meters, and divide by 10,000 to get hectares (2.5 ac. = 1 ha). If you do not have a metric rule, you can convert from square feet to square meters by multiplying by 0.0929, then dividing by 10,000 to convert to hectares.

Round Ponds

If your pond is circular, or nearly so, you can measure its total perimeter by tape (in sections) or by pace, if your pace is accurate. This determines the circumference of the pond. Square the number obtained and divide by 547,390 to arrive at the surface area in acres. This formula will also hold true for ponds that are close to round, but the more egg-shaped the pond is, the more errors will be introduced in the computation.

Determining the Depth of the Pond

The easiest way to accomplish this is by making soundings in a regular fashion over the entire pond surface. This task is done by boat, using a weighted rope marked off in one-foot (0.3 m) intervals lowered to the bottom of the pond or lake. Averaging at least fifteen of these readings will yield a close approximation of the average depth of your pond.

Pond Volume Calculations

a) Where soundings have been taken on a built pond, the volume is simply the surface area multiplied by the average depth (the result of the 15 readings average suggested above). The acre-feet parameter was often useful in the past to estimate chemical-treatment dosage or fish stocking capacity and is easily arrived at if you take your soundings in feet. (See Formula 1)

b) A more accurate prismoidal formula to determine cubic yards of excavation required for a rectangular pond needs a more complex calculation, which involves using ground level, mid-depth, and bottom depth measurements. (See Formula 2)

FORMULA 1

Volume in acre-feet = $\frac{\text{Surface area in square feet}}{43{,}560}$ x average depth in feet

or if you wish to use metric measure:

Volume in hectare-meters = $\frac{\text{Surface area square meters}}{10{,}000}$ x average depth in meters

FORMULA 2

Volume in Cubic Yards = $\frac{[(TL \times Tw) + 4(ML \times Mw) + (BL \times Bw)]}{6 \times 27} \times D$

where

(TL x Tw) = length x width of excavation at ground surface in square feet
(MLx Mw) = length x width of excavation at mid-depth point in square feet
(BL x Bw) = length x width of excavation at bottom of pond in square feet
D = average depth of pond in feet
27 = conversion factor (cubic feet to cubic yards)
V = volume of excavation in cubic yards

For Volume in Cubic Meters: you can use the same formula inserting meters for all dimensions, dividing only by the digit "6" (no factor 27).

Or, you can simply multiply the volume "V" in cubic yards x 0.764,554 to arrive at cubic meters

Calculating gallons

From volume in cubic yards:

Imperial gallons - multiply volume in cubic yards x 168.178
US gallons - multiply volume in cubic yards x 201.974

From volume in cubic metres

Imperial gallons - multiply volume in cubic meters x 219.969
US gallons - multiply volume in cubic meters x 264.172

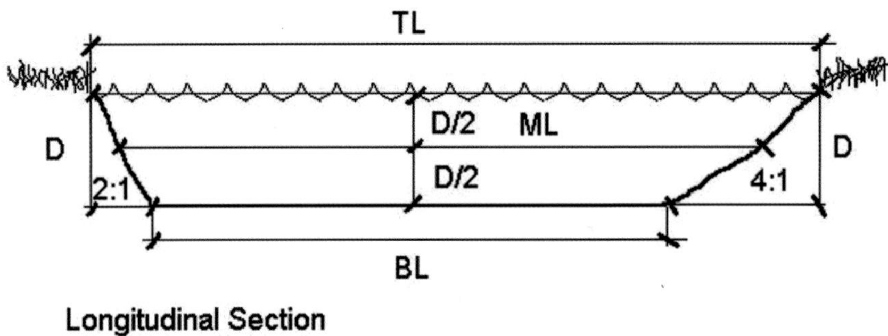

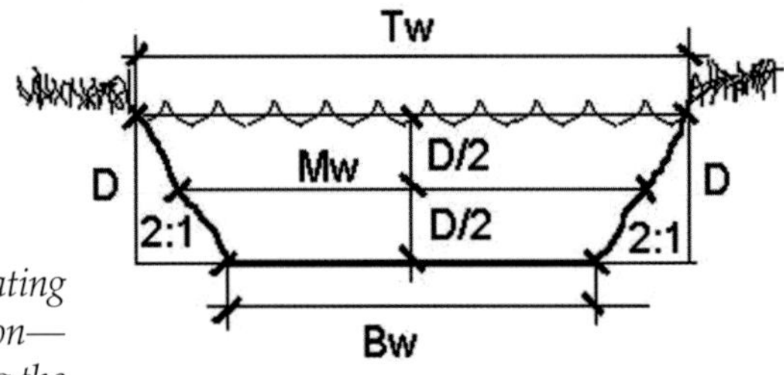

Figure 6.2 Calculating the excavation—diagrams illustrating the measurements required.

The most difficult factors to obtain in this formula are bottom length and width, and mid-point length and width. To calculate these, one needs to know the side-slope ratio at either end of the longitudinal section of the excavation, and the side-slope ratios on both sides. For instance, a side-slope ratio of 2:1 (a one-foot rise for every two feet horizontal) will produce a two-foot distance for every one foot of depth. A pond of 12 ft. (3.66 m) depth and 2:1 side slope would create a slope occupying 2 x 12 ft. = 24 ft. (7.32 m). Similarly, a side slope of 4:1 would create a slope occupying 4 x 12 ft. = 48 ft. (14.63 m). These two slopes are subtracted from the length of the excavation at ground surface (or top of the pond) to yield the bottom length and width. The mid-point length and width uses the same slope ratios, but with the depth (D) cut in half, since it's the midpoint.

This estimate will serve primarily as a basis for soliciting bids from a contractor who will want to know the volume of earth he has to remove. Refer to Figure 2.3 in Chapter 2 for the Pond Storage Capacity Table.

Types of Ponds

Bypass Ponds

Bypass ponds are highly recommended by departments of fisheries, fish and wildlife agencies and conservation authorities, because these ponds do not block the movement of fish in a nearby stream. They also do not raise stream temperatures as much as in-stream (or on-stream) ponds do. They reduce the opportunity for stream erosion and flooding damage, and if the excavated materials are kept within the flood plain, the exercise in creating the pond is essentially a balanced cut-and-fill operation. Most regulatory agencies require that all work done within the flood plain be a balanced cut-and-fill, thereby not changing the reservoir capacity (flood capacity) of the stream in that location. In-stream ponds eventually become full of silt from continuous sedimentation, due to the reduction in stream velocity through the body of the pond. Bypass ponds allow some measure of control—particularly during periods of high stream sedimentation from heavy rains, spring melt, etc.

Your pond site must be chosen carefully so that the pond can receive and discharge water from the adjacent stream/river. This means that attention must be paid to existing grades. In a low-gradient stream, the pond outlet pipe will have to be very long to attain the necessary gravity drain. A distinct advantage of the bypass pond is the owner's ability to shut the inflow pipe off during periods of high-flow and high-silt in the supply stream, saving the pond from silting and, possibly, contamination.

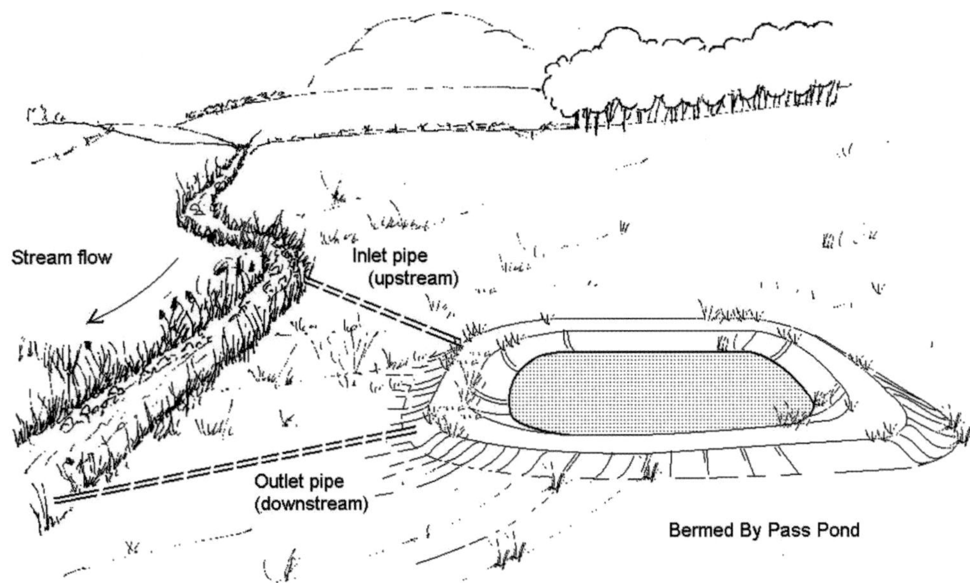

Figure 6.3 A typical bermed bypass pond.

Inlet and Outlet Controls for Bypass Ponds

Check-Dams

In some cases, it is advisable to install a low check-dam to increase the water level at your pond's inlet-pipe end. However, such an installation creates a small on-stream pond, which places the installation outside the recommended policy of the water management authority. Basically, damming up of rivers or streams invites flood damage, erosion, and warm-water infusion to downstream habitats, even though there are other beneficial advantages, such as fish-habitat creation, water conservation, and groundwater supplementation—at least at the pond location.

Choice of pond site is critical since it is not normally feasible to construct a bypass pond when stream banks are excessively steep or high. The lower the stream is below surrounding grade, the deeper the pond excavation will have to be to reach the water level predetermined by the inlet-pipe level in the stream.

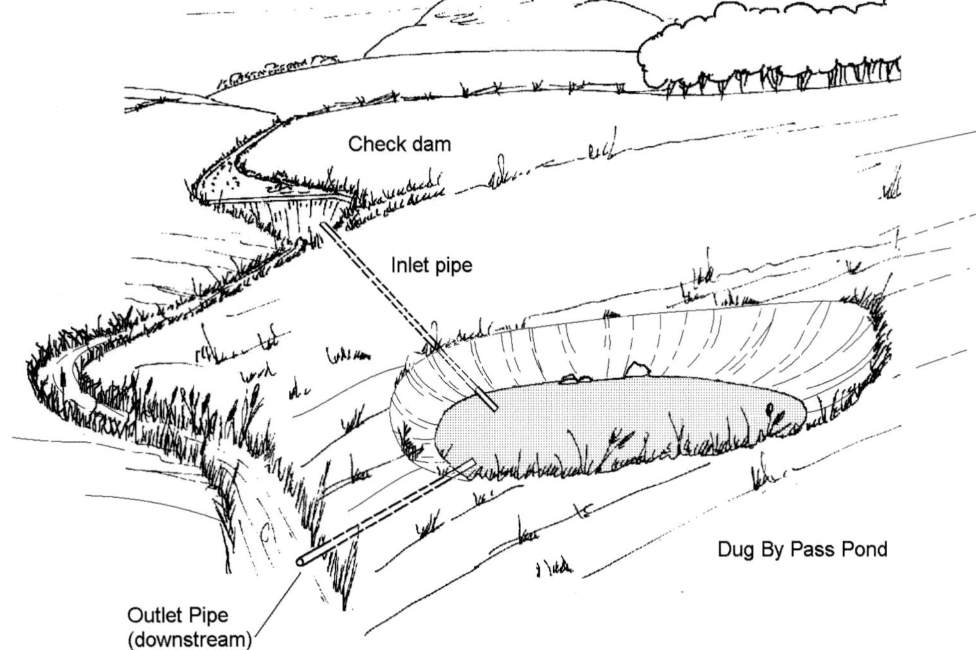

Figure 6.4 A typical excavated bypass pond with an upstream check-dam.

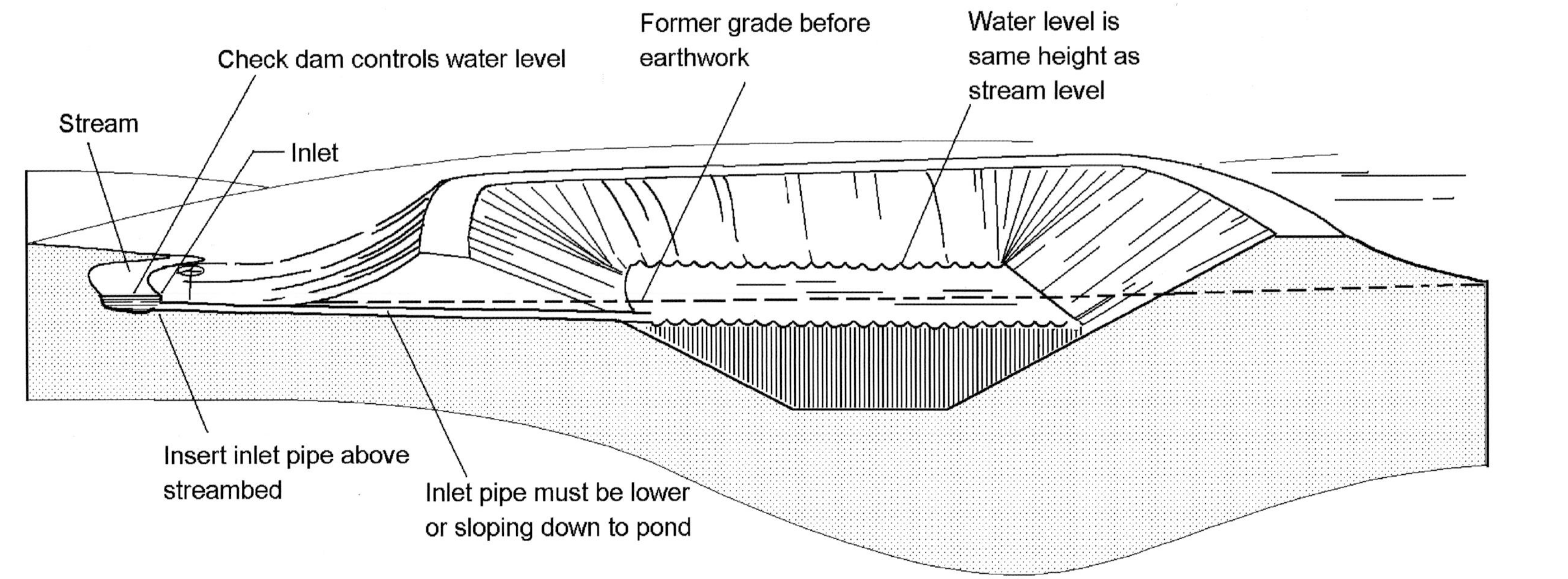

Former grade before earthwork
Water level is same height as stream level
Check dam controls water level
Stream
Inlet
Insert inlet pipe above streambed
Inlet pipe must be lower or sloping down to pond

Figure 6.5 A sectional view of a bermed Bypass Pond.

original grade prior to excavation
water level same as that behind check dam
Water level raises behind the check dam
2:1 slope maximum
Inlet pipe should lie above streambed
Inlet pipe must be level or sloping down to pond
If pond is located in the flood plain, it is wise to create a bermed area to prevent stream from flooding over into pond

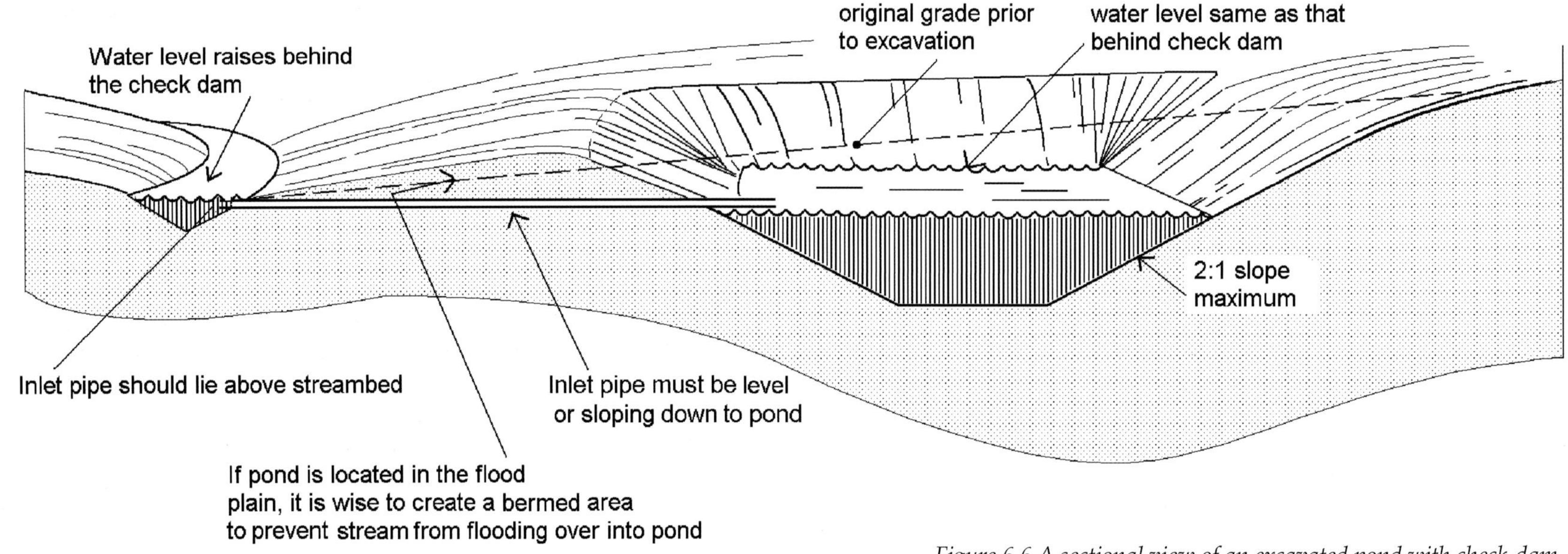

Figure 6.6 A sectional view of an excavated pond with check-dam.

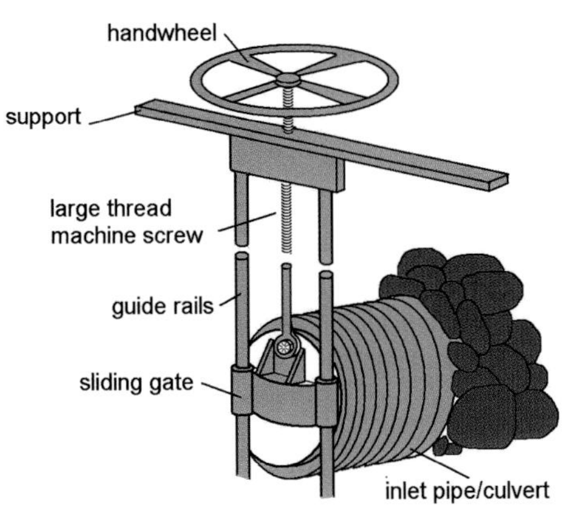

Figure 6.7 A slide-gate inlet-control device with a hand wheel—a bottom-draw operation.

hand wheel turns butterfly gate in pipe

support for wheel

tie rod welded to butterfly gate

supports for wheel welded to pipe

welds

gate cut from steel plate to fit inside diam. of culvert

embankment

culvert inlet pipe

stop

Figure 6.8 A butterfly-gate inlet-control device—also a bottom-draw operation.

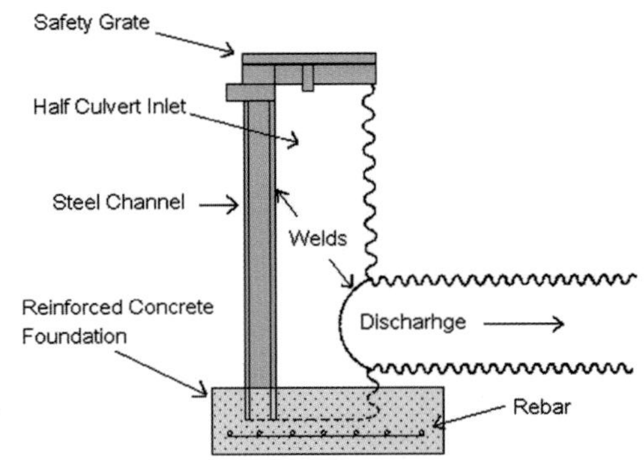

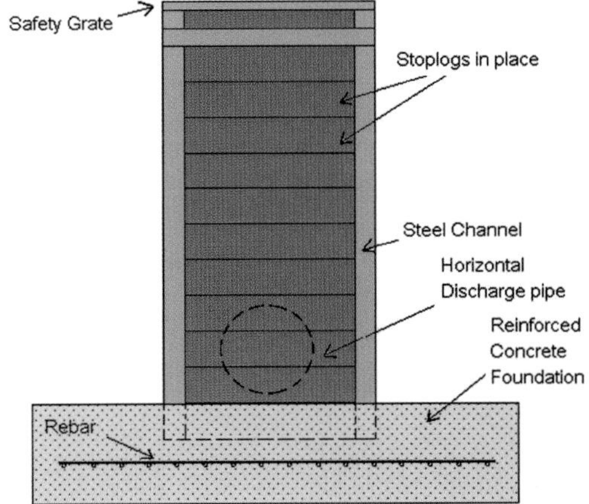

Inlet Pipes

The recommended size for inlet pipes is generally no more than one-third of the average summer flow of the stream. The inlet pipe should be raised above the stream bottom to avoid silt transfer into the pond, and also to avoid draw-down of the stream during periods of low flow, which worsens its drought condition. The pipe should not intrude excessively into the stream channel and its entrance must be protected with water-washed boulders and stone to prevent erosion at this vulnerable point. A concrete headwall, if constructed, will likely require approvals, and your local water management authority will probably discourage the building of such a structure. Grating must be placed over the inlet pipe at the stream end to prevent fish from entering or escaping from the pond. This also prevents any invasive species or oriental varieties from getting into the stream, should a care-

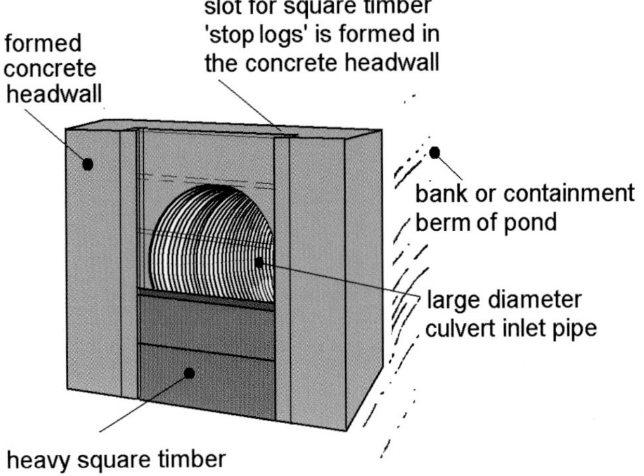

Above: Figure 6.9 (a) Two sectional views of a half-culvert drop structure often used as an inlet or an outlet structure. Left: Figure 6.9 (b) A concrete headwall with wood inserts is a simple inlet control. Both (a) and (b) structures will admit warm water to downstream habitats.

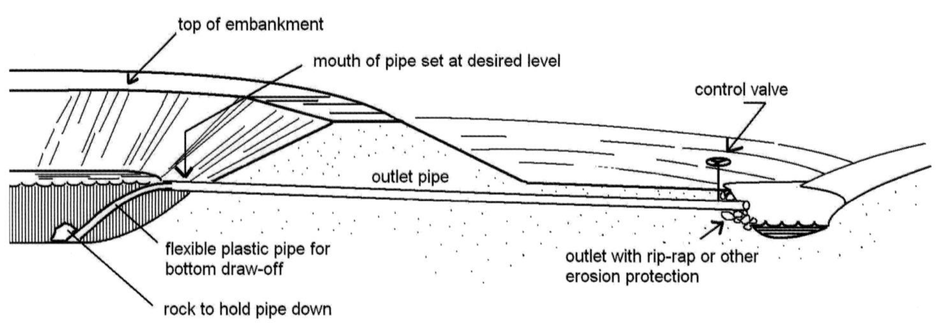

Figure 6.10 (a) An outlet pipe with a simple bottom-draw-off device and optional outlet control valve.

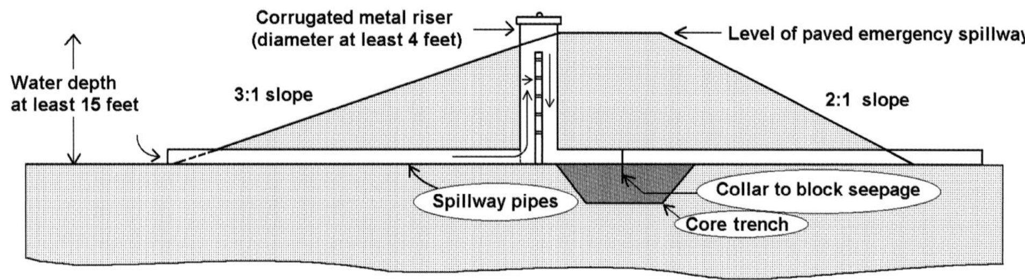

Figure 6.10 (b) A deeper, larger pond may require a dam with a riser pipe and buried bottom-draw-off spillway. Stop-logs are employed in the riser pipe to control water height.

less landowner stock the pond with an inappropriate fish species (an illegal activity).

Larger, deeper ponds may require several options for flow control: these may include a slide gate, butterfly gate, or a concrete/wood headwall.

Outlet Pipe

Outlet-pipe location is just as critical as the inlet because it controls water level in the pond and can also serve as a bottom draw-off device (to usher cool water downstream). The capacity of any outlet pipe should be at least 50 percent more than that of the inlet pipe to carry excess flow from rainfall, run-off, or spring-flood

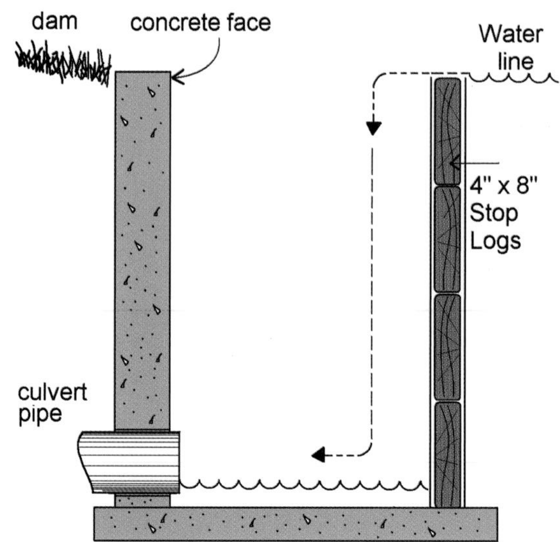

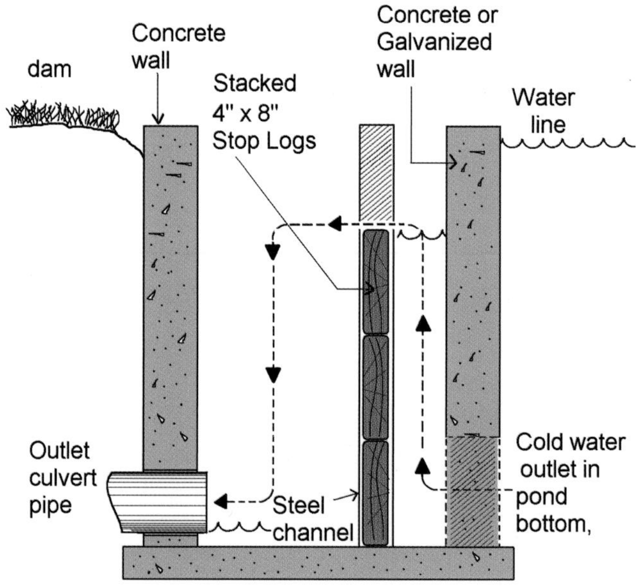

Figure 6.11 Cross-sections of typical bottom-draw-off structure versus top-draw structure. Both use stop-logs as water-level-control mechanisms

conditions. If water conservation is required within the pond, the outlet can be equipped with a valve or gate mechanism. To guarantee cold-water effluence from the pond, a flexible hose/pipe can be run from the mouth of the outlet pipe to the bottom of the pond and weighed down with rock so that it remains on the bottom. Deeper, larger ponds may require a drop-inlet type spillway with stop logs or heavy planks that also aid in controlling the pond's water level.

The outlet pipe should not project excessively into the stream and must also be protected with boulders and other natural erosion-control methods (plantings, fascines, etc.).

Isolated Dug-Out Ponds

Dug-out or simple, excavated ponds are the easiest to build, and usually are found in flat or nearly flat terrain. They have a moderate to slow rate of recovery following water removal for irrigation, fire protection, etc., but when dug deep enough, exposing a minimum water-surface area, they overcome evaporation losses quickly. Compared to off-stream bypass ponds and embankment ponds, these ponds are relatively flood-safe. Two types of excavated ponds exist, one fed largely by surface run-off and the other fed by groundwater springs or aquifers. Many dug-out ponds are replenished by both.

Locating an Isolated Dug-Out Pond

Dug-out ponds are often situated in or beside a drainage way, where run-off can be diverted into the pond. It is wise to avoid the lowest elevation in a natural drainage way or depression, otherwise excess pond water will not flow out and away during storms or after natural topping-up by rainfall. Do not locate a dug-out pond in a marsh, fen, or bog—this displaces valuable wildlife habitat and invites an algae or emergent aquatic-weed invasion from the former ecosystem.

Test Pits

To ascertain groundwater supply, presence of aquifers, or surface run-off potential, dig test pits in your chosen location before construction. After a day or two, water levels in these test pits will indicate the expected water level in your future pond. The difference in level between the water surface in the pit and the ground surface indicates how much overburden will have to be removed before the contractor reaches the potential surface of water in the pond. Check the recovery rate in the test pits by pumping them out and letting them refill with water. A slow rate of recovery renders the pond rather useless for irrigation or water-taking, since the rate of fresh groundwater inflow will be low. This will help avoid digging an expensive hole in the ground only to control a disappointingly low volume of stagnant water. Dig your test pits in midsummer to avoid false impressions resulting from a spring high-water table (usually attributed to snow melt and run-off).

The depth of soil to be excavated above the pond's

planned surface increases construction costs while contributing nothing to planned pond depth. Pond banks should not exceed depths of 6 ft. (1.88 m) for aesthetic and practical purposes, since their gradient will make access to the water surface difficult unless the banks are sloped back considerably (which again increases excavation and earth-removal costs). Steep pond banks also encourage erosion and silting, unless you have created erosion protection.

Soils

Fine-textured clays and silty clays, when they extend below the proposed pond bottom, usually assure a reliable pond site. These soil types also exhibit the best impervious qualities, discouraging seepage losses. Sandy clays reaching adequate pond depths are also suitable. Limestone bedrock, however, will exhibit a high degree of seepage, with cracks and crevices, as will coarse-textured sands or sand-gravel mixtures. Ponds with such permeable bottoms must be lined with rubber or butyl liners to retain water, an undertaking that is expensive and not very natural. Look for other finished ponds in your area; check soil type, run-off situation, and depths to get an indication of your soil's suitability.

Outlet/Overflow Pipes

An overflow/outlet system should be installed in dug-out ponds contained within an embankment on slopping lands. This prevents erosion and possible loss of the embankment in the event of a storm, rapid snow-melt, or extensive rainfall.

Burying long steel pipes at a slight angle in the embankment through to its downstream side allows excess water to trickle out. Three pipes, 4–6 in. (10–15 cm) in diameter, will be sufficient. The center (or outlet) pipe should be placed with its mouth at the proposed pond-water level, usually about 2 ft. (0.6 m) below the finished embankment grade. The other two pipes, acting as emergency "spillway" pipes, should be placed about 1 ft. (0.3 m) below the finished embankment grades. The pipes will normally be high and dry above the pond surface, never needed until a storm event. The outlet pipe has three functions: maintaining a continuous water outlet from the pond, forestalling the possibility of the water level reaching the higher elevation of the overflow pipes, and provoking a water intake from the aquifer(s) in the pond bottom, which adds cool, fresh water to the pond.

You should cut the inlet end of the outlet pipe at an angle to form a hood: install anti-seep collars if your pond is large. The inlet end of the outlet pipe should be screened, to keep fish in the pond. The easiest way to do this is to install a wire basket arrangement around the pipe. The top and bottom of the basket should be left open, but cut a hole in the side of the basket to the exact diameter of the outlet pipe. The basket is then fitted over the pipe inlet, with the pipe protruding into the basket through the pre-cut hole: the open bottom of the basket is thrust into the sloping pond bottom. The open top of the basket allows cleaning, to prevent debris and pond weeds from clogging the inlet. A long piece of plumbing pipe cut to fit the length of the outlet pipe, plus a foot or two (0.3–0.6 m), can be thrust up the pipe from the downstream side of the embankment to clean it out.

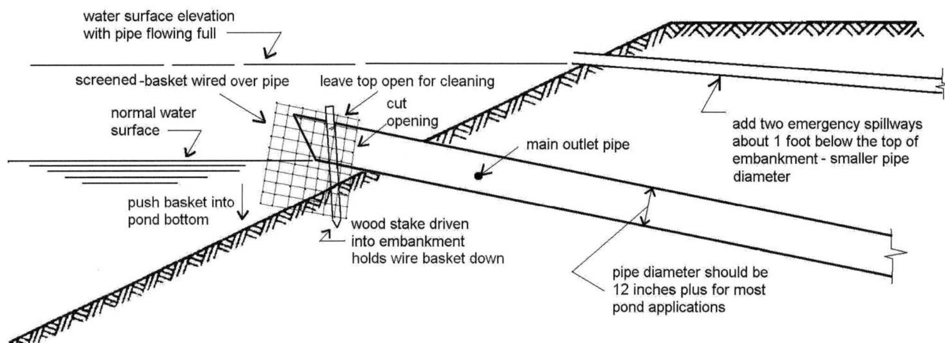

Figure 6.12 Cross-section of an embankment showing an emergency spillway pipe and hooded outlet pipe with screened inlet.

Excavation, Berming, and Distribution of Material

The use of excavated earth in a flood-plain environment may be a necessity depending upon the soil's characteristics. Muck and peat do not make good berming material because they are easily eroded by wind and water. Muck can also be eutrophic adding harmful bacteria to the flood plain. If, however, your excavated soil is suitable, it can be used for berming, and should be placed in layers about 1 ft. (0.3 m) thick, with each layer compacted after deposition. The foot or base of the berm should be at least 10 ft. (3 m) away from the stream or river source. The gradient of berm slopes should not go above the ratio of 2:1 (a rise of 1 ft. for every 2 ft. run, or 0.3 m for 0.6 m), for both erosion control and mowing purposes. Should the normal pond level be higher than the water surface in a nearby stream or river, your berm should be constructed in a soil with a high percentage of clay. The berm core must be of clay construction to avoid any rupture and leakage into the stream.

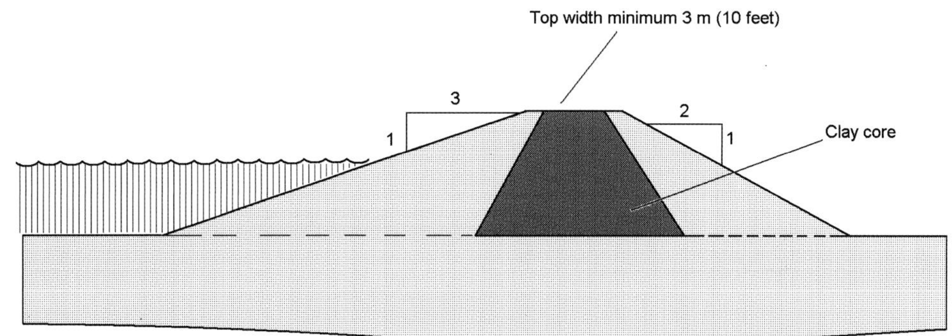

Figure 6.13 A pond berm showing its clay core.

Overall Considerations:

- No more than one-third of the normal stream flow should be diverted through the inlet pipe into a bypass pond. It is not good stewardship to take water from a stream during periods of drought or low flow.
- The owner should inspect the pond condition regularly, particularly after a heavy rainfall or flood condition, to relieve the pond of excess volume or to remove blockages from the inlet or outlet pipes.
- Grass and weeds on the berm containing the pond should be cut, but only to within 15 ft. 94.57 m) of

the water's edge (maintaining a natural filter and buffer for the littoral-zone habitat).

Embankment Ponds (Ponds with Dams)

Detailed Site Investigation and Engineering Surveys

Now that you have located the best site for your pond and its dam (or embankment), the location should be surveyed with a Dumpy level, or laser level, to determine existing grades and the extent of flooding which could occur. If you are not familiar with survey techniques, you will need to hire an engineer or engineering technologist to do this. The usual method consists of running a "profile" of the centerline of the dam and earth spillway, from which offsets are taken to estimate existing ground levels within the confines of the proposed pond structure. This step will allow an estimation of your pond capacity.

A complete topographical survey may be needed for larger ponds and reservoirs. This involves running a "line of profile levels" along the centerline of any proposed dam with offset levels up both sides of the containment and beyond the proposed top of the dam and earth spillway locations. A profile survey should also be undertaken along the centerline of the earth spillway. All significant changes in slope should be noted no more than 50 ft. (15 m) apart. These measurements will determine the volume of earth needed to build the dam and will establish the height of your earth spillway and "trickle tube." Begin your survey from a point on the upstream end, one that is well below the estimated water surface elevation. Existing elevations are determined on this line all the way downstream to a point where water will be discharged without damage to the dam structure. Locate a bench mark (or reference elevation point), which will remain undisturbed through the construction process. This mark will be used as a constant reference for existing and proposed elevations.

Soil Studies

Your choice of pond site for an embankment pond is dependent upon the ability of the soil to hold water. Clays and silty sands are superior, although sandy clays might be satisfactory. Coarse-textured sands and sand-gravel mixtures are too pervious and unsuitable. Lack of impervious material can be corrected by sealing with a well-graded, coarse-grained soil containing at least 20 percent clay, or by adding bentonite (finely-textured colloidal clay), thoroughly compacted. Limestone-bedrock sites are particularly permeable with crevices and channels below the upper-soil horizon; these are not visible on the surface. An inspection of surrounding rural and farm ponds in the area might reveal soil and sub-soil characteristics, avoiding soil-boring tests.

Dam-Core and Foundation Requirements

Your dam foundation must be stable and must provide

resistance to the pressure of a contained reservoir. It is essential to make soil borings at any such proposed site. Natural, undisturbed banks at the wings of the dam should also be investigated for structural characteristics. If a dam is to be built on rock, boring studies need to be done to determine rock thickness and any fissures or seams through which water can drain. A "cut-off core" of impervious material should be installed under the proposed dam, or on the upstream face of the dam; this must be composed of a leak-resistant material. Fine-textured silts and clays are not stable enough for larger dams. Some relief against water pressure can be achieved by flattening the dam's side slopes, although this will likely require more fill and regrading. You must remove all mucks, peat, and organic-matter soils from any dam-foundation area. Suitable dam-foundation materials possess both stability and imperviousness. A good mix of coarse and fine-textured soils fulfills both criteria. Such soils include:

- gravel/sand/clay mixtures,
- gravel/sand/silt mixtures,
- sand/clay mixtures,
- sand/silt mixtures.

The soils prescribed for dam foundations are usually suitable for fill material. Do not use organic silts and clays, which exhibit the characteristic of slippage or "slumping," in your foundation work. Optimal specifications for an earth-fill dam require material ranging from small gravel or coarse sand to fine sand plus clay, with 20 percent by weight of clay particles. Stay away from soils with a higher percentage of gravel or coarse sand; these are pervious and allow seepage through your dam. Too high a clay content will also result in swelling when wet and shrinking on drying. This situation creates dangerous cracks and potential leakage points.

Some foundation soil conditions require extensive construction methods not justified for smaller ponds and lakes. The best foundation situation is a thick layer of impervious consolidated clay or sand-clay. Removal of all existing topsoil provides a suitable bond with the clay or sand-clay subsoil. If there is no impervious clay layer at an economical depth, consult an engineer to design your dam, because the foundation soils must be reinforced to prevent seepage and failure. Similarly, a soil profile consisting of highly plastic clay or similar unconsolidated soil requires more extensive investigation and design for stability. Dams built on bedrock require anchoring into the rock and usually involve an entire cement structure to prevent slippage or seepage.

Cut-Off Trench

The possibility of seepage cannot be overlooked in situations where alluvial deposits of various previous sands and gravels exist at the surface, with rock or clay at a greater depth. You will need a cut-off trench to adhere to the rock or clay stratum and to join with the base of the dam. Compacted material with a high percentage of clay is most often

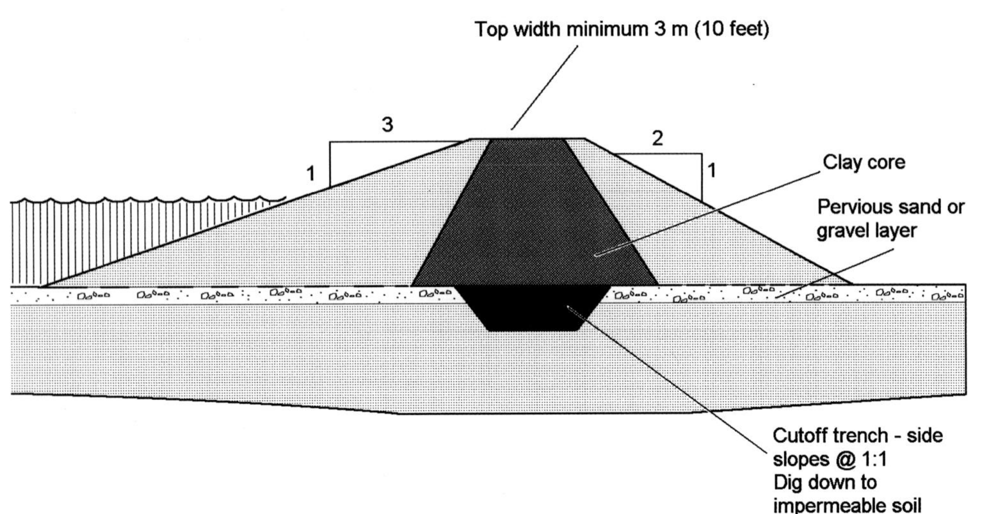

Figure 6.14 A cut-off trench beneath a typical dam structure.

used. A trench is dug along the dam's centerline down into the impervious layer, extending well into the proposed side abutments. The trench bottom should be no less than 8 ft. (2.6 m) wide with a 1:1 slope. Filling the trench with successive layers of sandy-clay or clay material and compacting each layer provides a good "core trench." Keeping these layers moist while compacting is essential.

Top Width

Dams less than 10 ft. (0.3 m) high require a top width of about 8 ft. (2.6 m), but as the height of the dam increases, this width also increases. The top width should be at least 14 ft. (4.6 m) if vehicular access is required across the dam; this will require a much wider base of the dam in order to maintain the same side slopes.

Side Slopes

The percent slope depends upon the stability of fill and foundation materials. Side slopes can be steeper with a more stable fill: unstable materials require a much-reduced percent slope—up to 4:1.

Freeboard

The added height of any dam above its water surface is called "freeboard." This height prevents wave action (produced by winds or floodwaters) from overtopping the dam, particularly when an emergency spillway cannot entirely handle flow. Heights of freeboard should be as in the table below.

LENGTH OF POND	FREEBOARD
Less than 650 feet (217 m)	+ 1 foot (0.3 m)
660 – 1,320 feet (217 to 440 m)	min. 1.5 feet (0.35 m)
Half a mile (1 km)	2 feet (0.6 m)

Longer ponds require the services of an engineer to calculate freeboard, because these water bodies are dependent on a much larger watershed.

Settlement of Fill

Your earth dam should be constructed somewhat higher than what's in your design specifications in order to allow for settlement of fill, although if the fill process involves compacting successive layers under good moisture conditions, there will not be an appreciable amount of settlement. Most uncom-

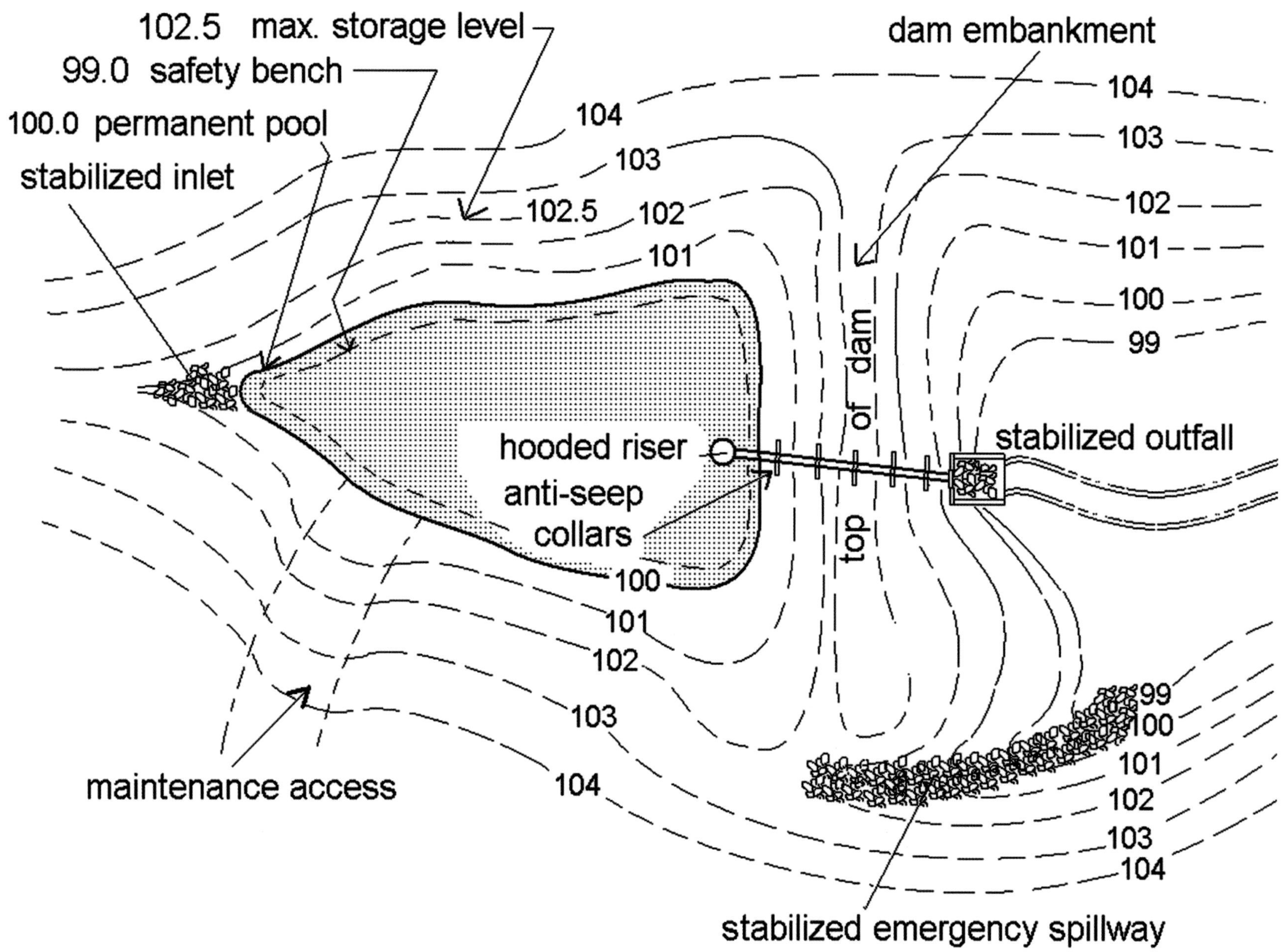

Figure 6.15 A simple contour plan of a pond with dam [Adapted from Site Engineering for Landscape Architects].

pacted foundations have a settlement range of 1–6 percent. Settlement rate for a compacted, layered dam will be about 5 percent of the designed dam height. This means that your dam must be built 5 percent higher in order to properly contain the final-design water level.

Earth Fill

After the design has been established, the number of cubic yards (cubic meters) of fill must be estimated to establish the cost of the project. The total estimate of volume will include allowance for settlement, volume required to backfill the cut-off trench, and all other holes or depressions in foundation. There is an efficient method in place to calculate the volume of earth fill called "the sum of end area method." It is published by the Natural Resources Conservation Service, U.S. Department of Agriculture, in Agricultural Handbook No. 387.

Plans and Specifications

An accurate plan for the pond or lake should illustrate all existing and proposed elevations with dimensions of the dam and cut-off trench. The location of the drop inlet pipe should be shown, along with a detailed drawing of its construction complete with dimensions. The plan provides an instrument for obtaining accurate bidding by contractors and a document to refer to as work progresses, verifying that work specified is being done properly. Sometimes, if a knowledgeable contractor has been hired, a simple contour plan of the proposed pond will suffice, but for larger ponds with more complex dam structures, it will be necessary to obtain the services of an engineer to arrive at a more detailed plan.

Staking Out the Pond

Prior to construction, the proposed waterline and the areas to be cleared of trees should be staked out by a

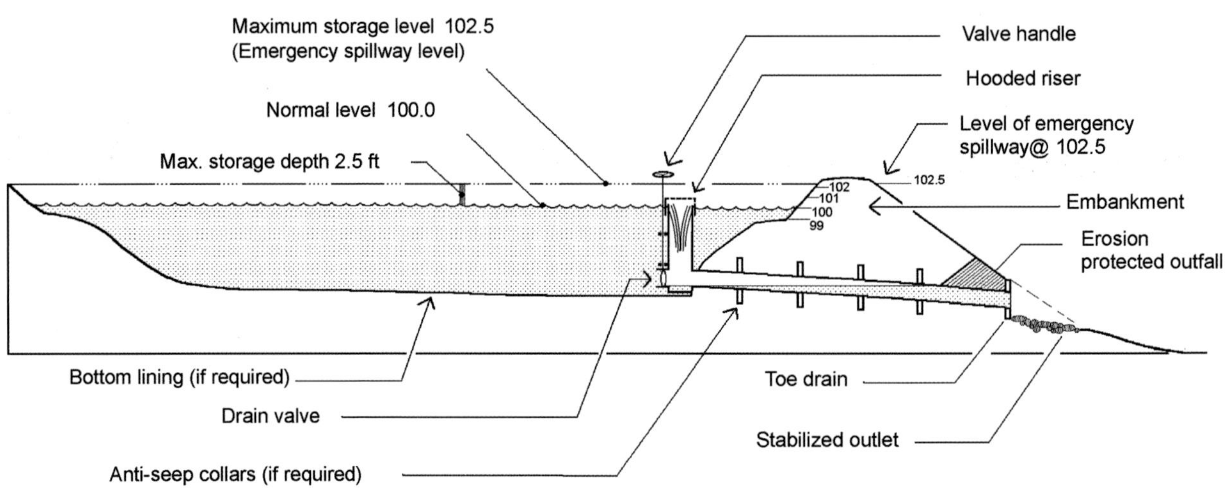

Figure 6.16 A cross-section of the pond and dam in Figure 6.15

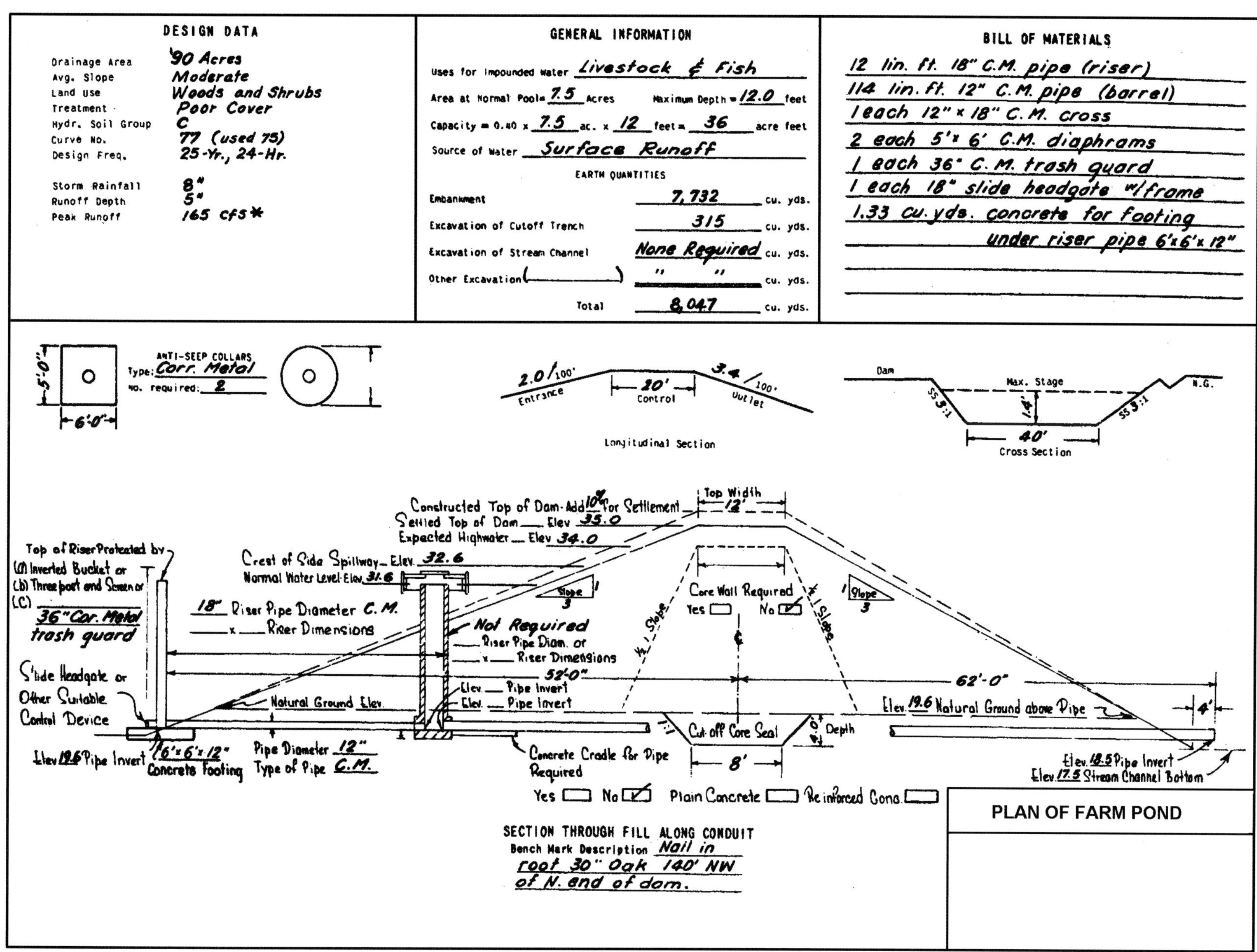

Figure 6.17 An engineer's drawing of a typical farm pond with dam [from Ponds for Water Supply and Recreation, Natural Resources Conservation Service, U.S. Department of Agriculture]

A vernal pond in spring on the edge of a sugar bush harbors seasonal frogs and nesting ducks, but dries up almost completely in the summer.

level survey. This usually involves the dam site, the spillway location, and the total area to be impounded. Stakes for clearing must be placed about 15 ft. (5 m) outside the waterline. Locating the dam involves setting stakes on its centerline every 50 ft. (17 m). Following this, fill and slope stakes should be placed upstream and downstream from the centerline stakes to locate the points where side slopes meet the ground surface, and to locate the outer limits of construction. Locating the earth spillway is done by first staking the spillway centerline, then setting the "cut" and "slope" stakes along the existing ground surface where the spillway side slopes will meet it. The drop inlet "trickle tube" location must be located later along its proposed course once the dam-foundation construction is complete enough. The drop inlet should be located on firm ground, preferably supported with a poured concrete footing.

Vernal Ponds

Importance of Vernal Ponds

Vernal ponds are a special type of seasonal pond or wetland. They are, by definition, a shallow, temporary pond usually quite separated from a river or stream, and most often inside or alongside a forest edge. Many landowners inadvertently drain them or fill them, feeling they have no importance to the ecosystem, often deepening them to create permanent ponds or lakes.

Vernal ponds are so called because they are often formed in early spring (vernal equinox) and dry up in late summer or early fall. The important fact is that they dry up annually or periodically, and do not contain fish. It is only recently that we have come to appreciate the ecological significance of these ponds or wetlands. It is, in fact, the temporary nature of these ponds that makes them valuable, because just as their seasonal nature prohibits fish habitat from being established, it also allows for the flourishing of amphibians, crustaceans, and all sorts of insects valuable to the ecosystem and forest. The periodic drying of vernal ponds creates a solid and firm bottom soil, which permits decomposition of leaf litter and dead vegetation accumulated during the pond's aquatic cycle. This allows easy walking access to most vernal-pond sites. Some vernal ponds will contain cattails, sedges, and bulrushes, all of which usually survive the drying cycle.

Unfortunately, the vernal pond's temporary nature makes it a target for destruction and replacement by man-made structures (roads, buildings, etc.) because such ponds are not protected by the legislation covering permanent wetlands or ponds. However, with careful site selection and planning, these ponds can be reintroduced into the same physiographic locations they once occupied.

In North America, up to one-half of the frog population and one-third of all salamander species depend upon seasonal ponds or wetlands for their growth and maturation. Two specific species that dependent upon vernal ponds are the wood frog and the spotted salamander, both of which can mature and arise from these fish-empty habitats. The vernal pond is much less likely to contain *saprolegnia*, a fungus harmful to frogs, toads, and salamander eggs. In addition, vernal ponds usually possess lower numbers of eastern newts, which kill amphibian eggs and larvae. Migrating waterfowl such as the wood duck and mallard species use vernal ponds, consuming insects, crustaceans, and aquatic plant seeds. Depending on their nature, vernal ponds are often visited by shorebirds (spotted sandpiper, lesser yellowlegs) which feed on the exposed mud flats formed as water levels decline. Reptiles (eastern box turtle, snapping turtles, and eastern garter snake) also inhabit vernal ponds, moving from one to another as water levels decline. Bat populations are often seen flying over the surfaces of these ponds, seeking for insects, a fact that makes them attractive to land-owners trying to reduce mosquito larvae populations. Salamanders, dragonflies, damselfly larvae, and many predatory insects (water strider, backswimmer) will prey heavily on adult mosquitoes. In all, the species normally inhabiting the vernal pond will effectively take care of the mosquito population.

A small vernal pond between trees in a bay forest ecosystem in Georgia, U.S.A..

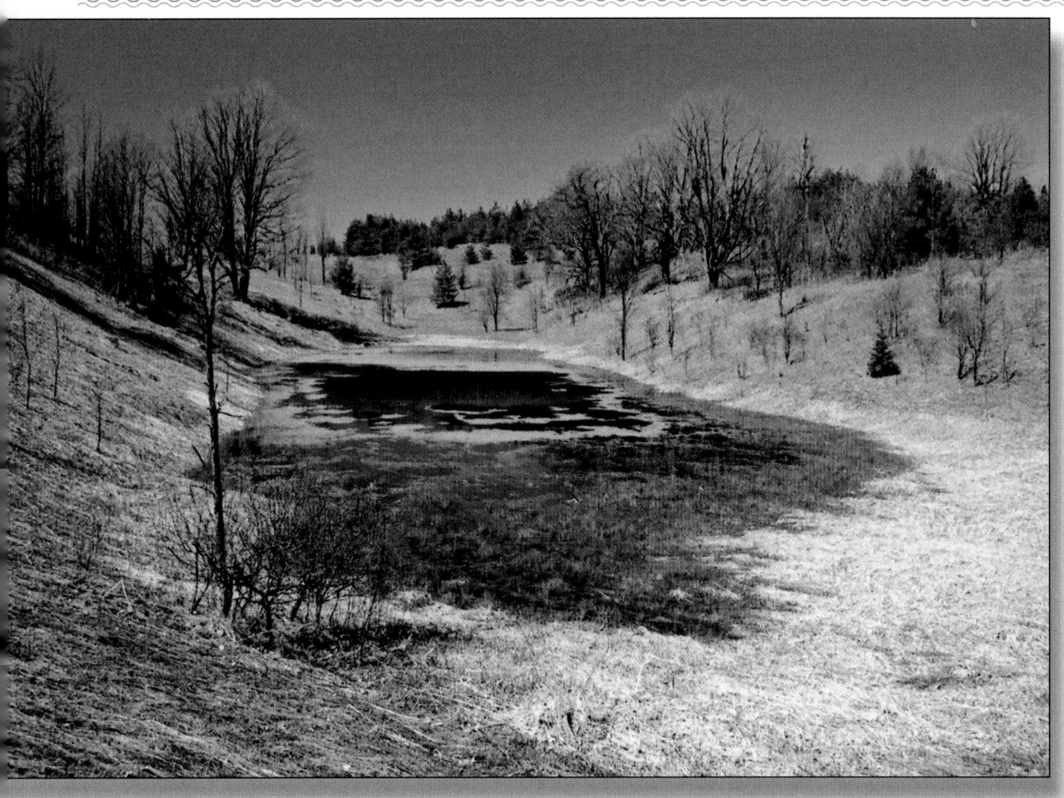

A large vernal pond nestled between two drumlins in Forks of the Credit Provincial Park. Although it seems large and deep, it is very shallow, forming annually from snow-melt and rainwater. Sustained only by a small watershed, this pond starts to dry up in late summer—an essential condition for vernal ponds.

The water-retention capability of vernal ponds, although only seasonal, still contributes to the overall groundwater recharge function across the landscape. Natural seepage into subsoil assists water conservation by reducing the amount of sheet run-off, thereby reducing erosion and flooding downstream.

Preparing for Construction

The general problem with most constructed vernal ponds is that they do not hold water long enough for aquatic plants or larvae to become established. This is largely the result of either improper site selection or permeable soil types under the pond or within the core of the dam. Insufficient soil compaction on the dam site can also be blamed for such failures. It is wise to consult a local conservation authority field officer or natural resource technician before embarking on siting. Such help is also offered also through landowner assistance programs within local stewardship councils or natural resource departments. Construction methods range from blasting to heavy equipment use. For practical reasons and because of potential damage to the ecosystem, I am limiting my recommended construction techniques to those involving heavy equipment. Contact your natural resource authority or conservation authority to determine if a permit is required, particularly if you choose to excavate what appears to be a wetland. Also contact your local gas, electric and cable companies to determine if a buried utility line search needs to be done before you commence the dig. The easiest and most practical excavation equipment is either a bulldozer or a tracked backhoe, depending on the water table of the site.

Once heavy equipment has moved the amount of soil required to form your pond, the site will appear disturbed and rather ugly with newly exposed soil. It will take several years to heal these "scars" unless some form of groundcover replanting occurs with species that will provide protection and erosion control.

A Cautionary Note

If you plan to reinstate a former vernal pond, use

aerial photos to identify suitable wet areas. These usually show up as darker textures on black-and-white photos. You can also enquire of local farmers or rural landowners if they know about any historical vernal pond sites or wet areas retaining water for at least part of the year. Such areas need to be scrutinized for construction debris, which may have been used as fill. Rocks, stumps, and logs create a permeable soil that will not retain water for long unless a synthetic pond liner is used. Hire a contractor to dig a test pit to locate the presence of any foreign materials before you determine a particular location.

Avoid natural wetlands whose wet habitats are already established. Disturbing these sites is counterproductive. Signs that a particular location harbors an existing vernal pond or wetland include the following: dark stained leaves, pond-edge vegetation such as cattails or sedges, clams, and snails. Sites like these are already precious, and are possibly established habitats for endangered or rare species. Consider consulting a biologist for assistance when choosing your location. Miniature vernal ponds can be formed by water bars, which direct water across roadways: they often help to trap sediment, and because they are off-road, remain sustainable.

Top: A man-made vernal pond full of water after spring melt and rainfall. Arnold C. Matthews Nature Reserve, Lake Simcoe, Ontario [Photo by John Hicks].

Bpttom: The same pond is functioning as a true vernal pond by late summer [Photo by John Hicks].

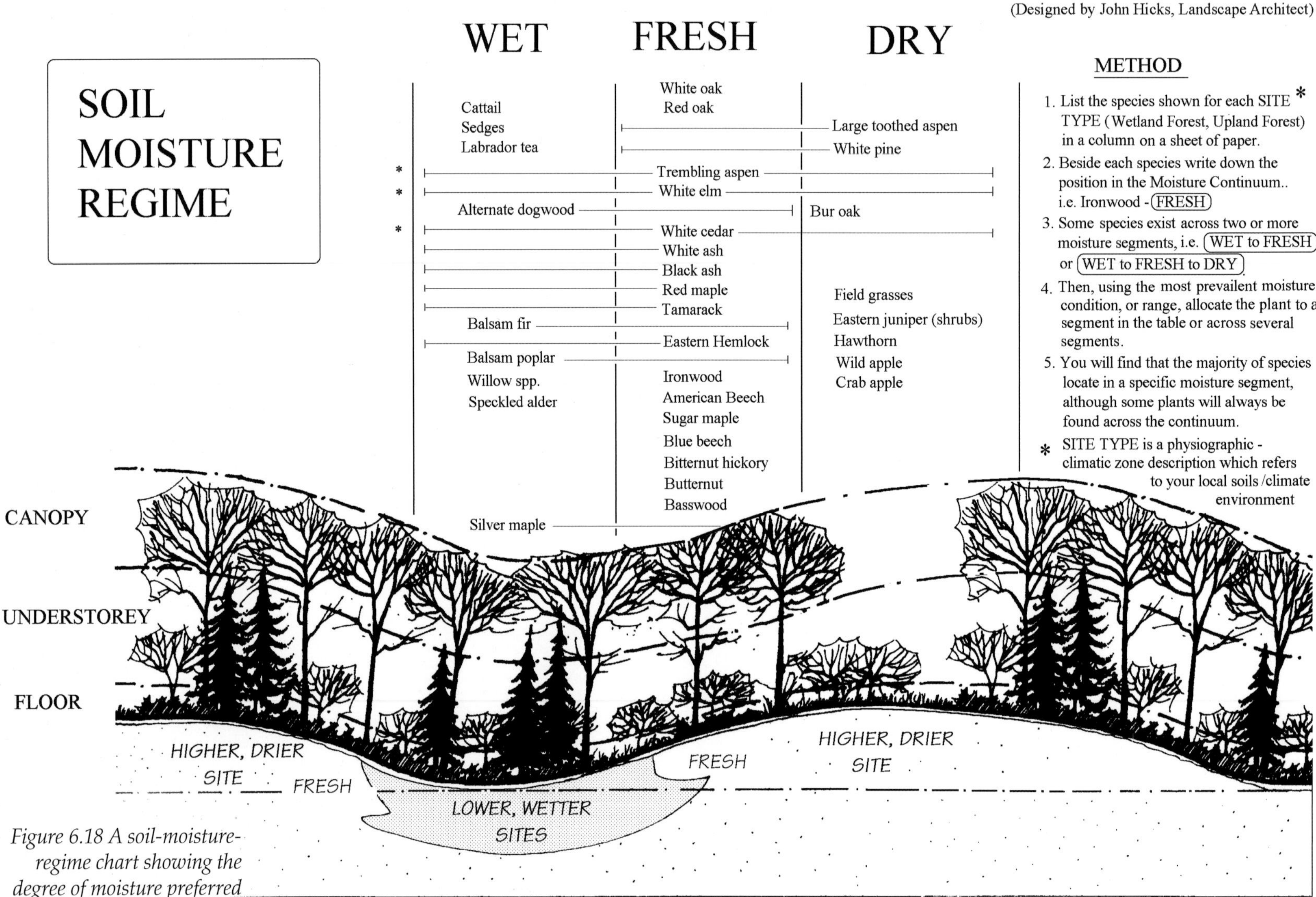

Figure 6.18 A soil-moisture-regime chart showing the degree of moisture preferred by selected trees and shrubs.

Location Considerations

Locating a vernal pond on slopes with a gradient of less than 3 percent (a three-foot drop in every hundred feet or 1 m in every 34 m) is recommended. When there are large trees present, a small wetland may be possible between them, but you must ascertain whether the tree species are tolerant of a flooded environment. Removing large trees for a vernal pond destroys one habitat for another, and is not recommended. Try to locate a new vernal pond near others,

A southern Florida vernal pond in the process of drying up. Notice the grass and hard-stem aquatic rushes growing in exposed clumps. Ponds like this one with twenty inches (500 mm) of water or less, exposed to full sunlight, will dry up quickly on hot summer days.

or close to wetlands. This will allow a continuity of habitats, which shorebirds and waterfowl prefer. Avoid areas where livestock destruction cannot be controlled (such as unfenced pasture or partial woodlands). Also avoid locations frequented by humans who lack understanding of what a vernal pond is (and may try to stock these sites with fish).

The Wet-Dry Cycle

Vernal ponds hold water, but dry up occasionally or even annually. Development of insects and larvae requires ninety or more consecutive water days during winter and spring. There must be a balance between shallow wetland (likely to dry up too soon) and deeper wetland (with a large watershed which never dries up).

The following factors regulate the wet-dry cycle in a vernal pond:

- Water depth
- Annual precipitation and evaporation
- Evapo-transpiration of water by aquatic and waterside plants
- Soil permeability
- The size of the watershed supplying water to the pond
- Amount of direct sunlight (not sheltered by trees)

Water Depth

Digging a pond too deep creates a wetland which holds water most of the year. Examine other wetlands in your area during the fall or the driest season to see how deep they are, and find watersheds that appear to support them. Look for water lines along the shore, and attempt to measure the water level fall. Note the degree of shade or sunlight present, along with the soil type (you may need a small shovel for this). This is how you can estimate expected evaporation in your area.

Water Table

Some sites experience a seasonally high water table. Such locations usually have a permeable soil type, which allows infiltration from surrounding soils. Check the height of water in your chosen site during various seasons of the year to determine more precisely how much variation there is in the water-table depth. You should dig a test pit well below the topsoil layer(s). When water infiltrates the test pit, it will rise nearly to the surface, an indication of a high water table. On land that has had little human alteration (such as a natural forest), it is often easy to predict soil moisture conditions just by the tree species growing there. Native trees locate themselves on soil-moisture conditions that favor their growth. Some species thrive across the complete soil-moisture continuum from wet to dry; most, however, have a specific hydrological requirement. Figure 6.18, based on species and soil moisture regime, displays this adaptation well, and it should be your first indicator of wet or dry soil conditions requiring further scrutiny.

Check for crayfish burrows around your site, and

for water close to the top of the burrow, as a crayfish digs down until it reaches water. Dry crayfish burrows likely indicate the presence of deep permeable soils, and thus, water loss. Building a vernal pond on such a site may require a liner or special construction practices. Contact your local state or provincial natural resource agency before creating a vernal pond on a site with saturated soils, since there is often legislation to prevent alteration of an existing wetland.

A large watershed is not a required for your pond and, in fact, may be a negative factor, ushering in copious amounts of water and silt on occasion that can fill the vernal pond with sediment. Situations with little or no watershed are preferred.

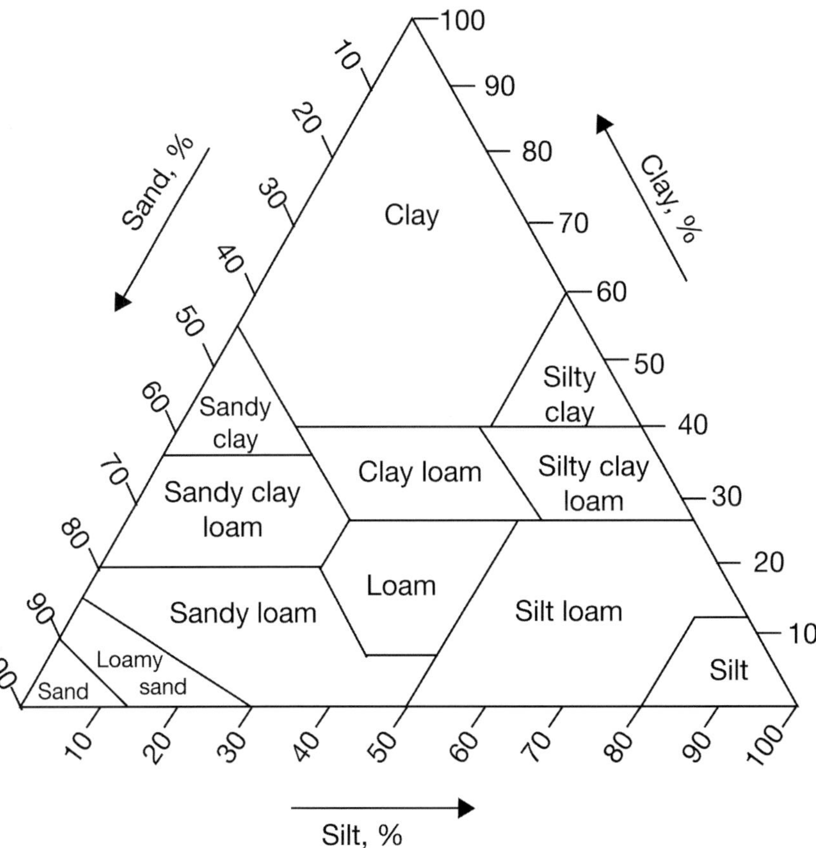

Figure 6.19 A soil-texture chart helps you to evaluate your site's specific soil characteristics.

SUN

Greater aquatic plant diversity.

More likely to dry up annually.

May contain dense growths of cattail species found in wetlands.

Pond warms up earlier in spring and promotes rapid growth of amphibian larvae.

Less leaf fall results in less bottom muck essential for nutrients.

More attractive to redwing blackbirds and yellowthroat warblers seeking nesting habitat (rushes, cattails, etc.).

SHADE

Less aquatic plant diversity.

Less likely to dry up annually.

Likely to contain grasses and sedges.

Growth could be curtailed by cooler water temperature combined with a falling water table.

Windblown leaf litter mulches into an organic muck—a food source for salamanders.

Less attractive to songbirds without aquatic plant habitat.

Sun Versus Shade

Locating a site with the optimum qualifications (soil type, water depth, size, etc.) may be difficult enough without the priority of sunlight. The table (on the left) outlines the effects of sun and shade on vernal pond development.

Soil-Type Preferences

Clay and silty loam soils hold water best because of their fine textures, and are ideal for a vernal pond. Coarse-textured soils such as sand and gravel are much more permeable, allowing water to percolate into the ground, and therefore require improvement to hold water. The coarse-textured class of soils permits too fast a draw-down in a vernal pond, and therefore, is generally not recommended for ponds without a liner.

Test the soil before beginning construction. Dig a test hole at least 4 ft. (1.25 m) deep. You should dig several test holes within the selected site to ensure uniform soil conditions. The simple test to determine clay or silt-loam content involves collecting a sample of soil between the thumb and forefinger. Add a little water if necessary, and squeeze the soil between your thumb and forefinger to form a ribbon. If you can form a ribbon at least 2 in. (5.08 cm) long, your soil should hold water.

Gravel Substratum

Also examine the soil texture under existing topsoil at your site location. If you detect a layer or bed of gravel you may run into real problems even if this layer is at considerable depth (up to 8 ft. or 3 m below the surface). Such conditions, which often exist under silt-loam and other soil types, make them unable to hold water without liners or special construction techniques; these are usually applied to the core of the dam.

Construction Techniques

Designing a Vernal Pond

Try to make the pond's perimeter irregular, or at least round. Most natural wetland ponds have a very gradual slope from the water depths to the shoreline edge, allowing emigration of developed amphibian larvae. Such gradually sloping pond banks also provide shoreline mud flats as water recedes during the pond's drying cycle. These exposed banks offer advantageous feeding areas to shorebirds.

Vernal-Pond Dam Construction

Unless your site is level, you will require some sort of dam to trap run-off. The maximum height of your dam is usually calculated as the difference in elevation between the high and low elevations on the chosen site, usually averaging between one to three ft. (0.3–1 m). Larger vernal ponds may require the use of a Dumpy-type survey level to measure the slope accurately. Make a drawing of your design before beginning construction. Revisit your site with a tape measure, lay out the design, and stake out the perimeter. Once you have the final elevation of the dam's top figured out, use a level to mark a line at that height on a tree bole (or drive in a pole outside the periphery of the dam). This will be used as a benchmark later on. The optimum time for vernal pond construction is during the driest season of your climatic zone (which is usually in the fall). There are two construction methods:

- Create a shallow depression in the soil to contain rainfall, utilizing a liner to contain the water.
- Create a shallow depression that fills with groundwater (if a high water table is present).

Site soils must have a low permeability; silt-loam or clay-textured soils are the most desirable. Try to find a local bulldozer operator experienced in building ponds, since he will be familiar with soil textures and soil-moisture conditions in your area. Most vernal ponds require construction techniques that compact soil within a shallow depression. This is most easily accomplished with bulldozer tracks.

Pile the topsoil near your pond site, as it will be re-spread around the finished project. Do not construct a dam with this material. Often, topsoil can be spread over the pond bottom before it fills up, providing a rich medium for the establishment of aquatic plants.

The next step is constructing a core under the proposed dam which blocks water movement under it. The core is usually as wide as a bulldozer blade, and should extend well below ground. The bulldozer operator should excavate the length of the dam down to an impervious layer of silt-loam, clay, or rock (if silt-loam or clay is already present, there is no requirement to remove it entirely only to shift and pack it back under the weight of the bulldozer). Permeable soils such as sand or gravel must be removed and replaced with impermeable soil (silt-loam or clay). If you find a large amount of sand or gravel, employ a synthetic liner or locate the pond elsewhere on your property. Building a dam on top of soil not properly excavated for a core will result in a failed pond, as the weight of the dozer and its blading action compresses excavated and shifted core soil, which remains porous. Watch for surface holes due to crayfish burrows and mammals. Tree roots or debris such as logs or fill can also present drainage problems when removed. Your core must extend to the bottom of any holes, and you should make every attempt to collapse and fill these prior to building. A single crayfish burrow left under a dam will drain an entire pond.

Making the core is a vital part of pond construction. Even when a dam is not required, a pond core should be built around the entire perimeter to prevent seepage out into surrounding soil. A core need only be 2 ft. (0.6 m) deep if no holes or crayfish burrows are present. Your core trench need only be as wide as the blade of your bulldozer, and soil needs to be excavated down to an impermeable layer. Repacking the excavated material in layers is essential to compact the soil and decrease porosity while increasing density. Soil layers should be about 6 in. (15 cm) deep, with each layer packed down firmly with the treads of the bulldozer blade before the addition of a new layer. The operator may have to run the dozer back over each layer several times. When finished, check with the Dumpy level to establish that the top of the dam is level and that a spillway point will not be created. The front and back of your dam should have a 10:1 slope, allowing for planting on the inside and mowing on the outside. A low slope discourages muskrats from creating a den entrance in your dam.

Vernal ponds or wetlands with dams over 3 ft. (1 m) high require a spillway to prevent washouts in periods of high water and storm flows. This spillway is usually placed next to the dam, preventing any area of the dam itself from being breached. The spillway depth for vernal ponds should be 6 in. (15 cm) to 1 ft. (30 cm) lower than the top of the dam, and generally as wide as a bulldozer blade. The spillway surface should be re-vegetated as soon as construction is finished. A grassed spillway is often sufficient, but a rock-lined spillway guarantees erosion protection and longevity. Use the Dumpy level again to excavate your spillway depth from 6 in. to 1 ft. (15–30 cm) below the lowest elevation in the dam (usually just next to the junction of the dam with the surrounding bank). Try to conceive how the water will flow out from this location by positioning yourself down-slope from the dam and judging the "lay of the land."

A drainpipe allows the pond owner to manage a pond—it can be used to lower the water level for repairs, to remove unwanted species, or just to control the wet-dry cycle. Install a horizontal section of 6 in. (15 cm) PVC drainpipe on top of the completed core before the layers of compacted soil are added. Anti-seep collars are normally not required on the drainpipe as vernal ponds have low hydraulic pressures. Compact all the soil layers on top of the pipe and add a 90° elbow to the inlet section in the center of the pond (or in its deepest section). Calculate the depth at this point and cut a vertical section of the same diameter PVC pipe for a riser. If you wish to control the water depth in your pond, purchase a 90° elbow gasketed such that the vertical section can be swiveled down into the water to the depth you choose to draw down to.

Spread all excess soil (removed and stockpiled earlier) around the perimeter of your pond, tapering it down to the existing grade of the surrounding soil. Do not create a "donut" around the entire vernal pond, for this will prevent run-off from entering it. Complete the earthwork by spreading topsoil (also stockpiled) on the pond bottom and up over the banks, shaping with a bulldozer and raking to blend with the shorelines. Introduce native aquatic and terrestrial plant species, planting them in and around the pond. Unless your pond is fully exposed in direct sunlight with little shade, the choice in plants will fall in the soil-moisture regime of wet-to-mesic shown on the chart in Figure 6.18.

If you discover your pond site has a layer of gravel beneath the upper soil horizon, or if you wish to create a larger vernal pond, you will need to use a tracked back hoe (or an industrial back hoe or track-hoe). This is used to dig a wide trench to form the dam core as wide as a bulldozer blade. (Some back hoes come with a blade also installed). Store the silt-loam upper-soil horizon along the inside edge of your vernal pond, but place the excavated gravel layer outside the pond perimeter. Back hoe excavation should go down as far as is practical or until an impermeable soil layer is encountered (clay or bedrock). Use the bulldozer to fill the trench with a clay-loam mixture, packing each successive 6 in. (15 cm) layer with bulldozer treads until you reach the height determined with the Dumpy level (remember the benchmark in the tree bole).

Sites with sand-and-gravel upper-soil horizons or buried fill require the installation of a liner. Since liners are a considerable expense, the size of your vernal pond will be limited (usually less than 30 ft. or 10 m wide and 40 ft. or 14 m long). Make sure the liner you purchase is "fish grade," or classified as a commercial liner used for landfills. Two types of liner are in common use for ponds—EDPM (ethylene propylene monomer) and PVC (polyvinyl chloride). EDPM liners are about 1.75 in. (45 mm) thick, while PVC liners are just over an inch (30 mm). Tarps or plastic drop cloths are not suitable. You should protect the liner with a fabric pad called a "geo-textile" or "geo-pad" to prevent puncture by sharp rocks and debris that may be in the fill. Liners should last 30 years or more. A bulldozer is required to excavate the shallow depression. This should be 6–8 in. (15 to 20 cm) deeper than the desired pond depth, since soil must be placed over the liner. A dam of some sort may be required at the lower grade of the site to maintain a level perimeter.

Place the geo-textile pad on the floor of the excavation, and carefully lay the synthetic liner on top, smoothing out all wrinkles. When you are satisfied that the liner is

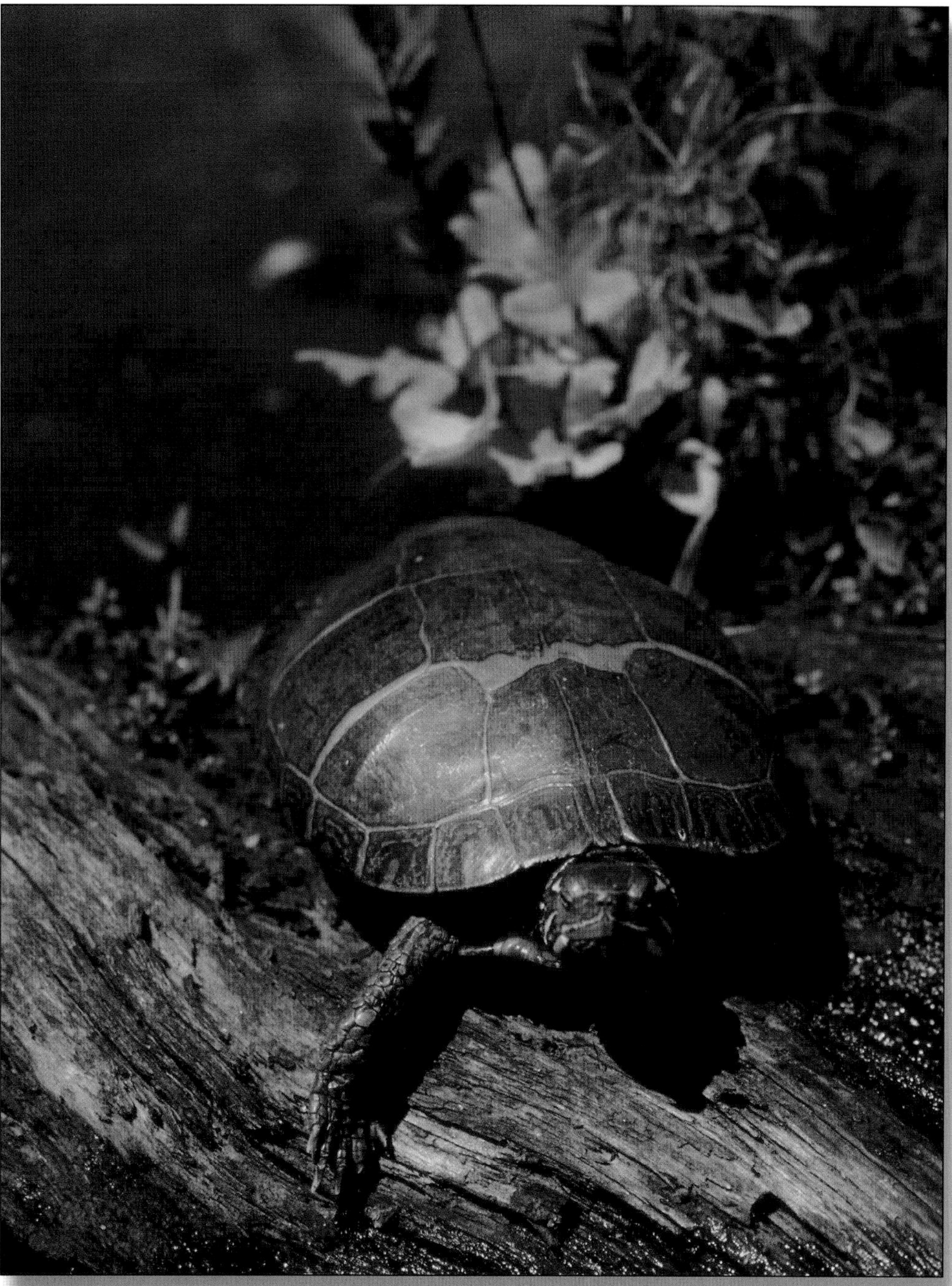

A mature painted turtle takes advantage of a log in a vernal pond to catch some sunshine.

as smooth as possible, place another geo-textile pad on top of it. Anchor the uppermost rim of the liner plus the geo-textile with wire pins or large spikes with washers 24 in. (60 cm) apart. These pins prevent the liner from being dislodged and pushed down into the excavation once soil is dumped into it and graded.

Carefully cover the liner-plus-geotextile by pushing soil back into the excavation, making sure the bulldozer travels on at least 6–8 in. (15–20 cm) of freshly deposited soil. Do not turn the bulldozer on the fresh soil over the liner as the treads will move it and tear it. Soil over the liner protects it from damage by limbs and deer hooves, while preventing deterioration from ultraviolet rays. Adding soil over the liner also provides habitat for amphibians and insects, in addition to being a medium for plant growth. Seed and mulch the exposed soil around your pond perimeter with an erosion-control species such as crown vetch or bird's-foot trefoil.

Sites with a High Water Table

Using heavy equipment around saturated wetland soils is risky—and expensive if the machinery gets stuck. A tracked back hoe is essential, but a large area free of trees is required to allow an operator room to swing the bucket away from the excavation site. The tracked back hoe will dig the entire vernal pond basin when it is in a stable area. Test the location first by backing the machine carefully in and out of the site before commencing work. If the soil underneath is soggy, the machine will embed itself when loaded. This is to be avoided. A good operator will slope the sides gradually by drawing the bucket toward the machine, leaving the vernal-pond profile relatively smooth. Without a bulldozer, the banks and surrounding area must be graded smooth by hand using shovels and rakes to make the site look less disturbed. Seed the banks and surroundings with a good erosion-control species as above.

Creating Habitat

You can attract wildlife by using logs from trees cut down during construction. Turtles will utilize these for basking. Natural vernal ponds within forests usually contain woody debris, such as fallen branches or trees; this debris increases the number of wildlife species occupying and using the pond. Salamanders attach eggs to tree branches in the water, beneath logs on the banks, or under leaf litter when the pond is dry. Autumn rains aid the hatching of these eggs, giving them a headstart over other amphibians breeding in the pond. Emerging salamanders also find protection in the logs near a vernal pond as they wait for suitable conditions to migrate from water to forest cover. Salamanders are a very valuable species within the forest ecosystem.

Maintaining the Vernal Pond

Your vernal pond should be inspected at least once a year. Carefully examine the dam sides and a short section downstream from your spillway to make sure there are no underground seepage points. The spillway should also be cleaned out annually, removing logs and branches that may have fallen onto it. The perimeter of any vernal pond should be mowed once a year with a bush hog, or manually with a brush scythe, to remove live trees growing on the dam. (If left to mature, their roots will offer channels for leakage, eventually undermining the dam.) You may also want to reduce any cattail or bulrush growth which invades your the pond, particularly if it occupies too large an area of water surface. Hand-pull the stems but remember this often leaves small sections of tubers which re-propagate the next spring. A light application of Roundup applied directly (and very sparingly) to any stem will kill the roots. I hesitate to recommend the use of chemical herbicides, since it is very difficult to prevent contamination of the water body, but when applied with great caution, they assure a permanent stem kill. Do not use a spray but apply the chemical with a small paintbrush, making sure no drips get onto the water surface.

Use of Explosives to Create Vernal Ponds

I have omitted outlining the use of explosives for vernal-pond excavations for reasons of habitat destruction, the danger to nearby residences, and the difficulty in obtaining permits to use them. They may be applicable in more remote areas, but for the general citizen, the use of explosives is not recommended.

Insert a log into the depths of a vernal pond leaving one end on the bank, for turtles and other invertebrates to use for sunning on above and for shade below.

Chapter Seven

Spillways, Water-Control Devices, and Erosion-Control Materials

Earth spillways

Building an adequate spillway is essential, as most spillways are destroyed during the first severe storm. The spillway is designed to usher excess floodwater around your dam, preventing water from overtopping it. The downstream slope of any dam erodes easily once it is overtopped with storm water at high velocity and volume. Earth-type spillways should be used only where discharge of peak flow is well downstream from the dam. When expected outflow exceeds 100 yd.^{3} (76 m^3) per second, you will need to hire an engineer to design a structural (cement) spillway. An excavated or preformed spillway has three sections: approach channel, control section, and exit channel.

Water enters the spillway through the approach channel. The central level portion controls flow rate, ushering water through the control section and the control point, which forms the downstream edge of the spillway. Then the flow discharges through the exit channel. The direction of the sloped exit section should not allow outflow onto any part of the dam, or else scouring will occur. Satisfactory operation of these three sections will guarantee that your spillway functions as designed. When the end of the dam meets the side slope abutment, this should be well protected with rip-rap or other suitable erosion-control surface materials. The channel entrance should be 50 percent wider than the control section's bottom width. The approach channel must be gradually curved (no sharp angles). A negative slope no less than 2–3 percent must be constructed to ensure proper drainage into the spillway. The control section should lie upon the centerline of the dam, running fully across it. The control point on the downstream edge of the control section should be level and about 20 ft. (6.1 m) long. Make sure that the exit section has

Overflow spillways on dams are put to the test under snow melt and spring run-off conditions.

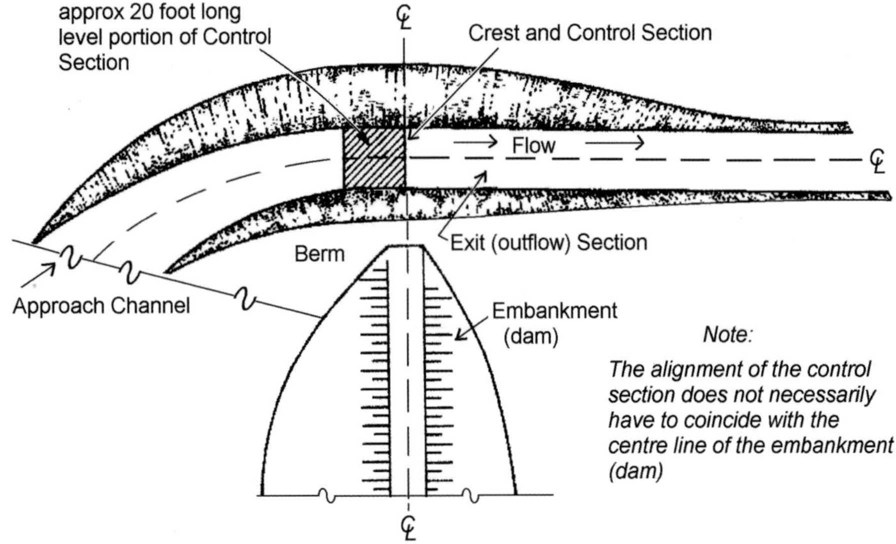

Figure 7.1 A plan view of an excavated earth spillway [adapted from Ponds for Water Supply and Recreation*].*

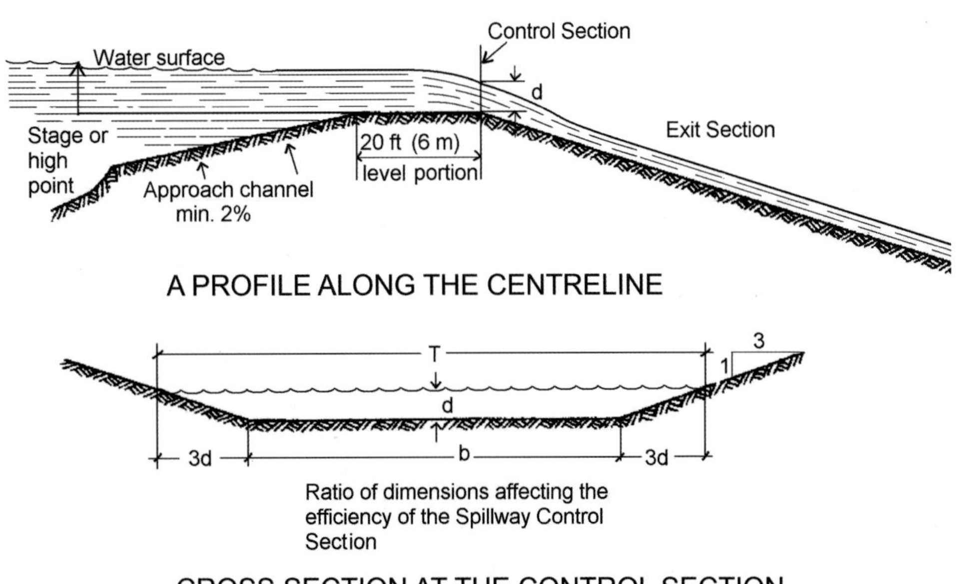

Figure 7.2 A centerline profile and cross section of the earth spillway in Figure 7.1.

enough slope to discharge peak storm flow within the channel confines. This slope must be no steeper than permitted by the soil type and its erosion-control cover, considering the maximum velocity of water expected. (Permitted velocities are usually less than 5.5 ft.[3] (1.5 hectoliters) per second for earth spillways.)

The spillway exit channel should be designed relatively straight, with side slopes in a ratio of no greater than 3:1. The entire spillway must be protected by stonework. I prefer a mixture of large boulders and assorted medium-sized water-washed stones, hand-placed to simulate a natural stream boulder-bed. Rip-rap, or blast rock, is usually employed by road departments on adjacent dams, but is neither aesthetic nor environmentally friendly. Carefully assembled stone work should look natural. Some pond owners install "wing-dykes" beyond the control point with heavy-gauge wire mesh strung between them to retain fish in the pond—another required management practice requested by river authorities. With good erosion-control materials, your spillway should require little maintenance and add an element of "flow" to an otherwise still pond.

Drop-Inlet Trickle-Tube Spillways

A drop-inlet trickle-tube spillway is typically a spiral steel pipe under or through the dam, and connected to a "riser" at the upstream end of the pipe. This tube usually protects the emergency spillway channel from being used, because it ushers excess flow out under the dam itself. Crest elevation of the riser should be 12 in. (30 cm) or more below the top of the flat control section of the earth spillway (note that some dams do not have an emergency spillway). The trickle-tube must be large enough to carry flow from springs, snowmelt, or rainstorms. It can also be used to drain a pond if a valve is installed at the upstream end of its horizontal submerged section. There are tables for calculating required pipe sizes for adequate discharge capacity (see endnotes). The diameter of the riser is usually specified to be larger than the diameter of the barrel below it in order that the tube may flow-fill. Smaller diameter pipes are easily clogged with trash, rodents, and sticks; use a 6 in. (15cm) diameter pipe as a barrel, with the riser approaching 1 ft. (30 cm) in diameter.

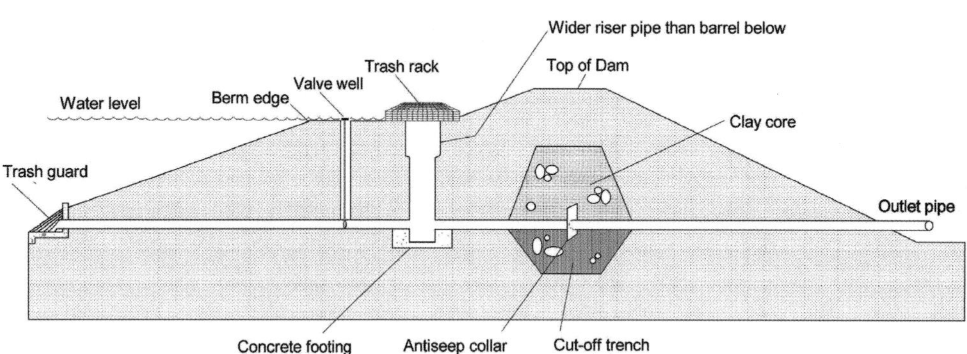

Figure 7.3 Cross-section of a typical surface-overflow dam with a drop-inlet spillway and optional bottom-draw tube [adapted from USDA Agricultural Handbook #590*].*

Other Water Control Devices

Anti-Seep Collars

To prevent seepage along the surface of the trickle-tube through the dam, it is essential to install anti-seep collars. Steel collars are suitable for smooth steel pipes and special metal diaphragms are available for corrugated metal pipes (culvert pipes). Concrete collars 6 in. (15 cm) thick are often used with concrete and cast-iron pipes. The collars should extend into the fill about 24 in. (60 cm) perpendicular to the pipe. Usually two or more collars are required, equally spaced between the centerline of the dam and the upstream end of the pipe.

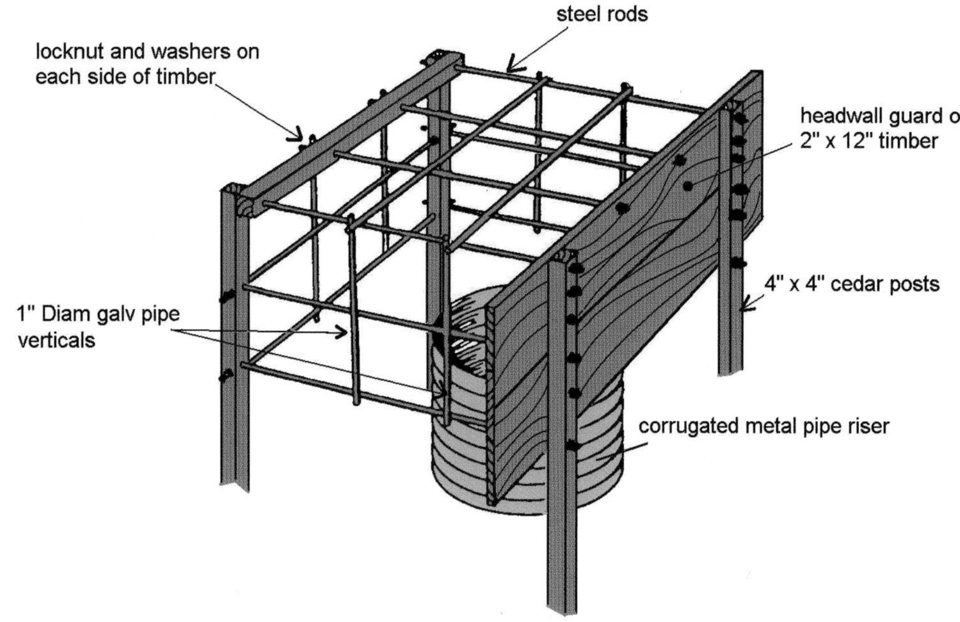

Figure 7.4 A self-fabricated timber headwall and trash rack used in drop-inlet trickle-tubes [from Ponds for Water Supply and Recreation*].*

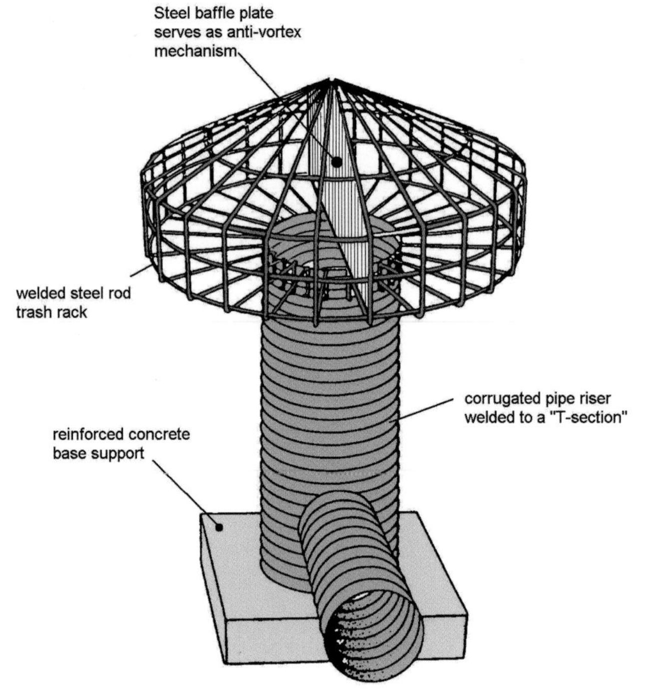

Figure 7.5 A conical wire trash guard with a baffle built in for larger corrugated metal culvert risers [from Ponds for Water Supply and Recreation].

Trash Racks

These are devices attached to the top of the trickle-tube riser to prevent trickle-tubes from being clogged with debris. The designs shown in Figures 7.3 and 7.4 have proven successful.

A satisfactory trickle-tube trash rack can be fabricated from fence posts 5–6 in. (13–15 cm) in diameter, and woven-wire fence. Steel posts can be used as long as they are braced. The fence "cage" should extend above the highest-expected water level. For tube diameters greater than twelve inches (30 cm), specially designed trash guards as shown in Figure 7.5 are necessary.

Drawbacks in Using Piping for Spillways

Many pond owners have a distrust of underground spillways, preferring a simple earth spillway across the dam. A lot of money can be invested in building underground spillways, and they are prone to leakage. A bottom-drain spillway offers an instant tap-type control of pond volume, fast-flushing the pond for habitat alteration, or facilitating a draw-down to harvest fish or undesirable aquatic weeds. The spillway standpipe also maintains a steady water level in the pond as long as incoming water is sufficient. This sounds good until a leakage occurs, and one must remember the whole underground system, including all steel piping in contact with earth, is prone to leakage. Two types of drain pipe are usually considered: iron and culvert-style steel (spiral pipe). The double-riveted spiral pipe, when tar-coated and spot-welded in the trench (versus at the plant) is more trustworthy than pre-welded material trucked to the site. This latter pipe is usually several pieces welded together; and flexure during transportation can open up an unnoticed seam. Iron pipe available from a scrap yard is less expensive, but care must be taken during installation. The base under the pipe must be packed firm before the pipe is lowered in, or settling will eventually break the joints. When an overflow standpipe couples to the drain, the drainpipe should be tilted downward to achieve a clean flow and prevent sediment clogging.

Anti-seep collars along the drain pipe are a must, but still provide no guarantee against leakage.

The drain plug or gate at the forward (upstream) end of the drain pipe can be another headache. Usually buried in sediment or weeds at the very bottom of the pond, this fixture is hard to remove or release, although it may be dependable enough when controlled by a hand-wheel (which must be operated frequently to assure its performance). Water at 62 lb. per ft.^{3} (28 kg per 0.3 m^3) has a powerful influence on gates, gears, and iron devices. Deep anaerobic water has a tendency to corrode metals quickly.

"Uncorking" a simple softwood stopper by punching it out with an iron pipe has its merits, but there's no closing it. Earth ponds naturally degenerate without constant management, and any pond owner must

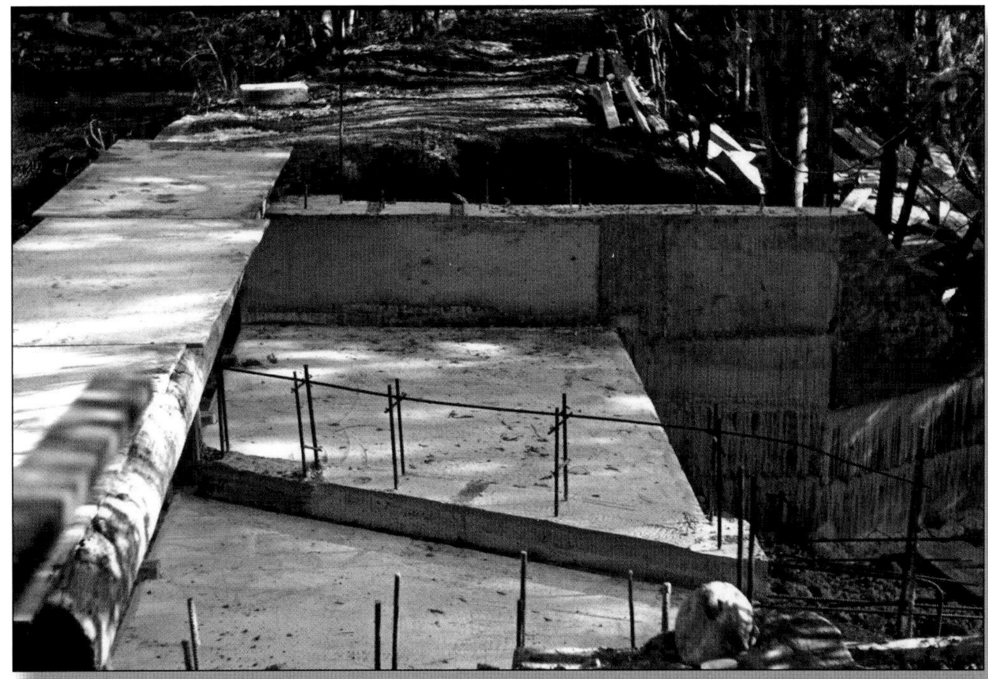

Top: A typical overflow spillway under construction as an integral part of the dam—notice the thickness of cement on the sides and the spillway apron. This type of spillway requires good engineering and construction skills. A separate emergency spillway should also be built to handle a regional storm. Failure of this single spillway due to undercutting could result in the loss of the dam in a storm. The dam in this photo is accompanied by another that the owner maintains for security. They both usher warm surface water downstream—often a necessity in dams like this with large water volumes [Courtesy of Valorie Levens, Udora Mill, Udora, Ontario].

Bottom: An older dam with an overflow spillway creates a beautiful mill pond beyond its waterfall. A unique footbridge spans the top of the dam. This structure is the third dam of the series, all three engineered to handle flood waters and control the millrace water level which runs downstream to the mill [Courtesy of Valorie Levens, Udora Mill, Udora, Ontario].

take a careful look at the simplest ways to achieve a reliable draw-down system without damaging the pond's earth structure.

I'm inclined to agree with the natural earthen alternative, except for the fact that it gives the owner no ability to flush the pond. An earth spillway cannot donate a cooler column of water either, because the spillway is at the pond's warm-water surface.

A roll of hose line used as a siphon, pushed through the single outlet pipe to extend into the bottom of the pond, serves as a viable alternative to an expensive "trickle-tube riser." The siphon will drain cooler, low-strata, high-sediment water from the pond. This achieves three objectives stream authorities promote:

- Cold water is contributed to downstream environments.
- Silt build-up in the pond is prevented.
- Bottom eutrophication in the pond is reduced.

Using an earth spillway (without a drop-inlet riser) keeps a pond overflowing constantly as inflow augments the water volume. In low-flow creek or drought conditions, the spillway rests empty. When the channel is lined with rip-rap over a thick geo-

Top: A steel lift-gate–type dam spillway with concrete side walls and hand wheel to lift the gate [Pefferlaw Brook, Udora, Ontario].

Bottom: The discharge side of the dam above. Note the strong flow resulting from a spring run-off. Water pressure on the steel gate is much too high to move the gate by hand, hence the hand wheel and gear assembly to manipulate it [Pefferlaw Brook, Udora, Ontario].

textile fabric, it usually resists erosion. Owners often use concrete slabs or granite blast rock over heavy-flow spillways, although a well-lined grassy spillway will suffice for most normal conditions. One has to watch out for storm-created flows, where scouring can result in failure of the pond. The probability for failure depends upon the size of the watershed, surface conditions, and gradient. A simple dug-out pond with a sub-surface spring outflow will probably only overflow in a heavy rainstorm, whereas a pond in a gully or a dammed pond will likely sustain structural damage.

The spillway for a small dug-out pond should be filled with compacted soil and seeded in grass. Spillway side slopes should be no steeper than 3:1 to prevent slumping: the spillway banks should be mulched to protect against erosion.

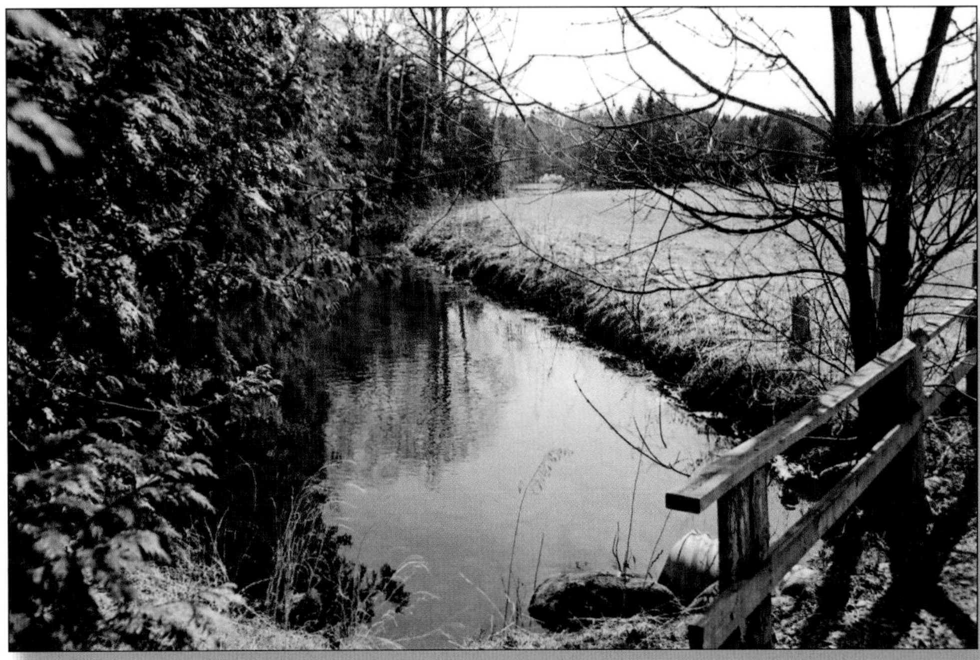

A natural emergency spillway issues a constant slow flow of water through a stream course on the quiet side of the impoundment on page 130. This emergency spillway adds security to the dam structure and will carry away any excess storm water the dam cannot control. It also could serve as a fish-way to allow fish upstream if no impediments, such as a perched culvert or drop structure that fish cannot migrate over or through, exist [Pefferlaw Brook, Udora, Ontario].

Use of Erosion Control Materials

Protecting the Pond Environs

Once you have graded and established the planned water level of your pond, its banks should be seeded in erosion-proof product such as bird's-foot trefoil, which is quick to establish and acts as a good nurse crop. If you saved topsoil from the initial excavation, it should be spread evenly across the embankment and dam area and the site thoroughly raked either manually or with a tractor-drawn rake (such as a York rake) to loosen up soil surface in preparation for seed. If you choose to apply trefoil seed, which is hardy enough

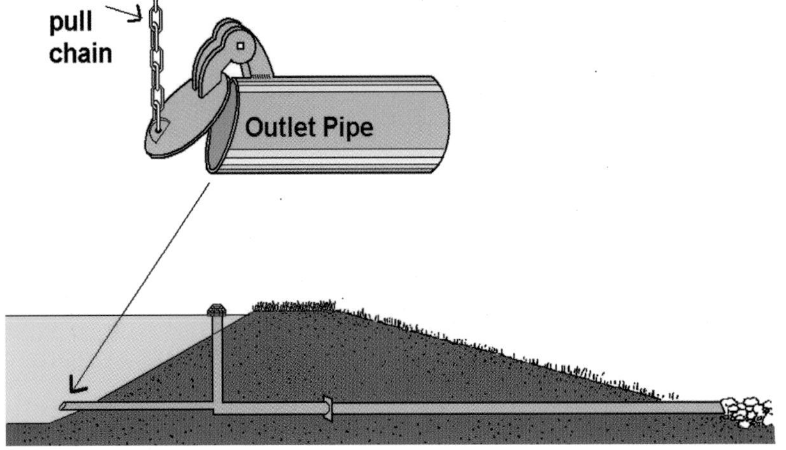

Figure 7.6 A simple, fabricated flap valve operated by a chain is attached to the bottom-draw pipe outlet, allowing easy draw-down and valve-closing [adapted from Earth Ponds*].*

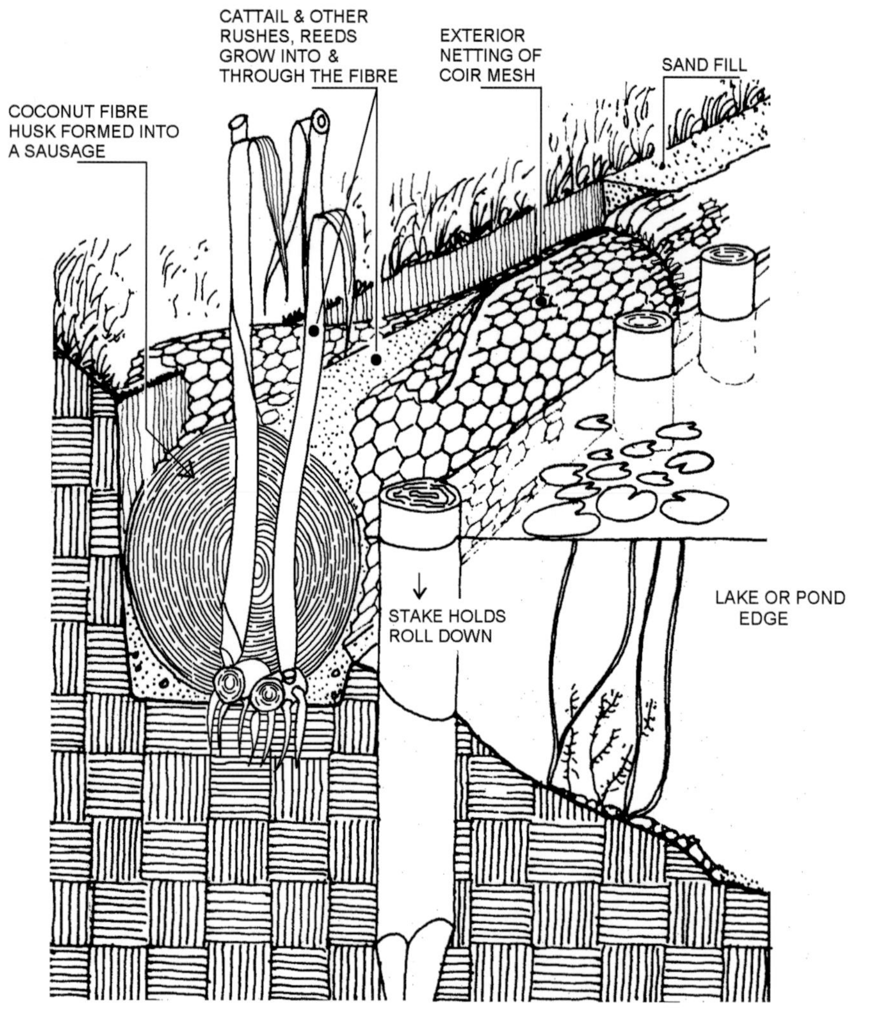

Figure 7.7 A Waterlog roll, usually composed of coir or jute, installed along the margins of a pond or lake, quickly becomes naturalized with emergent aquatic plants and is unnoticeable as a synthetic product. [Courtesy of Maccaferri Limited].

to grow on almost any soil condition, spread a thin covering of topsoil to speed growth.

Immediately following seed application, cover the ground with an organic-type erosion-control blanket consisting of woven straw and string. Verdyol and North American Green both manufacture excellent products of this type. The blanket aids in retaining moisture while shading developing seed from sun,

A coconut-fiber biodegradable blanket. [Courtesy of North American Green Inc.]

wind, and rain erosion should a rainstorm occur before the plants establish themselves. Remove the blanket before the trefoil gets too high and entraps it; alternatively you can leave it to biodegrade by ultraviolet light as it is designed to do. (Should you cut the trefoil some time later by machine, be aware that the blanket will catch in the rotating blade and wind up thicker than rope, stalling the engine). If the blanket is left intact, set mower deck high and maintain the trefoil no less than 6 in. (15 cm) high. These plants serve as a good wildlife food source and habitat preferred by deer, rabbits, and other rodents.

Jute- or coir-fiber rolls such as Waterlog can be applied to eroding pond edges. Stake them in at the water line lest wave action begin to chew away at the pond. These rolls are easily handled and easy to fix with wooden stakes along the margins of your pond: they form a barrier to wave action and promote vegetative growth either within the roll or adjacent to it. Waterlog ends are tied together with coir twine. Plants are plugged in along the top of the Waterlogs between the coir netting, or in the soil alongside. The product will biodegrade over time, leaving a pond margin lush in natural emergent aquatic plants. This is a quick and healthy way to aid nature in establishing a pond littoral edge.

Top: Pre-cast interlocking concrete blocks (Terrafix) shown lining the face of a water-quality pond spillway. Grass has completely filled the voids in the turf stone blocks, providing excellent erosion protection [Keswick North Subdivision, Town of Georgina].

Center: A close-up of Terrafix concrete blocks forming a heavy erosion-proof mat, installed using a crane or industrial backhoe. [Courtesy of Risi Stone Inc.]

Protecting the Dam and Spillway Surfaces

The spillway and face of the dam at the downstream end of the pond are exposed to the rigorous current and wave action, and must be protected against erosion. Log booms cabled together and anchored to each end of the dam are a good means of breaking wave action while also warning boaters of the pond's dangerous end. Logs should be coupled together no more than 2 ft. (0.61 m) apart by chain, leaving enough slack to allow the booms to adjust to fluctuating water levels. The optimum position for your boom should be about 6 ft. (2 m) upstream from the dam face. The ends of the chains should be linked to steel posts driven deep into the banks of your pond.

Rip-rap is normally applied to the margin of the pond at the face of the dam. This offers good protection, but is hard to walk on or fish from. It should be placed over a fiberglass geo-textile blanket fabricated for erosion control. Stretch the geo-textile blanket out on the face of the dam and stake it securely before applying rock to a depth of about a foot (0.3 m). It is important to use crushed-stone rip-rap or blast rock, which are rough and irregular, so that they lock together. Rounded stone, although much more natural and aesthetic, tends to roll and dislodge from

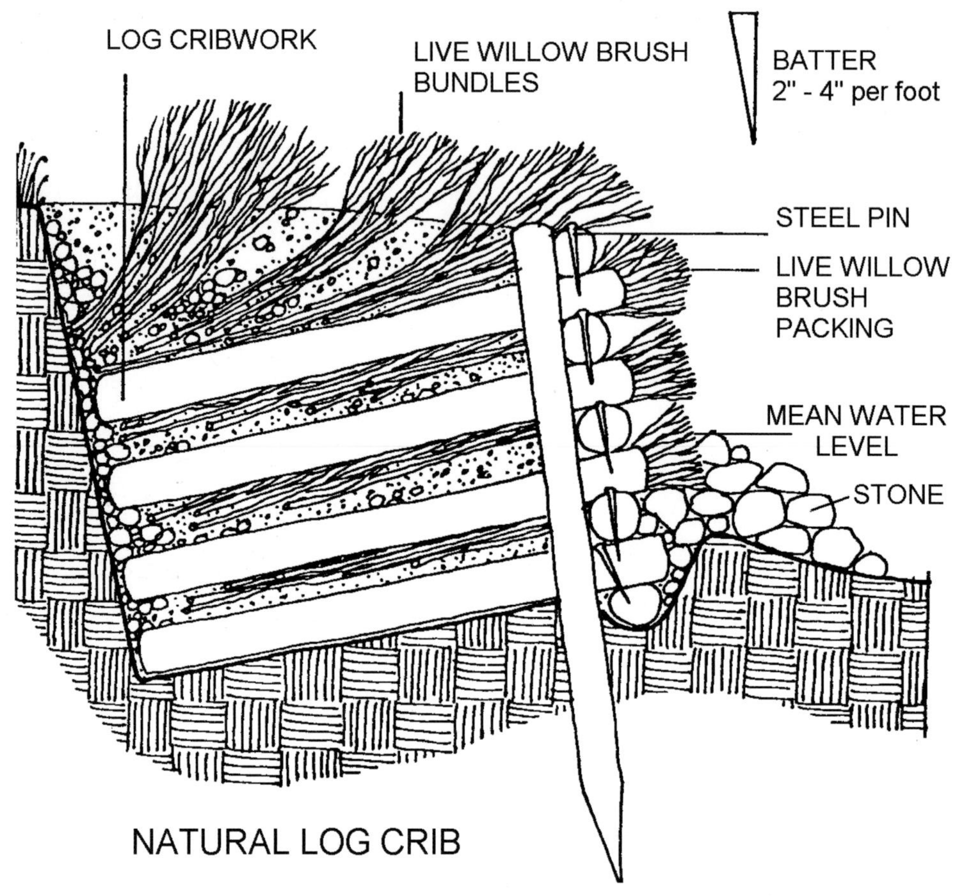

Figure 7.8 Installation of log cribs and willow brush serves as a bioengineered deterrent to erosion in moderately turbulent areas of a pond or lake where current or wave action is damaging the shoreline.

the dam's sloping face. The rip-rap and blanket should extend from the dam crest to approximately 3 ft. (1 m) below the expected water level; it is imperative to apply the blanket before the pond is filled with water. Other products on the market can be substituted very well for rip-rap. These include turf stone or a precast concrete-stone slab with openings for turf establishment. Lay the stones on a fiberglass filter cloth over the compacted sub-grade and place one against the other by hand or crane. Again, the stones must fill the entire area on the exposed dam face to approximately 3 ft. (1 m) below expected water level. Voids in the turf stone can be filled with an earth mixture above the water level and seeded with a natural grass mixture such as Pickseed's Wetland Mixture. Apply the seed after adding soil to about one-half the depth of the voids in the turf stone, then top up the voids with soil. Filling protects the seed below the stone slab surface and prevents it from washing away in rain. Other types of articulated concrete units can be applied as "mats," interlocked with steel wire. These are very heavy and usually installed by crane.

Maintenance and Inspection

Your pond should be inspected regularly, particularly after heavy rains and in winter, when ice-cover may block outflow pipes and spillways. If immediate damage repair is not undertaken, the situation usually worsens. Washouts or rills in side slopes of the dam or spillway require the most attention and repair. Application of a coir blanket (a tougher blanket made from coconut fiber) may be necessary. Pin this down temporarily to prevent further damage. Later, you can lift it off and reseed. Cut the vegetation on the dam top and slopes occasionally to prevent the growth of woody plants, which undermine your dam as their root systems create seepage channels. Check regularly for burrowing animals such as muskrats or bank beavers along the waterline or just below it. If you find evidence of these creatures, reduce the damage by burying heavy-gauge mesh fencing along the face of the dam or its banks. If you used turf stone or rip-rap on the dam face, that area is probably adequately protected. Trickle-tubes, trash racks, outlet pipes, and valves need to be constantly cleared of debris. This requires at least a weekly inspection of larger ponds, particularly those with embankment dams.

A spring-fed pond will usually freeze under winter conditions, blocking the outlet pipe. Most spring-fed ponds also suffer a reduced inflow rate in winter. Deep frost and snow cover reduce the groundwater recharge rate until spring melt. A rapid melt, which often happens in spring, causes the inflow rate from springs and run-off to create standing water over the pond's ice surface. Excess water unable to escape through an ice-clogged overflow or outlet pipe collects over ice and can quickly overtop the embankment or dam of the pond. Time your inspections for this event so that you can chop free any ice surrounding the overflow or outlet pipes.

When you discover damage through seepage in the dam structure, you should consult an engineer. Owning a pond is a management responsibility if you want to keep it intact and operating smoothly.

A beautiful, well-kept dam and pond is a tremendous asset to any rural property [Pefferlaw Brook, Udora, Ontario].

Chapter Eight
Ponds for Fish

General Ponds for Fish

The following guidelines are ideal if you are considering a warm-water fish or trout population in your pond or small lake:

- Surface area of 0.5 ac. (0.2 ha) or larger
- Side slopes minimum 1 ft. (0.3 m) vertical to 3 ft. (1 m) horizontal
- Depth of pond bed approximately 12–15 ft. (4–5 m) (ponds over 15 ft. or 5 m in depth are not recommended due to the possibility of low levels of oxygen which will result in fish kills)
- Concentration of dissolved oxygen above 5 ppm, even in deep water
- Low infiltration of nutrient chemicals, at the level at which they would enter the pond normally when the drainage basin was covered by natural, undisturbed vegetation. Inflow that occurs only by groundwater normally keeps nutrient levels low and avoids the consequent high algae growth.
- Water supply from ground water seepage rather than run-off from overland sources
- Dissolved mineral content of 150–250 ppm
- pH scale acid-alkalinity rating from 7 to 8
- Moderate amount of submergent, emergent, and floating aquatic plants, including algae. Less than a quarter of the pond bed should be covered by plant growth.
- Site location with fertile soil (versus sterile soil)
- Provision of a bottom draw-off device to reduce summer and winter oxygen depletion and subsequent fish kills, while maintaining colder water temperatures downstream
- Avoidance of run-off from barnyards, pastures, and fertilized or eroding farmland
- Avoidance of high levels of nitrogen (Have your water source tested before planning a fish pond, as high levels of nitrogen cause gas bubble disease in fish.)

One of the perks of owning a pond is the joy of catching your fish.

- No livestock in or near the pond (Livestock fencing is a must.)
- No leachate beds from septic tanks within 300 feet (100 m) or more in pervious soils
- Kidney-shaped design, with the long axis oriented north-south to minimize wave action and erosion

Over-enrichment of ponds with nutrient phosphate will reduce a pond's potential for fish production. Algae and other aquatic plants become a nuisance when excess phosphorus enter the pond. Many ponds have low to moderate amounts of aquatic vegetation, even though overall conditions are perfect for plant production, because little phosphorus enters from surrounding land. Phosphorus is deemed the limiting factor for algae and leafy-plant production, and is the basis of the pond's food web. Increasing the phosphorus load does not always result in greater production of fish, because usually only a portion of algae production is useful to fish. The size of that portion depends upon the water's *alkalinity.*

Conditions such as the concentration of dissolved mineral content in ground water would be impractical to try and regulate, and the pond owner should not be discouraged from proceeding with a fish pond just because the water supply might have mineral levels of only 50–100 ppm. Other factors—such as very low-volume water supply from stream water, or, more critically, run-off from land sources— might be more serious. A perfect cold-water pond for trout will differ from a warm-water pond for bass mainly in its greater inflow of well-oxygenated ground water, which will maintain a lower water temperature in summer.

Investigating Suitability for Fish

Seek the assistance of a professional biologist who will make measurements of factors such as alkalinity, pH, dissolved oxygen, inorganic nitrogen, phosphorus, temperature, and dissolved solids (conductivity). These are usually best done in spring just after ice leaves the pond or lake. Your expert should offer advice on adjusting the balance between alkalinity and phosphorus for the best fish production. Kits are available for these tests, but interpretation of the results requires professional experience as will any design alterations required to improve the conditions. The following indicators are essential:

- Maximum water depth
- Abundance of water plants
- Sources of phosphorus
- Dissolved oxygen (DO)
- Water temperature

Dissolved oxygen tests require a DO meter; a minimum survey should involve sampling in mid to late summer after hot weather, and in winter when ice and snow have rested on the pond for about a month. Summer measurements should be taken before 6:00 a.m. and again at 3:00 p.m., after maximum sunlight. Sampling should take place throughout the water column where the pond is deepest. The results of temperature and DO should be recorded as tables. Samples/readings must be taken at the bottom of the pond, and at a medium depth. Additional reading or a course in pond biology is recommended if you are intent on taking these readings yourself.

Cold-Water Species Requirements

Ponds planned for trout production require a constant supply of cool, clean water. Spring-fed ponds can usually support a healthy trout population, whereas ponds fed by run-off water from overland sources will be much more vulnerable to low flow, high temperature, and turbidity. A pond outflow rate of up to 2 $ft.^3$ ($0.6\ m^3$) per second is ideal, although some situations with lesser outflow will still maintain an adequate fresh-water replenishment. Water temperature is the most important condition on the critical-factors list: best growth for trout occurs between 10°C (50°F) and 18°C (65°F). Some portion of your pond should supply this temperature range for best fish production. Surface-water temperatures may reach as high as 27°C (80°F) or more, provided deeper bottom temperature does not exceed 21°C (70°F). Dissolved oxygen levels should be well above 5 ppm throughout the year, even in the deepest part of your pond. Ponds with lower deep-water temperatures often take advantage of the insulating effect of chara. In trout pond management, it is beneficial to maintain a carpet of chara on the pond bottom, particularly in deeper ponds where it will not reach the surface. Deep-water temperature is a useful criterion in assessing the suitability of a pond for trout. (M. G. Johnson, Toronto and Region Conservation Authority). Turnover period and inflow temperature, both somewhat uncontrollable, are undoubtedly the most important factors influencing pond temperature. Since much success depends upon pond depth and water supply, the deeper your pond is, the better for trout.

Trout may attempt to spawn in pond areas where a spring upwells, exposing gravel or coarse sand. Normally, however, they spawn in gravel beds under flowing stream water and rarely reproduce successfully in ponds.

Trout prefer zooplankton, insect larvae and crayfish. Although you can supplement this diet by feeding (particularly if there is a large trout population in your pond), it is not normally recommended.

Cold-water fishes include trout, whitefish, salmon, and grayling, but normally, only trout are considered suitable for managed ponds or small lakes. Other cold-water fishes such as northern pike, muskellunge, walleye, and perch usually do not flourish in smaller bodies of water, preferring larger lake bodies. These spaces are only recommended for lake environments.

Warm-Water Species Requirements

When cultivating warm-water fish, much of your pond should be warmer than 21°C (70°F) throughout the summer months. This should be measured about a foot (0.3 m) below the surface in the pond center. If you find the temperature is below 21°C (70°F), smallmouth bass might be a logical species choice as they prefer water cooler than that inhabited by their cousin, the largemouth bass. Dissolved oxygen in this case can go as low as 3–4 ppm in summer, but should be above 5 ppm most of the time. If your pond is 15 feet (5 m) deep or more, oxygen will be more plentiful in summer and winter as long as aquatic plant nutrients are low and a build-up of ooze does not happen in the benthic zone. Do not feed your fish with pellets, as this will accelerate the growth of algae and other aquatic plants, resulting in an accumulation of organic matter, which ultimately causes oxygen depletion and fish die-off.

Bass thrive on worms, frogs, insect larvae, small fish, and crayfish. You can always supplement this, if you find that your bass need additional food.

Fish Stocking and Restocking

Fish stocking and restocking depends on a plethora of conditions, including the amount and size of fish present, fishing pressure expected, available food, whether reproduction is occurring, and the pond owner's budget. You should decide whether catch-and-release fishing or outright harvest will be your ongoing practice. Common sense dictates that the larger the pond size, the greater the percentage of fish will survive being caught.

Trout

An existing pond destined for trout should be purged of other fish, with inlets and outlets screened to prevent entry of the smallest species. This practice applies both to an existing pond and a new pond. It may also be wise with an existing pond to combine a re-digging operation with a fish-removal draw-down to eliminate excess vegetation. Reducing organic matter from the benthic zone aids habitat conditions for trout, although an exception to this rule would be removing a fine carpet of chara. Chara helps maintain low temperatures. April, May, and early June are good months to stock because water temperatures have increased slightly and natural organisms (fish food) are plentiful. September and October are less favorable because the pond cools down and the chance for growth lessens; as winter approaches, there is less time for the new imports to adjust. Stocking trout in summer exposes them to thermal shock, which can cause fishkill. Start out with less rather than more; the latter risks the food supply. It might be wise initially to stock only 100–200 fingerlings to determine the suitability of your pond environment. Avoid fishing until the next year. For immediate fishing, stock yearlings 6–7 in. (15–18 cm) long. When restocking a pond within a native or established population, use fingerlings a minimum of 5–6 in. (12–15 cm) long to prevent cannibalism.

Bass

Before stocking bass (largemouth or smallmouth) to a warm-water pond, add minnows to it, or just wait and see if they are really needed. Only one stocking should be necessary to establish a perpetual colony, particularly if you are practicing catch-and-release fishing. Bass reproduce well. Normal stocking involves 100 fingerlings 1–3 in. (2.5–7.6 cm) long, with 25 yearlings 5–7 in. (13–18 cm) long (consisting of 6–12 adult pairs). No attempt should be made to fish until these have spawned. When stocking fingerlings, you should wait two or three years before fishing, and one to two years when using yearling. Wait one year following construction of a pond before stocking to give vegetation and insect life a chance to establish. The best time to stock bass is in the spring (April, May) when temperatures are moderate. Avoid the higher temperatures of summer.

Beware of stocking bass alongside bluegills: bluegills will overpopulate a pond; as a result, both bass and the bluegills will show stunted growth. If the species are mixed, it is advisable to give bass a one-to-two-year headstart so they will have more effect on the bluegills. If you want to establish a panfish pond, stock only fingerlings initially, giving the pioneer population time to grow before they have offspring to compete with for food.

Have your fish transported directly to you by special transport vehicles. Sport fish, particularly trout, are very susceptible to changes in water temperature, and fish containers may need to be cooled with packed ice. Make sure to "temper" packed fish by placing the bags or containers in the pond until the water in the fish-bag is the same temperature as your pond. Note that ponds in the flood plain with no connection to public waters are still considered high risk by fisheries authorities. These may be connected to an adjacent or downstream water body during a flood event, a burst dam, or discharge from a pond cleaning, and should not be stocked with species not present in adjacent waters.

Regulations, Permits, and Licensing for Fish Ponds

General fishing-license requirements are complex and vary considerably for different countries, provinces, and states. It is imperative to contact your local Natural Resource Ministry, or State Fish and Wildlife Department for more information. The regulations that follow provide an example of the present requirements in Ontario. Specific regulations for the pond owner are included.

Fishing Licenses in Ontario—General Requirements

Resident: Definition

You have lived in Ontario or Canada for six consecutive months out of the last twelve immediately before applying for the license.

(Note: If you are an Ontario or Canadian resident

17 years old or younger, or 65 years old and older, you are *not* required to purchase a fishing license.)

Non-Resident: Definition

You are neither a Canadian nor an Ontario resident, and you are 18 years old or older. You must purchase a fishing license; there is no exemption for persons over 65 years of age.

(Note: Non-Canadian residents 17 years old and under do not have to purchase a fishing license if they fish with an adult who has a valid fishing license. Any fish they catch go towards the quota of the person who holds the license.)

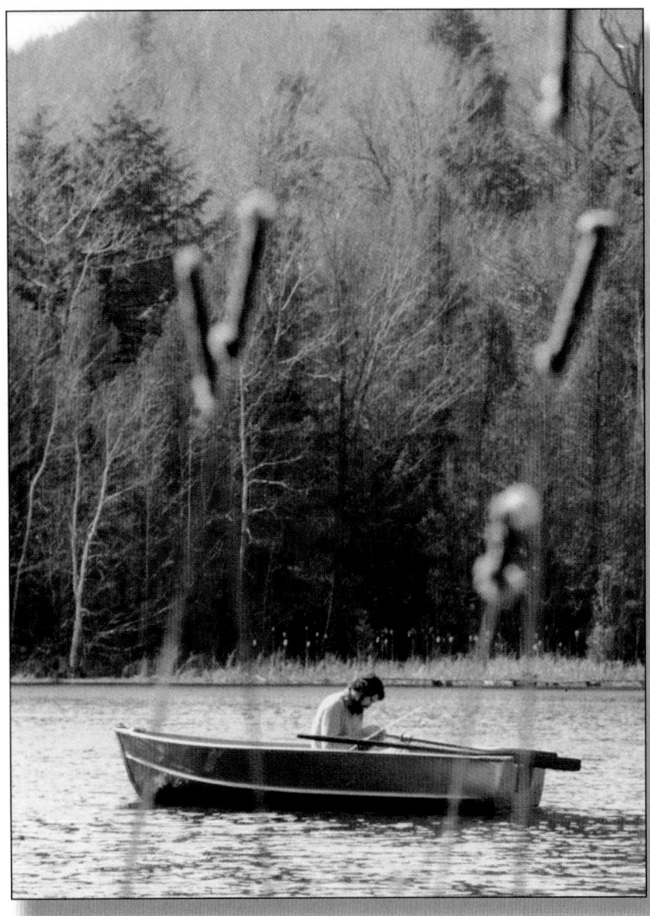

When fishing in a new location make sure you check the fishing regulations for the area— the new regulations can vary from lake to lake in some counties and municipalities.

Both residents and non-residents should familiarize themselves with fishing regulations, must only fish in season, and should adhere to daily catch limits.

Ontario Fishery Regulations do not apply if the pond or lake meets the criteria below. The owner does not need a fishing license if he/she is:

- Fishing in waters to which the National Parks of Canada Fishing Regulations apply
- Carrying out activities under an Aquaculture License
- An employee of the Ontario Ministry of Natural Resources carrying out aquaculture activities
- Fishing in artificially created waters, into which only fish obtained from either the holder of an aquaculture license or the holder of a commercial fishing license have been released for non-commercial purposes

Note that the above regulations do not apply to fishing and related activities carried out under a license issued under the Aboriginal Commercial Fishing Regulation.

Obtaining an aquaculture license

An aquaculture license is required in Ontario for owners wishing to be exempt from closed seasons and daily catch limits under the Ontario Fishery Regulations. In the past, these were called fishing reserves, where fish were propagated for angling purposes. The holder of an aquaculture license may:

- Culture those fish specified in the license from among the species of fish set out in the license for any location set out in the license
- Buy fish of the species specified in the license for any location set out in the license and may deposit such fish only in that location
- Sell fish of the species specified in the license taken from any location set out in the license [Ontario Regulation 664/98, s 20 (1)]

Fishing Clubs

Fishing activity in Ontario must be in accordance with the Ontario Fishery Regulations as above.

Selling Fish

For the most part, it is illegal to sell fish in Ontario if you are a pond or lake owner.

As you can see from the regulations above, the exemptions are quite specific and the pond or lake owner must contact his/her local Ministry of Natural Resources or State Fish and Wildlife Department for particulars.

Chapter Nine
Fish Biology Profiles

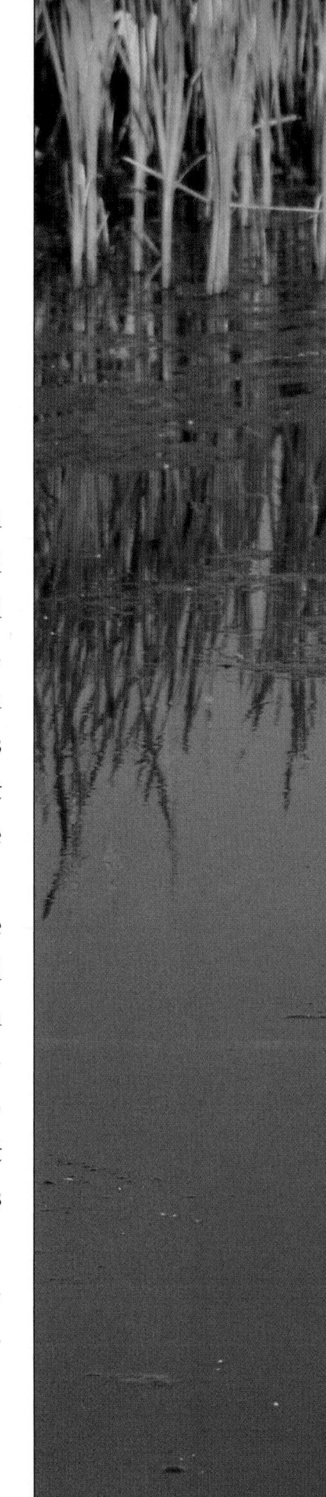

Common Pond Fishes: Life History and Angling

The prime cold-water fishes recommended for colder, deeper ponds are in the trout family: brown, speckled, and rainbow. Owners of shallower, warmer ponds, should restrict species to members of the bass and sunfish family—smallmouth and largemouth bass along with smaller fishes, including bluegills and pumpkinseeds. Pay attention to potential problems associated with mixing bass and bluegill species.

I have also included pike, muskellunge, yellow perch, walleye, whitefish, black crappie, and rock bass for management purposes in lake environments. These lakes could be man-constructed, formed naturally by beavers, or already existing. Fish profiles for these species will give the lake manager an indication of their requirements and preferred habitat.

I have, in my own pond, stocked rock bass, left to mature in a clay-bottom environment that was entirely unsuitable for them. They were caught on a fly, transported from a nearby lake in the sixties, and shipped to my pond in a bucket. They all survived well, but looking down into the depths of the pond, I've always felt some regret that I removed them from their chosen environment. One should always have respect for a living creature's choice of habitat and attempt to replicate that at all costs, or leave the species out of one's plans.

Don't attempt to mix pike and muskellunge, as one is predatory on the other and they compete for food and habitat. In any case, you will have difficulty in obtaining either species from fish suppliers, particularly the muskellunge, because it is particularly difficult to raise to maturity, providing a management challenge even for provincial and state fisheries professionals.

The black crappie, prolific in Grenadier Pond, Toronto, was a favorite fly-fishing challenge for me.

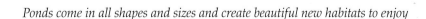

Ponds come in all shapes and sizes and create beautiful new habitats to enjoy

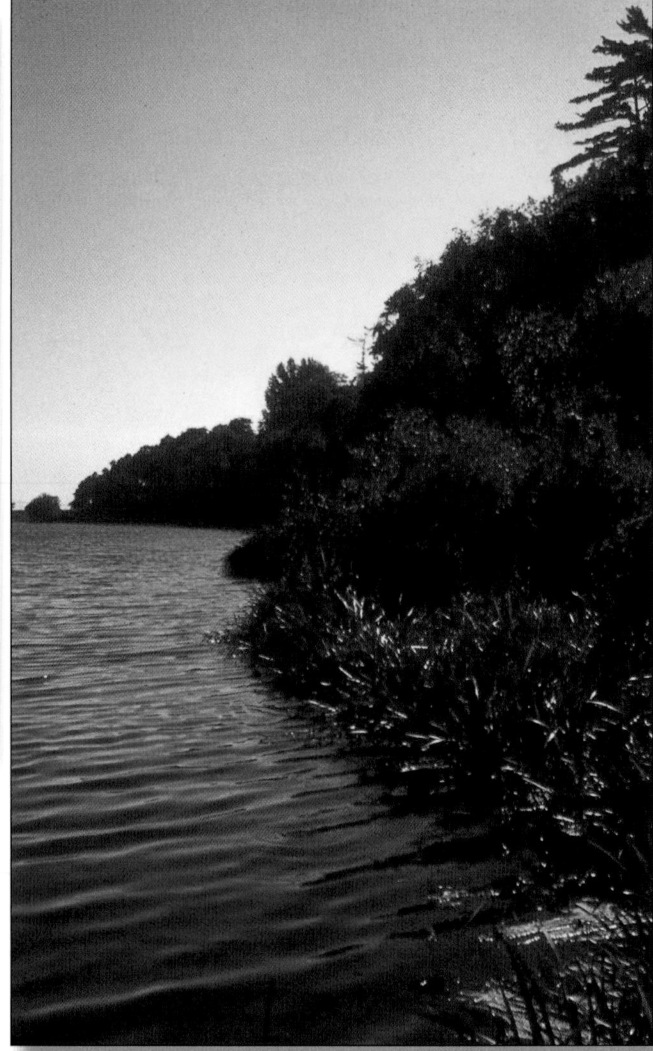

Finding perfect habitat in a deep, warm-water, weedy pond, it became prolific. The pike and smallmouth bass didn't seem to suffer; they too appeared plentiful. I have never forgotten the joy of seeing the flash of the black crappie alongside sunken logs in the shallows of the Grennie. Knowing the habits of these freshwater fish will aid the pond or lake manager in providing suitable habitat. The smallmouth bass that I stocked in my own pond became pets, cruising the shoreline whenever I approached—always waiting for the frog or grasshopper I would throw in. The following fish profiles outline identification, size, range, habitat, spawning habit, and angling opportunity for each of the species I feel are candidates for small lakes and ponds. Since I have ventured into many northern lake habitats, I felt inclined to include the more common lake species encountered over my lifetime of fishing.

A pond in Algonquin Park, Ontario, formed by beavers, which could develop into a natural reservoir for fish.

The littoral zone along the west shoreline of Grenadier Pond in Toronto, Ontario. It is the perfect habitat for smallmouth bass and black crappie.

Brown Trout (German Trout)

Family Salmonidae Scientific Name *Salmo trutta Linnaeus*

Identification

- Golden-brown color, a more pale color in lakes
- Large brown and black spots on its sides, back, and adipose and dorsal fins
- A few orange spots with pale haloes on sides
- Tail is squared-off rather than forked (like those of the rainbow and brook trout)

Size

- Weight ranges from 2–11 lb. (1–5.4 kg)
- Range
- More successful in southern Ontario than in more rapid rivers of the north
- Occurs in North America as a result of extensive introduction
- Native to Western Europe

Habitat

- Prefers cold, clean water at 18°C (65°F), but is tolerant of warmer water
- Favors slower stretches of water, eddies in rivers, pools with overhead cover
- Feeds on insects, fishes, worms, and spawn
- Surface feeds more than other trout
- Preferred feeding times are dawn and dusk
- Often attains large size
- Usually does not survive in ponds as well as rainbow trout or brook trout

Spawning Habits

- Spawns in rivers from October to February, in shallow depressions made in gravelly bottoms
- Eggs hatch in spring
- Does not die after spawning

Angling

- In streams, takes wet and dry flies, worms, spawn, and spinners
- A more difficult trout to catch
- In lakes, is found closer to the shore than other trout and salmon
- Most often caught by trolling spoons

Brown Trout [Courtesy of Duane Raver / U.S. Fish and Wildlife Service and Tracy Lee]

Rainbow Trout (Steelhead Trout, Kamloops Trout)
Family Salmonidae Scientific Name *Salmo gairdneri Richardson*

Rainbow Trout [Courtesy of Duane Raver / U.S. Fish and Wildlife Service and Tracy Lee]

Identification

- Numerous small, dark spots on the dorsal fin and caudal fin as well as most of the upper portions of the body
- Often has a conspicuous reddish stripe running from the head down the side of the body to the caudal fin
- Back is greenish-blue, and sides are silvery

Size

- Averages 0.5 lb. (0.25 kg) in small streams, and 2–15 lb. (1–7 kg) in large bodies of water

Range

- Was introduced into many parts of eastern Canada
- Native to the waters off Pacific coast of North America, from California to Alaska
- In Ontario, a permanent resident of Lake Superior, Lake Huron, Georgian Bay, Lake Simcoe, and Lake Ontario

Habitat

- Can be found in small to medium streams, most public lakes, slower stretches of water, eddies in rivers
- Prefers cold clean water around 13°C (55°F)
- Requires an abundance of aquatic insects and their larvae for food, plus invertebrates (leeches, crayfish, and minnows)
- Surface feeds more than other trout
- Prefers feeding at dawn and dusk

Spawning Habits

- Spawns in the spring, but also enters river systems in the fall
- Does not die after spawning
- Requires fast water over gravel to spawn and does not reproduce successfully in ponds (may reproduce if pond is spring-fed)
- Normally matures at age two or three with high mortality rate due to predation by aquatic animals; usually grows to 12–14 in. (30–35 cm) at three to four years and does not survive beyond
- Widely available from commercial hatcheries
- More tolerant than brook trout of varying temperatures

Angling

- In lakes, taken with minnows, worms, spawn, spinners, and spoons
- Takes wet or dry flies
- In lakes, found closer to shore than other trout

Speckled Trout (Brook Trout, Aurora Trout)
Family Salmonidae Scientific name *Salvelinus fontinalis Mitchill*

Identification
- Large mouth, strong teeth on jaws, tongue, and roof of mouth
- Caudal fin is square-cut, not forked
- Breeding male fish develop an upward curving hook at the forward end of the lower jaw
- Back is green to dark-brown
- Heavy, dark, wavy lines extend onto the dorsal and caudal fins
- Sides are well-peppered with small, well-pronounced red spots surrounded by a blue halo
- Prominent milky-white border on leading edge of lower fin

Size
- Usually weighs under 1 lb. (0.5 kg); occasionally 2–3 lb. (1–1.5 kg)

Range
- Central and eastern Canada, introduced into all central and western parts of North America

Habitat
- Rests under submerged logs or rocks, occasionally sunning in mid-stream
- Prefers cool, clean streams and lakes below 20°C (68°F), colder than the temperature preferred by rainbow trout
- Feeds on insect larvae, adult insects, small fish, crustaceans, and worms
- Has a high mortality rate, few live beyond age four

Spawning Habits
- Reaches adulthood at two to three years
- Spawning occurs in late autumn in shallow, gravel-bottomed headwaters of streams, and occasionally, lakes
- A shallow pit is hollowed out in clean gravel, usually by the female
- Eggs are deposited, fertilized, and covered with gravel
- No parental care is given except to scare off intruders
- The young live during winter on their yolk sac

Angling
- Regarded as the finest of game fishes
- Delicious flavor
- Accepts wet or dry flies, small spin-casting lures, and live bait

Speckled Trout (Brook Trout) [Courtesy of Duane Raver / U.S. Fish and Wildlife Service and Tracy Lee]

Whitefish (Lake Whitefish)
Family Salmonidae Scientific Name *Coregonus clupeaformis Mitchill*

Whitefish [Courtesy of Robert J. Eakins]

Identification

- Deep-bodied, laterally compressed
- Mouth overhung by snout with two flaps of skin between nostrils
- Back is pale-green to brown, becoming silvery on the sides
- Fins are light

Size

- Normally weighs 2–4 lb. (1–2 kg)
- In inland lakes, fish are often 1–3 lb. (0.5–1.5 kg)

Range

- Lake species occur throughout eastern Canada, in all of the Great Lakes, up to Hudson Bay. Also found in Newfoundland

Habitat

- Though adapted to bottom-feeding, they also eat plankton, snails, aquatic insect larvae, and small fish
- Strong swimmers, often moving about in schools

Spawning Habits

- Spawns November to December
- Female scatters eggs over rocky, gravelly, or sandy shoals
- May journey inland up streams to spawn
- Adults do not protect eggs, which hatch over winter
- Rate of growth is rapid, a weight of 2 lb. (1 kg) can be attained in four to five years.

Angling

- Once the most valuable commercial species in Ontario, now thinned out by pollution and predation by sea lampreys
- Important food for lake trout
- Fished for all winter in Lake Simcoe (largely in ice huts)

Walleye (Pickerel, Yellow Pickerel)

Family Percidae Scientific Name *Stizostedion vitreum Mitchill*

Identification

- Elongate and full body
- Strong, sharp, canine-like teeth in jaws
- Large eyes
- Olive-brown to dark-brown in color
- Numerous spots of gold or yellow sprinkled over the body and on the head
- Spiny dorsal fin is smoky in nature—has a distinct blotch on the membrane between last two or three spines
- Creamy-white pelvic fins
- Lower lobe of caudal fin has creamy-white margin

Size

- Average weight is approximately 3 lb. (1.5 kg)

Range

- Occurs throughout Ontario and Quebec, northward to Hudson Bay, and westward to British Columbia and the Northwest Territories

Habitat

- Most of the year, inhabits the shallow waters of many lakes and rivers
- Seeks deeper, cooler waters in late summer
- Food consists of other fishes (i.e., yellow perch, various minnows such as suckers, and, in deeper waters, ciscoes)
- Also eats a large number of mayflies in summer

Spawning Habits

- Spawns in spring just after ice break-up
- Often ascends streams, spawning in shallow water over gravel
- Also spawns in shallow water of sandy, stony, or gravelly shoals of lakes

Angling

- Summer lake-fishing in deeper beds, or shoals and weed beds

Yellow Pickerel [Courtesy of Duane Raver / U.S. Fish and Wildlife Service and Tracy Lee]

Northern Pike (Great Northern Pike, Jackfish)
Family Esocidae Scientific Name *Esox lucius Linnaeus*

Northern Pike
[Courtesy of Robert J. Eakins]

Identification

- Elongate, laterally compressed body
- Large head with flat dorsal surface
- Large mouth with many long, sharp, backward-pointing teeth on flattened "duck-like" jaws
- Patches of teeth on roof of mouth
- Cheek and upper half of gill covers covered with small scales
- Ten sensory pores or holes on underjaw
- Green or dark-green back, shading to lighter green on sides, to white below
- In adults, sides have elongate light-colored spots
- Young fish 6–7 in. (15.2–17.8 cm) long, with light-colored bars

Size

- Averages 2–4 lb. (1–1.5 kg), but occasionally in excess of 15.5 lb. (7 kg)
- Females live longer than males and grow larger

Range

- Throughout Ontario, Quebec, Labrador, New Brunswick, and northwest to Alaska
- Absent from the highland areas in Ontario (Algonquin Park, Haliburton County)
- Occurs throughout the northern hemisphere in northern Europe and Asia

Habitat

- Prefers weedy shallows of lakes in summer, moves to deeper waters in autumn
- Frequently hangs motionless below the surface
- Feeds primarily on other fish (suckers, yellow perch, minnows)
- Devours aquatic insects, leeches, crayfish, frogs, snakes, mice, small muskrats, and ducklings

Spawning Habits

- Spawning takes place in early spring shortly after ice break-up
- Prefers weedy shallow bays and flooded, marshy areas for spawning
- Eggs are scattered and deserted

Angling

- Popular game fish
- Bony flesh is flaky and white

Muskellunge (Maskinonge, Tiger Musky, Musky, Lunge)
Family Esocidae Scientific Name *Esox masquinongy Mitchill*

Identification

- Pike-like appearance
- Long body with long flattened head
- Large mouth, strong jaws
- Strong, sharp, canine teeth on jaws, smaller teeth on the tongue and roof of mouth
- Has dark vertical bars or dark spots on light background (pike has the reverse coloration). Coloration varies by locale—Ontario species have barred pattern; in Quebec, spots predominate
- Background color of sides is pale-green to grey

Size

- Typically over 20 lb. (9 kg); some are over 40 lb. (18 kg)
- Average size caught is between 6–10 lb. (2.5–4.5 kg)

Range

- Native only to eastern North America
- In early years, Lake Simcoe had a good muskellunge population, but numbers have fallen drastically. Efforts are underway to improve habitat and spawning opportunities

Habitat

- Prefers water bodies of medium size, and is often found in association with northern pike
- During warm summer weather, moves out into deeper water
- Frequents edges of weed beds, rocky shoals, and shallow margins of lakes in fall
- Is predatory
- Yellow perch and white suckers provide a large part of its diet, although many other species are eaten, including pan fish

Spawning Habits

- Spawning occurs in spring, one to two weeks following pike spawning, in low-lying, marshy areas inundated by spring flooding and upper tributary areas
- Eggs deposited in shallow waters over vegetation, stumps, and other bottom debris
- Spawning often accompanied by rapid swimming about and rolling
- No nest is made, and no parental care given
- Eggs hatch in ten to fourteen days, dependent upon water temperature
- Eggs deposited on inundated land likely to be exposed and killed by rapid recession of water (vulnerable reproduction)

Angling

- Enjoys the highest popularity among sports fishermen due to its fighting tactics and endurance
- Taken on plugs and spinners much like those used for pike

Muskellunge
[Courtesy of Robert J. Eakins]

Smallmouth Bass (Black Bass, Smallmouth)
Family Serranidae Scientific Name *Micropterus dolomieui Lacepede*

Smallmouth bass [Courtesy of Duane Raver / U.S. Fish and Wildlife Service and Tracy Lee]

Identification

- Robust, deep, and laterally compressed body
- Large head and mouth
- Numerous small teeth on jaws and roof of mouth
- Mouth extends to below the eye
- Spines on dorsal fin are short (on the spinal portion)
- Distinct vertical bars on sides of fish sometimes broken to produce a spotted effect on upper body portion (eight to fifteen vertical bars)
- Coloration varies with environment—fish in large, weedy lakes are usually green, while those from small, peat-stained waters of inland lakes are brown to golden-brown with a cream-colored belly

Size

- In Ontario the average weight is 2–3 lb. (1–1.5 kg)
- Four-pound (2 kg) specimens are not uncommon

Habitat

- Best habitat is found in clear, rocky lakes with depths of 25–30 ft. (8–9 m) containing sparse aquatic vegetation, and rocky or gravelly shoals
- Lakes or ponds with summer temperatures over 27°C (80°F), and weedy, mud-bottomed lakes not well-suited to this species
- Food includes aquatic insects, crayfish, frogs, leeches, and fishes (yellow perch)
- Reaches adulthood in three to six years

Spawning Habits

- Spawns in temperatures of 15°C–20°C (60°F–70°F), June to July
- Nest built by the male on stony or gravelly bottoms
- Male sweeps nest clean with caudal fins, carrying silt, leaves, and debris away until a rocky, gravelly, shallow depression is created
- Female enticed over the nest until she deposits the eggs, which the male will fertilize; then she is driven off
- Male zealously guards the nest; is very susceptible to angler's baits during this period and will attack anything moving near the nest

Angling

- Takes plugs, flies, spinners, and spinner-baits
- Can be caught by still-fishing with worms, frogs, crayfish, leeches, and minnows
- Has superb fighting qualities
- Extra readiness to strike baits or lures during summer months

Largemouth Bass (Largemouth Black Bass, Green Bass)
Family Centrarchidae Scientific Name *Micropterus salmoides Lacepede*

Identification

- Similar to smallmouth bass but deeper-bodied
- Larger mouth extends beyond the eye (end of maxillary bone reaches past the eye)
- Spiny dorsal fin higher than smallmouth's dorsal
- Has a broad, lateral, dark band instead of vertical bands as in smallmouth species (this may be inconspicuous on larger adults)
- Body is dark-green on the back, becoming lighter on the sides and even lighter below
- Average size is 2–3 lb. (1–1.5 kg), maturing at three or four years of age, reaching lengths of 8–12 in. (20–30 cm)
- Fish weighing up to 5 lb. (2.5 kg) are common
- Lifespan is about seven years, most do not survive beyond five years

Range

- Common in North America in warm, weedy inland lakes

Habitat

- Prefers warm water of depths less than 20 ft. (6 m)
- Found in weed beds, under logs, around stumps, and in other sunken debris
- Is more tolerant of turbid waters and silt conditions than smallmouth bass
- Food consists of crayfish, frogs, insects, and smaller fish

- Similar to smallmouth bass in feeding habits, growth, and reproduction

Spawning Habits

- Spawning occurs in May or June
- Chooses a nesting site on mud or marl bottom, often on water lily roots
- Male exposes the roots by sweeping debris away
- Eggs and young are guarded zealously, then abandoned

Angling

- Can be caught along weed beds and around sunken objects
- Takes surface plugs, spinners, spinner-baits, and flies
- Still-fishing bait includes worms, leeches, frogs, and crayfish

Largemouth Bass [Courtesy of Duane Raver / U.S. Fish and Wildlife Service and Tracy Lee]

Bluegill (Bluegill Sunfish, Blue Sunfish)
Family Centrarchidae Scientific Name *Lepomis macrochirus Rafinesque*

Bluegill [Courtesy of Duane Raver / U.S. Fish and Wildlife Service and Tracy Lee]

Identification

- Deep, laterally compressed body
- Back is blue-green to olive-green, becoming lighter on the side
- Gill flap (opercular flap) is short and dark, sometimes with a purple hue, no scarlet margin
- Has a small mouth
- Throat and breast are often orange to yellow
- Has series of vertical bars on the sides
- Also has a series of oblong blotches on the membrane between the last few rays of the dorsal fin (these may merge)

Size

- Attains a length of 10–12 in. (25–30 cm)
- Is the largest of the sunfishes

Range

- Found in the Great Lakes, Upper St. Lawrence drainages, St. Clair drainage system, Rideau Lakes and in Quetico Provincial Park

Habitat

- Inhabits warm, weedy waters of protected bays, ponds, and lakes

Spawning Habits

- Spawns in spring
- Male constructs a nest on gravelly bottoms in shallow water
- Male guards eggs and nest
- Principal foods are aquatic insects and small crayfish

Angling

- A more popular game fish in the U.S.A. than in Canada
- Strong fighter

Pumpkinseed (Sunfish)
Family Centrarchidae Scientific Name *Lepomis gibbosus Linnaeus*

Identification

- Laterally compressed body, more round in outline than other sunfishes
- Mouth is small, extending only to anterior edge of eye
- Small teeth
- Streaks or lines of brilliant blue on cheeks and opercules; more prominent in males
- Dark opercular flap with brilliant scarlet spot on posterior margin (note absence of this in the bluegill)
- Body sprinkled with rust-colored scales
- Several vertical bars frequently occur on the sides of young fish and mature females
- Clear pectoral fins with pointed tips
- Most fins dusky with brown spots, particularly the dorsal fin

Size

- Lake sunfish might reach length of 8–9 in. (20–23 cm)
- In smaller ponds where they are sometimes over-populated, length limited to 4–5 in. (10–13 cm)

Range

- Most common, widely distributed sunfish
- Occurs throughout southern Ontario, from Quebec to Sault Ste Marie and Temagami
- Also found in New Brunswick

Habitat

- Found most frequently in weedy ponds, lakes, slow-moving rivers
- Food is mainly aquatic insects, snails, and other invertebrate animals
- Occasionally feeds on smaller fish

Spawning Habits

- Male sweeps away gravel and debris on bottom using his caudal fin like a whisk, creating a shallow depression
- Once eggs are laid by female, male guards them up until a short time after hatching

Angling

- Not considered a game fish but provides good sport
- Delightful to see in a pond due to its color
- Easy to maintain

Pumpkinseed [Courtesy of Duane Raver / U.S. Fish and Wildlife Service and Tracy Lee]

Black Crappie (Calico Bass, Speckled Bass, Oswego Bass
Family Centrarchidae Scientific Name *Pomoxis nigromaculatus LeSueur*

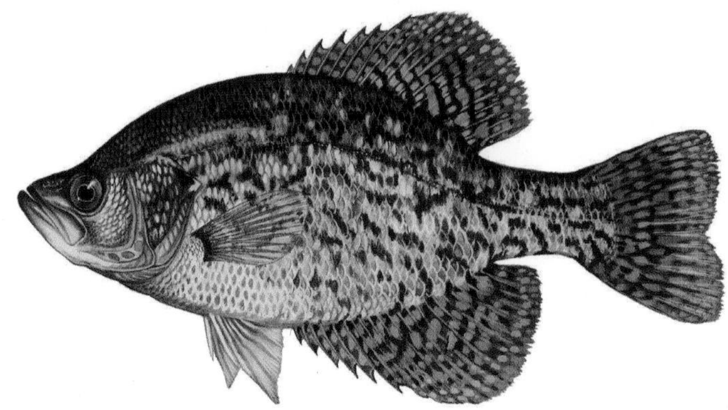

Black Crappie [Courtesy of Duane Raver / U.S. Fish and Wildlife Service and Tracy Lee]

Identification

- Deep-bodied, laterally compressed
- Has a forehead depression just above the eyes
- Dorsal spines are seven to eight in number
- Dark-green to black on the back
- Sides are silvery with irregularly arranged dark-green or black spots
- Also dark-green speckles on dorsal, anal, and caudal fins

Size

- May weigh up to 2 lb. (1 kg), reaching 12–14 in. (30–35 cm) in length
- Average weight close to 0.5 lb. (0.25 kg), and length at 7–10 in. (18–25 cm)

Range

- Found in Upper St. Lawrence, eastward into Quebec and the Ottawa River, Lake Ontario, Lake Erie, and Lake St. Clair
- Common in Rideau Lakes
- Recently established in northern Lake Superior bays

Habitat

- Likes quiet waters of lakes, ponds, and slow-moving streams
- Prefers a good growth of aquatic plants
- A gregarious species, often traveling in schools
- Prefers to eat small fishes and aquatic insects

Spawning Habits

- Spawns in late spring or early summer
- Constructs nest in 3–6 ft. (1–2 m) of water, on sandy or silted bottom among rooted plants

Angling

- Provides excellent sport
- Caught on live minnows and loves flies (Yellow Sally is a favorite)
- Flesh is exceedingly sweet and has good flavor

Rock Bass (Redeye, Northern Rock Bass)
Family Centrarchidae Scientific Name *Ambloplites rupestris Rafinesque*

Identification

- Laterally compressed, but not as much as sunfishes
- Eyes large and red in color
- Body olive-brown with dark mottling
- Scales on sides have a large, dark spot fading toward the belly
- As many as six spines in the anal fin (sunfish has only three)
- All fins (except pectoral and pelvic) dusky and spotted

Size

- Lengths up to 12 in. (30 cm) have been reported
- Usually grows to 6–8 in. (15–20 cm), with average weight being approximately 0.5 lb. (0.25 kg)

Range

- Found in all Great Lakes, north to Lake Abitibi, southern Manitoba, and west to southern Saskatchewan
- Abundant in Lake Ontario and Georgian Bay

Habitat

- Most often found in rocky shallows of lakes
- Adults often move in schools
- Commonly found in some waters with small-mouth bass and pumpkinseeds
- Food is largely aquatic insects, crayfish, and small fish

Spawning Habits

- Spawning occurs in spring or early summer when temperatures reach 15°C–21°C (60°F–70°F)
- Male builds a circular nest in gravelly bottom in shallows
- Eggs are deposited by the female and guarded for a short time by the male

Angling

- Usually caught accidentally while fishing for another species
- Provides a good fight on the line
- Flesh is white, flaky, and of good flavor

Rock Bass [Robert J. Eakins]

Yellow Perch (Perch, Lake Perch)

Family Percidae Scientific Name *Perca flavescens Mitchill*

Yellow Perch [Courtesy of Duane Raver / U.S. Fish and Wildlife Service and Tracy Lee]

Identification

- Distinctly deeper than wide, laterally compressed
- Fine teeth on jaws, no canine-type teeth
- Body is yellow-green
- Sides have seven to eight broad, dark, vertical bars extending almost to the belly
- Membrane between spines of first dorsal fin smoky in color; pectoral fins light in color
- Pelvic fins pale to bright orange

Size

- Medium to small size
- Weight usually in the range of 0.25–0.625 lb. (0.1–0.3 kg), sometimes exceeds 1 lb. (0.45 kg)

Range

- Found throughout North America, especially common in Great Lakes drainage basin

Habitat

- Although found in small bodies of water, it is a lake fish
- Principal food is animal plankton, aquatic insects, and fishes

Spawning Habits

- Spawns in shallow water in the spring (April or May)
- Eggs are expelled in rope-like strands embedded in a gelatinous sheath
- No parental care is given by adults; eggs hatch in approximately three weeks at a temperature of 8°C (45°F)

Angling

- Takes worms, flies, and small spinners
- Flesh has delicious flavor, highly esteemed
- Of considerable importance to commercial fisheries in the Great Lakes

Wil Wegman and friends land a large muskellunge [Courtesy of Wil Wegman]

Chapter Ten

Managing the Pond for Wildlife

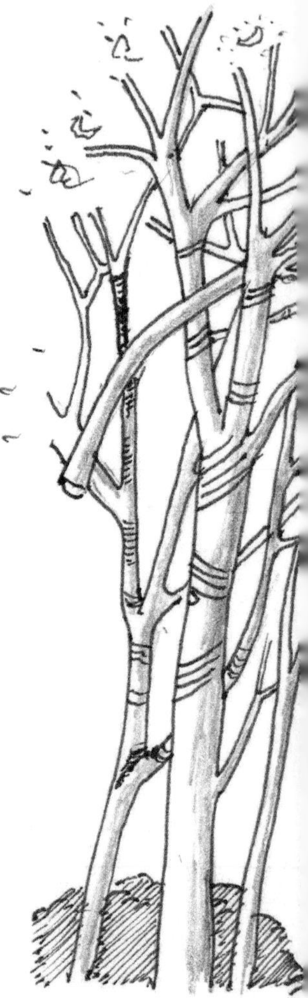
Deciduous Canopy (perching & nesting)

Layers of Life

The diagram on the opposite page illustrates a range of terrestrial plant layers that provide both habitat and food for specific animal types. Plant species can be grouped into recognizable layers on the basis of height. High canopy, intermediate canopy, and groundcover attract specific animal and bird species. Along with the "edge" factor, these plant levels provide protection, food, nesting places, and escape or prey opportunities. When planning your pond, utilize these levels to create a planting scheme that provides some degree of habitat. This may only be in one part of your pond, preferably in a location that uses a linkage to adjoining hedgerows or forest tracts. Such a junction establishes a wildlife corridor to your pond.

Soil-Moisture Regime

The soil-moisture regime (or the amount of permanent water in the soil) in your chosen pond site will be indicated by the vegetative species you find growing on it, providing it has not been man-altered. Most species naturally locate on one, sometimes two, segments. A few species, such as cedars, most elms, and some poplars, can be found right across the spectrum of moisture content and are not reliable indicators of a specific soil-moisture requirement. The soil-moisture regime table for your region is a useful tool for listing the species that you wish to install around your pond. Researching the trees and shrubs listed in the following section will help you to understand their form, growth, and light requirements, along with moisture preference. You can then place the species you wish to grow in their respective categories in the table (see Figure 6.18). This process will help you select your plant species on the basis of an important ecological parameter, assuring success in your planting program. The suitability of any site for planting success depends upon many factors: soil type, porosity, texture, and, of course, the existing water table.

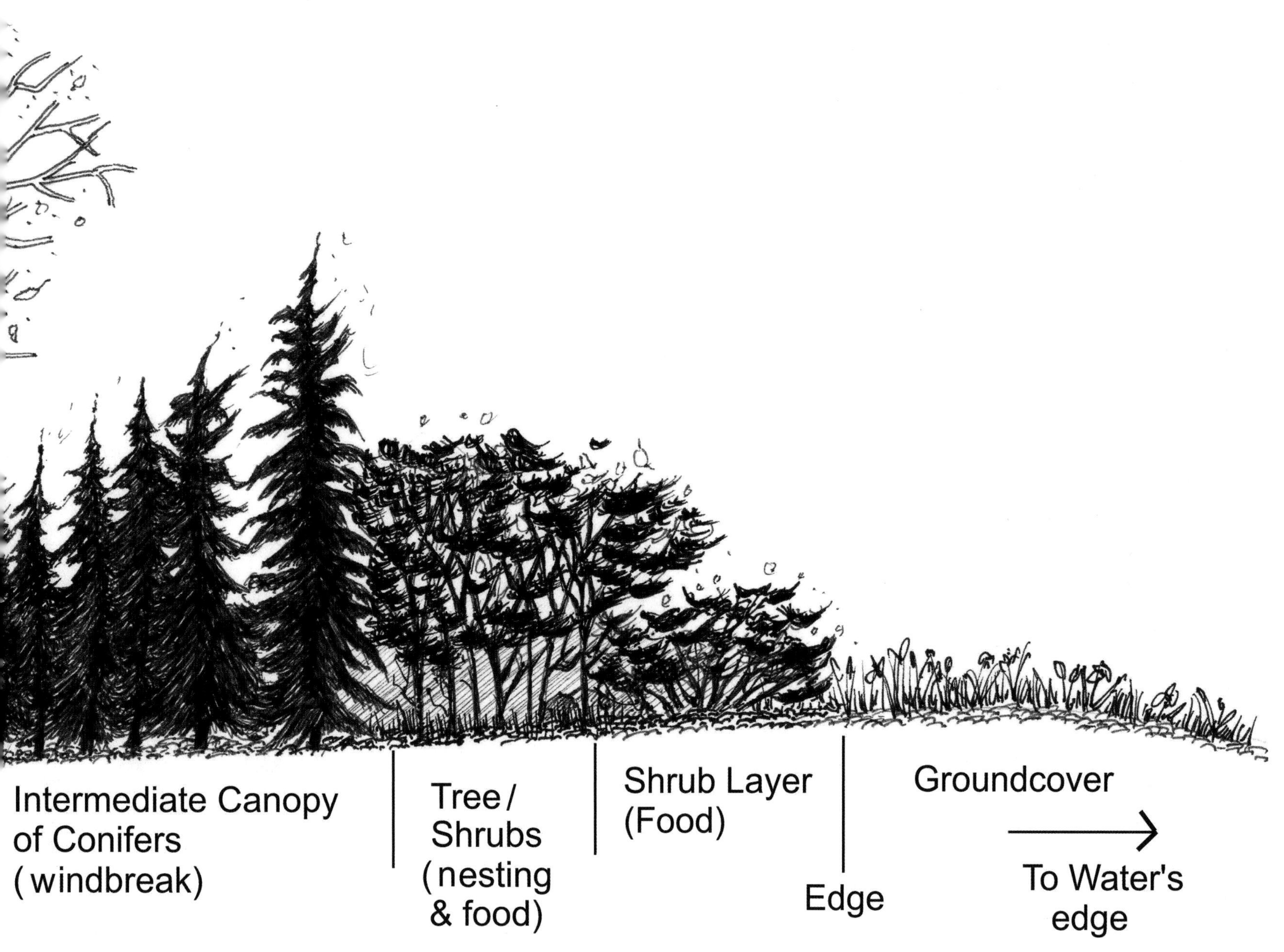

Figure 10.1 Layers of Life Diagram—This cross-section through a typical conservation buffer next to a pond shows the layers of life supported when habitat, food and erosion protection are provided [Adapted from Buffers Protect the Environment*].*

Recommended Plants to Attract Wildlife to the Pond Environment

Plant Perimeters Above the Shoreline

Plantings around your pond should always involve plant species native to your area; these will adapt best to weather conditions on your site, particularly as regards the number of annual frost-free days, moisture, pH, and soil texture. Figure 10.2 provides aid in planting native species in the right soil and moisture conditions.

If one of your objectives is to establish wildlife habitat, Figure 10.3 illustrates food and cover opportunities offered by native trees, shrubs, vines and grasses.

Explanation of Symbols

Forest Regions	Moisture Preference	Soil Types
(G) Great Lakes and St. Lawrence Valley	**(A)** All (wet, moist, and dry)	**(B)** Broad range of tolerance
(D) Deciduous Carolinian Forest	**(D)** Dry	**(C)** Clay
(B) Boreal Forest	**(M)** Moist **(W)** Wet	**(L)** Loam **(P)** Peat **(S)** Sand

FIGURE 10.2 NATIVE TREES, SHRUBS, VINES, GROUNDCOVER & AQUATIC PLANTS SUITABLE FOR POND & LAKE ENVIRONMENTS

Species are listed under regional location with moisture and soil preferences [Table adapted from *The Urban Outback – Wetlands for Wildlife*].

CONIFERS	REGION	MOISTURE REGIME	SOIL PREFERENCE
Balsam fir (*Abies balsamifera*)	G	MW	LS
Eastern red cedar (*Juniperus virginiana*)	GD	DM	CL
White cedar (*Thuja occidentalis*)	GDB	A	CS
Eastern hemlock (*Tsuga canadensis*)	GD	MW	LS
Eastern white pine (*Pinus strobus*)	GDB	A	CS
Red pine (*Pinus resinosa*)	G	DM	LS
Black spruce (*Picea mariana*)	B	W	CLS
White spruce (*Picea glauca*)	GDB	DM	CLS
Tamarack (Larch) (*Larix laricina*)	GDB	A	CLS

BROADLEAF TREES (DECIDUOUS TREES)	REGION	MOISTURE REGIME	SOIL PREFERENCE
Black ash (*Fraxinus nigra*)	GDB	DMW	CL
White ash (*Fraxinus americana*)	GDB	MW	CL
Green ash (*Fraxinus pennsylvanica*)	GDB	DM	CL
American mountain ash (*Sorbus americana*)	GDB	DM	CLS
Bigtooth aspen (*Populus grandidentata*)	GDB	DMW	CLS
Trembling aspen (*Populus tremuloides*)	GDB	DMW	CLS
Balsam poplar (*Populus balsamea*)	GDB	MW	CLS
Cottonwood (*Populus deltoids*)	GDB	DM	CLS
Black cherry (*Prunus serotina*)	GDB	DM	CL
Choke cherry (*Prunus virginiana*)	GD	A	B
Pin cherry (*Prunus pennsylvanica*)	D	DM	CLS
Crabapple (*Malus coronaria*)	D	DM	CL
Hackberry (*Celtis occidentalis*)	GD	A	B
Hop hornbeam (Ironwood, *Ostrya virginiana*)	GD	DM	CL
Red maple (*Acer rubrum*)	GDB	MW	CLS
Silver maple (*Acer saccharinum*)	GD	MW	B
Sugar maple (*Acer saccharum*)	GD	DM	B
Bur oak (*Quercus macrocarpa*)	GD	DM	B
Swamp white oak (*Quercus bicolor*)	GD	M	CLS
White oak (*Quercus alba*)	GD	M	CLS
Shagbark hickory (*Carya ovata*)	GD	DM	CLS
White birch (*Betula papyrifera*)	GDB	MW	CLS

VINES AND GROUNDCOVER			
	REGION	MOISTURE REGIME	SOIL PREFERENCE
Bearberry (*Arctostaphylos uva-ursi*)	GD	D	CLS
Bittersweet (*Calustrus scandens*)	GD	DM	B
Virginia creeper (*Parthenocisuscinquefolia*)	GD	DM	CLS

FIGURE 10.2 (CONTINUED FROM P. 164)

SMALL TREES AND SHRUBS			
CONIFERS	**REGION**	**MOISTURE REGIME**	**SOIL PREFERENCE**
Eastern red cedar (shrub) (*Juniperus virginiana*)	D	CL	CLS
DECIDUOUS	**REGION**	**MOISTURE REGIME**	**SOIL PREFERENCE**
Speckled alder (*Alnus rugosa*)	GDB	W	CLPS
Common elderberry (*Sambucus canadensis*)	GDB	A	CLS
Red mulberry (*Morus rubra*)	D	MW	CL
Serviceberry (Shadbush) (*Amelanchier canadensis*)	GD	MW	CL
Beaked hazel (*Corylus cornuta*)	GD	M	CLS
Nannyberry (*Viburnum lentago*)	GD	DM	B
Red osier dogwood (*Cornus racemosa*)	GDB	MW	B
Alternate-leaf dogwood (*Cornus alternifolia*)	GDB	MW	CL
Staghorn sumac (*Rhus typhina*)	GD	D	CLS
Wild rose (*Rosa rugosa*)	GD	DM	CL
Pussy willow (*Salix discolor*)	GDB	MW	CLS

FIGURE 10.3 TREES, SHRUBS, VINES & GRASSES THAT PROVIDE WILDLIFE FOOD (F) & COVER (C) IN POND ENVIRONMENTS

[Adapted from *Best Management Practices*, Fish & Wildlife Habitat Management, Ontario]

PLANTS	Hawks & Owls	Songbirds (Uplands & Treed Ponds)	Marsh Birds (Bittern, Grebe, Coote, Heron)	Waterfowl (Dabbling Ducks, Wood Ducks)	Cavity Nesters (Chickadees, Nuthatches, Woodpeckers)	Bobwhite Quail
TREES, SHRUBS & VINES						
Hemlock	C	C	C		F, C	
White Pine	C	F, C	F, C		F, C	C
Red Pine	C	F, C			F	
White & Norway Spruce	C	C	C			C
White Cedar	C	F, C	F, C			C

Tamarack	C	F, C	C		F, C	C
Poplar & Aspen	C	F, C	F, C			
White Birch	C	F, C	F, C	F, C		C
Red & Silver Maple	C	C	C	C	C	C
Sugar Maple	C	C		C	C	
Red & White Oak	C	C		F, C	C	F, C
Hickory, Beech	C			C	C	
Pin Cherry, Serviceberry		F			F	F
Wild Apple		F				
Alders (speckled green)		F	C		F	
Willows (scrub species)		F, C	C	C	F, C	
Red Cedar		F, C				
Juniper		F, C				
Sumac		F				F, C
Dogwood		F, C	F, C			F, C
Buttonbush				F, C		
Am. Highbush Cranberry		F, C			F	
Hawthorn		F, C				F
Raspberry, Blackberry		F, C			F, C	
Elderberry, Currants		F, C	F		F, C	F
Wild Grape		F, C			F, C	C
Virginia Creeper						

FIGURE 10.3 (CONTINUED FROM P. 167)

PLANTS	Hawks & Owls	Songbirds (Uplands & Treed Ponds)	Marsh Birds (Bittern, Grebe, Coote, Heron)	Waterfowl (Dabbling Ducks, Wood Ducks)	Cavity Nesters (Chickadees, Nuthatches, Woodpeckers)	Bobwhite Quail
UPLAND GRASSES						
Clover, Timothy, Fescue		C		C		F, C
Switchgrass				C		C
Big Bluestem, Indian				C		C
LOWLAND GRASSES						
Reed Canary Grass			F, C	C		
Bluejoint Sedges			F, C	C		

PLANTS	Ring-Necked Pheasant	Ruffled Grouse	Wild Turkey	Woodcock	Chipmunk & Squirrels	Hares & Rabbits	Beaver	Deer
TREES, SHRUBS & VINES								
Hemlock		C	C		C			F, C
White Pine	C	C	C	C	F, C	F, C		C
Red Pine		C			F, C			C
White & Norway Spruce	C	C		C	F, C	C		C
White Cedar	C	C	C	C	F	F, C		F, C
Tamarack		C				F, C		F, C
Poplar & Aspen	C	F, C	C	C		F, C	F, C	F, C
White Birch		F, C	C	C		F	F, C	
Red & Silver Maple	C	C	C			F, C	F, C	F, C
Sugar Maple	C	F, C			F, C	C		F
Red & White Oak	F	F	F, C		F			F
Hickory, Beech			F, C		F, C			F
Pin Cherry, Serviceberry	F	F	F	C		F, C		F

PLANTS	Ring-Necked Pheasant	Ruffled Grouse	Wild Turkey	Woodcock	Chipmunk & Squirrels	Hares & Rabbits	Beaver	Deer
TREES, SHRUBS & VINES								
Wild Apple	F	F	F	C		F	F	F
Alders (speckled green)		F		F, C		F	F	C
Willows (scrub species)				C		C	F	C
Red Cedar								F, C
Juniper		C		C		F, C		C
Sumac	F, C	F	F	C		F, C		F, C
Dogwood	F, C	F	F	C		F, C	F	F
Buttonbush				C				
Am. Highbush Cranberry	F	F						
Hawthorn	F	F, C	F	C		C		F, C
Raspberry, Blackberry	F	F	F	F, C			F, C	F
Elderberry, Currants	F	F	F			F		
Wild Grape	F, C	F, C	F			F, C		
Virginia Creeper		F			C	C		
UPLAND GRASSES								
Clover, Timothy, Fescue	F		F	C	C	C		F
Switchgrass	C		F		C	F, C		F
Big Bluestem, Indian	C		F		C	F, C		F
LOWLAND GRASSES								
Reed Canary Grass	C		F		C	F, C		F
Bluejoint Sedges	C		F		C	F, C		F

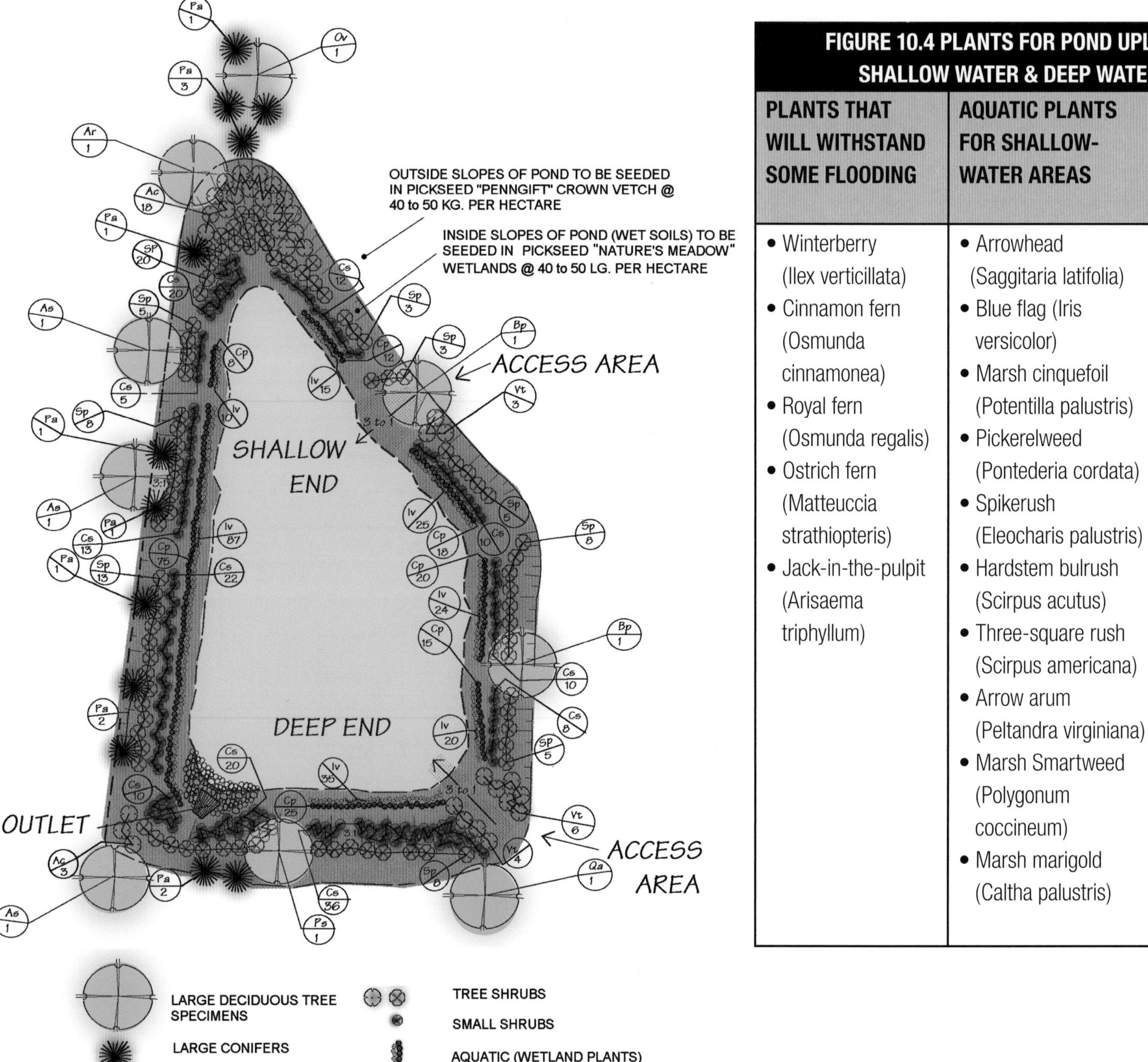

Figure 10.5 A typical wildlife planting plan for a small rural pond [Design by John Hicks]

FIGURE 10.4 PLANTS FOR POND UPLAND SITES, SHALLOW WATER & DEEP WATER AREAS		
PLANTS THAT WILL WITHSTAND SOME FLOODING	**AQUATIC PLANTS FOR SHALLOW-WATER AREAS**	**AQUATIC PLANTS FOR DEEPER POND AREAS**
• Winterberry (Ilex verticillata) • Cinnamon fern (Osmunda cinnamonea) • Royal fern (Osmunda regalis) • Ostrich fern (Matteuccia strathiopteris) • Jack-in-the-pulpit (Arisaema triphyllum)	• Arrowhead (Saggitaria latifolia) • Blue flag (Iris versicolor) • Marsh cinquefoil (Potentilla palustris) • Pickerelweed (Pontederia cordata) • Spikerush (Eleocharis palustris) • Hardstem bulrush (Scirpus acutus) • Three-square rush (Scirpus americana) • Arrow arum (Peltandra virginiana) • Marsh Smartweed (Polygonum coccineum) • Marsh marigold (Caltha palustris)	• Floating-leaf pondweed (Potamogeton natans) • White water lily (Nymphaea odorata)

Typical Wildlife Planting Plan for a Pond

The Advantages of Riparian Buffers

A riparian buffer of trees, shrubs, and groundcover forms a barrier against wind-blown soil and a living filter that reduces run-off from nearby fields entering your pond. A strategically placed buffer can also prevent movement of nutrients, pesticides, and pathogens produced by adjacent farming operations from reaching your pond environment.

Buffers provide protective cover and habitat for a variety of birds, mammals, and other wildlife that feed, breed, and rear young near water. They also can provide habitat improvement for fish by shading and cooling the water, as long as higher-canopy trees are planted within this buffer.

Your pond-conservation buffer should be planted as a border 30–50 ft. (9–15 m) wide. If an existing fencerow of trees or a forest edge is not available next to your pond, plant a row of broadleaf trees outermost in the buffer—this creates the required high canopy and hunting perches for shorebirds such as herons and bitterns that prey upon pond minnows. The high-canopy row should contain important mast species such as hickory, ash, walnut, and butternut which provide nuts for small mammals. Existing wild apple trees in hedgerows are equally valuable, if you are lucky enough to have them, as these offer soft fruit for a variety of mammals. Plant several rows of conifers next to the broadleaf high-canopy buffer to form the majority of windbreak and provide additional nesting opportunities. These trees should be lopped annually, to maintain height at 16–20 ft. (5–6 m), creating the denser, intermediate conifer forests which wildlife favors.

Tall, then shorter shrubs should follow next—species that flower and yield fruit at different months of the year and produce annual growth and buds. This intermediate canopy provides the "browse" layer, essential for various birds and mammals for nesting and feeding.

The ground cover layer follows. This should be composed of a grass-legume mixture about 16–20 ft. (5–6 m) wide; mowed lightly in summer to 6–8 in. (15–20 cm)—the right height to maintain a good filter and provide cover for small mammals and shorebirds. Many wetland wildlife will use this grassy cover next to the pond as a forage area (see Figure 10.1)..

FIGURE 10.6 A PLANT LIST FOR THE POND IN FIGURE 10.5

POND PLANTING LIST

DECIDUOUS SHRUBS	KEY	NO.	COMMON NAME	GENERIC NAME	ROOT	SIZE
	Sp	86	Arctic Willow	Salix Purpurea	Pot	
	Cs	166	Red Osier Dogwood	Cornus Servicea	3 Gal	50 cm
	Vt	13	High Bush Cranberry	Viburnum Trilobum	3 Gal	50 cm
	Ac	21	Serviceberry	Amelanchier Canadensis	W/B	200 cm

AQUATIC EMERGENTS	KEY	NO.	COMMON NAME	GENERIC NAME	ROOT	SIZE
	Cp	173	Marsh Marigold	*Caltha Palustris*	5″–6″ pots	25 cm
	Iv	216	Blue Flag Iris	*Iris Versicolor*	4″–5″ pots	80 cm

TREES (DECIDUOUS)	KEY	NO.	COMMON NAME	GENERIC NAME	ROOT	SIZE
	As	5	Sugar Maple	*Acer Saccharum*	W/B	60 mm Cal
	Bp	2	White Birch	Betula Papyrifera	W/B	60 mm Cal
	Qa	1	White Oak	Quercus Alba	W/B	60 mm Cal
	Ov	1	Ironwood	*Ostrya Virgiana*	W/B	60 mm Cal
TREES (CONIFEROUS)	Pa	12	Norway Spruce	*Picea Abies*	W/B	250 cm Height

Chapter Eleven
Common Pond-Management Problems

Fish Kill

Winter Fish Kill

You should suspect a winter kill if you don't see (or catch) any fish in the spring after ice has left your pond. Following a winter kill, typically, you will not see any signs of dead fish on the surface.

Causes

Oxygen is produced by aquatic plants as long as sunlight can penetrate the ice on a pond or lake. When snow 4–6 in. (10–15 cm) deep blankets the ice, it prevents light from penetrating to vegetation in the pond depths. Bacteria then begin to grow on algae and other organic plant material, converting this biomass into inorganic material, which results in the release of substances and gases toxic to fish. Respiration—of fish and other aquatic animals—and the bacterial process deplete the supply of dissolved oxygen. The situation is more severe in shallow ponds with more organic matter. Fish will suffocate when the snow cover continues for an extensive period of time.

Prevention

- Reduce the quantity of weeds in your pond before winter, removing them far from the pond.
- Deepen the pond by dredging (an extreme measure).
- Install a bottom draw-off device in summer or early fall.
- Shovel off the snow cover from at least a quarter of the pond surface to permit more light penetration.
- Inject a stream of air bubbles into the deepest section of the pond with a small compressor, half-inch PVC pipe, and an airstone (or sprinkler head).
- Place the airstone or sprinkler head at least one foot (0.3 m) above the pond bottom by anchoring it with

With proper pond management a healthy pond can be achieved for all concerned.

a weight one foot (0.3 m) beyond the airstone.

- This will not disturb the benthic zone of ooze and decomposing bacteria on the bottom which should not be mixed with the upper strata pond of water.
- Water can also be pumped out from under the ice to an inclined area on the shore (either natural or man-made) that has ridges, baffles, or rocks on its surface to oxygenate the water, while releasing any toxic gases before it runs back into the pond. (Note that a simple hole cut in the ice will not suffice for introducing oxygen.)

Summer Fish Kill

In midsummer or after an extended period of cloudy, windless days, fish are sometimes observed on the surface of the pond, gasping for air. They might also exhibit listlessness or erratic behavior (such as floating on their sides). At night or in the early morning, these fish may be seen gulping for air at the pond's surface or inflow location. When oxygen is at its lowest level, dead fish may be observed with their mouths wide open, gill covers raised and separated, indicating their effort to obtain enough oxygen. Once fish begin to die, it's normally too late to remedy the situation, but understanding the causes can prevent a reoccurrence.

Causes

Over-enrichment by nutrients from barnyard wastes, septic systems, etc. causes aquatic plant die-off. Pond water turns turbid and often has an offensive odor. When algae die suddenly and are decomposed rapidly by oxygen-consuming bacteria in the pond, fish are begin to die. Summer fish kill can also be triggered if the weather is overcast for several days and surface conditions are calm, or by a period of persistent rainfall and strong winds that mix the volume of the pond, distributing the decaying material and deoxygenating pond water.

Aquatic growth that is fueled by nutrients, in combination with calm, cloudy weather, can initiate oxygen depletion. (The intensity of sunlight is reduced by cloudy conditions, lowering the rate of photosynthesis in aquatic plants, lessening oxygen production.) Respiration exceeds photosynthesis at night, resulting in fish kills the following morning. A temperature increase also lowers oxygen concentration, and dissolved oxygen may decline in the upper pond layers as they warm up excessively. Fish driven from deeper layers low in oxygen to the upper layers of the pond experience suffocation when they reach the surface, which is now also depleted in oxygen.

Prevention

- Control aquatic vegetation and algae growth by physically removing excess plants.
- Deepen the pond by dredging (extreme measure).
- Reduce the nutrient inflow into the pond by:
  - diverting local run-off from barnyard wastes, feedlots, and pastureland away from the pond with ditches, culvert or drains;

- keeping a buffer of vegetation around the pond perimeter to intercept local run-off and to catch leaves and other organic debris in a filter of high grass and marsh plants;
- not connecting your pond to a storm drain;
- clearing tree leaves, a massive source of organic matter that, once decayed, add nutrients to the pond bottom (A forest edge close to a pond can be an advantage for wildlife but a disadvantage for pond management.);
- using little or no fertilizer on land draining toward the pond;
- keeping the grass near the buffer zones high to absorb run-off;
- locating septic systems at least 300 ft. (100 m) from your pond, as eventually, wastes will percolate through soil layers into the water (The better your soil passes the "percolation test," the sooner it will become saturated with phosphorus, which will be ushered right to your pond.); and,
- locating your tank and tile bed on a down slope *away* from your pond.

- Add fresh oxygenated cool water from a well or spring.
- Install a bottom draw-off device.
- Aerate your pond with a compressor at times when summer kill might occur, at night, early morning, and particularly during persistent cloudy weather (better aeration techniques could include a surface water agitator or a high-volume surface fountain).
  - Avoid artificial feeding of fish to prevent excessive vegetation (feed as sparingly as possible and be aware you are making a trade-off in the quality of the pond environment).
  - Do not stir up water in the pond as a remedy until you determine the source of the problem: mixing cool bottom water low in oxygen and high in organic sediments with warm surface water will make your pond unhealthy for fish.

Turbidity

Influence on Fish

Turbid, muddy water does not in itself kill fish, but will produce the following damaging effects:

- Limit the penetration of light and, therefore, oxygen produced by aquatic plant life.
- Coat and smother fish eggs and bottom-dwelling animals that fish rely on for food.
- Coat fish gills, reducing oxygen uptake.
- Reduce fishes' ability to see and catch prey.
- Increases water temperatures' to 'Increase water temperature.

Origins

Turbid, muddy water is produced by fine clay and clay-silt particles in suspension. This condition can be caused by bank erosion, run-off from nearby agricultural operations, livestock trampling in unfenced stream-source areas, or burrowing beavers and muskrats within the pond environs. It is almost always produced in the pond construction process, where excavation creates a blue, hazy pond filled with clay or mud particles in suspension. Given time, these particles will settle down, coating the bottom of the pond.

Treatment

- If turbidity (cloudiness) is due to wind-blown particles, a wind-break planted on the windward side of the pond can reduce the problem.
- Eroding banks or dam areas can be stabilized with rock, vegetation, or erosion-control fabrics and techniques.
- If silt is coming from adjacent agricultural operations, suggest contour plowing to the landowner or reroute the effluent through ditches or drains.
- If turbidity is the result of soil type (chronic clay turbidity), it can be treated with powdered gypsum (hydrated calcium sulphate).[1] It should be applied evenly to the pond surface, but is only a temporary solution and must be repeated when conditions reoccur.
- If livestock are entering either stream-source areas or the pond itself (heaven forbid!), fence them out. Assistance programs are available from your local stewardship councils, agricultural extension departments, and conservation authorities.
- Remove undesirable bottom-feeding fish and control or eliminate muskrats if they are the source of the problem.
- Never use lime or alum in a fish pond as a cure for turbidity.

Pond Scums

Green Pond Scum

When green algae are overabundant in the pond, they cause the water to resemble pea soup. Excessive quantities of algae produce a greenish mat, or bloom, on the pond surface, which decomposes and results in oxygen depletion, offensive odors, and often, a fish kill. These filamentous algae are composed of a series of cells end-to-end, which gives them their fine, threadlike appearance. Filamentous algae may grow prolifically early in spring, often dying back naturally by summer's end.

Cladophora algae appears as filamentous strands growing on rocks underwater until broken off, when it washes up on shores to decompose, producing an offensive odor. Chara (muskgrass) and nitella (stonewort)—two species of algae that are mistaken for submergent aquatic plants—also become overabundant and float on the surface in smelly mats, producing the same undesirable effects.

Red Pond Scum

Red scum is an algae bloom that usually endures only for a few days. It is found in shallow ponds which have become too warm, stagnant, and nutrient-rich. There are about two hundred species of red algae that live only in fresh water. *Lemanea* is a listed freshwater

1. Such chemical applications are to be discouraged as "short-term cosmetic remedies" which cannot help the fish, phytoplankton or zooplankton kingdoms in the pond. All other methods must be explored before any chemical "cure" is resorted to.

genus, but nearly all are marine species. Red algae are red because of the presence of the pigment *phycoerythrin*, which reflects red light and absorbs blue. Some members of the class have very little phycoerythrin, and may appear green or bluish due to chlorophyll and other pigments present in them. Because of the varying amount of this constituent, some blue-green algae have different wavelength uptake patterns, resulting in their taking on other colors or appearing red. Classification and taxonomy of red freshwater algae appears slim, with little information available on species and their control.

Do not confuse red pond scum with the infamous "red tide," a saltwater toxic marine dinoflagellate. Certain dinoflagellates in high concentrations create a bloom that releases a poison, or toxin, into the water. This toxin can paralyze fish, causing them to stop breathing. In Florida, the most common marine dinoflagellate causing red tide is *Karenia brevis* (*K. brevis*). *Karenia brevis* toxins, called brevetoxins, attack the nervous system of fishes, paralyzing the nerves and suffocating the fish. Eliminating the red tide is difficult because the blooms occur over hundreds to thousands of square miles of water and are distributed throughout the water column.

Yellow Pond Scum

A yellow film occurring late in spring is most likely pine pollen that drifts on the air and is deposited on the surface of the pond. It will eventually decompose and vanish, doing no harm to your pond.

Photo of our pond completely infested with chara.

Blue-Green Pond Scum

Blue-green algae can also be just blue, green, reddish-purple, or brown in color. They are a group of photosynthetic bacteria also knows as *cyanobacteria*. Most species are buoyant and will float to the surface, where they form scum layers or floating mats. Blue-green algae blooms generally occur between mid June and late September, but have been observed in winter, even under ice. The most commonly detected species are *Anabaena* sp. and *Microcystis* sp. These make up only a portion of the phytoplankton in many ponds or lakes, and are not eaten by other aquatic organisms. Thus, they are not an important part of the food chain. Discolored water is only an aesthetic issue, but when blue-greens reach bloom densities, they reduce light penetration, which can adversely affect other aquatic organisms directly (phytoplankton and aquatic plants), and also indirectly (zooplankton and fish that depend upon phytoplankton and plants). Blue-green algae blooms can also be quite smelly, affecting the taste of drinking water that derives from surface waters undergoing a bloom. When the blue-green algae bloom dies off, algae cells sink to the bottom and are broken down by microbes. Such an event consumes oxygen and can create a biological oxygen demand (BOD). This will result in a decrease in oxygen concentration in the water, affecting fish and other aquatic life and culminating in fish kills.

Certain blue-green algae blooms produce potent toxins and pose a health hazard to humans and animals drinking pond water. The same species can interfere with the uses of pond water for swimming, fish production, crop irrigation, and livestock watering, and must be controlled. This is one of the infestations where chemical control might be warranted.

A new method of algae control has appeared on the market which involves injecting an infusion of zooplankton into the pond. A simple method of distribution is to drag a nylon stocking filled with a zooplankton "soup" through the pond.

Aquatic-plant and algae control

A major component of controlling aquatic-plant growth is the restriction of phosphorus and nutrient supply to your pond. Long-term aquatic-plant control through preventative measures is the best approach. It may involve several techniques or a combination of techniques, depending upon the species of aquatic plants present, the magnitude of the problem, local regulations (permits required, etc.), and how much you are willing to spend. Your pond might need a continuous program consisting of one or several of the temporary measures suggested on the next few pages, rather than a specific measure. Increasing circulation by inducing turbulence of surface water by a propeller-driven device (such as the Algae Mill) appears to be taking the lead in aquatic-plant-control techniques. This method allows Mother Nature to help cure the problem. However, not all ponds are serviced by the electrical power needed for this device. Best management practices involving preventative actions should always be your first consideration. For additional help and technical advice, contact your local resource agency, environment agency, or conservation authority.

Best Management Practices for Aquatic Plant Control

If your pond or lake is near an agricultural operation, there are several wise land-use practices that may eliminate your aquatic plant problems. You can reduce soil erosion and the supply of nutrients through the following techniques:

- Contour plowing
- Installation of grassed waterways
- Fencing livestock away from ponds, inflowing streams, and run-off channels that are upstream from or adjacent to your pond or lake
- Diverting livestock wastes from feedlots, barnyards, and pastures that are upland or adjacent to your pond
- Preventing silage leachate spills and infiltration into surrounding soils by installing curbed solid pads with run-off containment and by roofing over storage facilities
- Installing water- and sediment-control basins on run-off channels
- Building conservation buffers and earth berms
- Creating constructed wetlands upstream from your pond or lake

Most of these actions will require some persuasive discussions with adjacent farmers or landowners, and you may be asked to contribute to the cost of achieving them, but overall, prevention is probably the best measure. You might also become a significant player in improving local conditions through soliciting assistance from your local stewardship council, soil- and crop-improvement associations, or conservation authority. Many of these agencies are willing to contribute assistance in the form of one-half the installation costs or in-kind contribution (manpower hours).

It is important to scrutinize your site as it relates to all the land around it and all the operations carried out upon it. Housing-construction sites, for instance, can impact your pond site by issuing run-off through ditches, water-quality ponds, or tile drains. This occurs simply because construction activities disturb the topsoil layer, destroy turf, and expose loose soil laden with phosphates and nutrients to rainfall erosion. Storm-water effluent from water-quality ponds or ditches in subdivision plots are laden with phosphates from excessive lawn fertilization and will be the largest of the nutrient-addition threats to your pond. This will normally occur during a storm when excessive rainfall fills the municipal water quality ponds, which then spill the excess over into drainage ditches.

Septic systems also eventually leak phosphorus through infiltration into the surrounding soils for distances as great as 300–400 ft. (100–130 m). This distance will increase when sandy soils are predominant or if overland seepage occurs. If you suspect a leaky tile bed or tank, make a close soil inspection. Your system should be pumped out every three years to keep the level of solids low, allowing proper drainage of liquid. A plugged tile field resulting in overland seepage will be disastrous if it reaches your pond or lake. If a neighbor has a faulty tile bed or one connected to a field-tile drainage system, report it to the health authority, as such connections are illegal.

Physical Removal by Hand or by Machine

Perhaps the most practical temporary method of control is just to wade in and uproot nuisance plants by hand. This will work for cattails, rushes and many other emergent species when they grow as isolated plants and not in colonies. Some submergent plants can also be accessed this way in depths that are reachable. The first uprooting will be very hard, messy work, but follow-ups repeated when necessary will keep the numbers down. Frequent raking of the shallows can help to keep perimeter areas weed-free, but raking the depths will be entirely impractical, as I found out in the case of my own pond. Often a garden rake fitted with a long handle from a pool cleaner can be manipulated from a boat or raft. These are tools often fabricated from hollow aluminum shafts that float, making your work easier, or at least less tiring. This works well only to a certain depth, limited as it is by the weight and density of the weed mass.

A scythe or hoe on a similar long handle could also assist your weeding operation, but be careful of the blade in water; it is more dangerous than in air, so wear protective boots. Remove the cut plants from your pond environment as soon as possible so that nutrients will not run back into the pond.

In some farm ponds, a temporary way of reducing algae mats and submerged and emergent weeds involves dragging an underwater rake (made from a harrow, mattress spring, heavy chains, or a log loosely wrapped with multiple strands of barbed wire) through the body of the pond with chain and tractor. A heavy chain connecting the log or rake to the tractor helps to sink the device to the pond bottom. The rake is guided by a rope manipulated by a person on shore. In an attractively landscaped pond, this process would wreak havoc on the perimeter, what with the tractor and the effects of positioning the heavy chain and the improvised rake for each run. Great effort is required to disentangle the weeds caught in a bedspring rake, reducing its practicality.

Mechanized harvesters can be practical down to a depth of about 4 ft. (1.2 m), and are often mounted on a boat, using cutter bars like those found on hay mowers. After the weeds are cut, these must be raked off to a removal area on shore, amounting to some effort. Larger harvester units are impractical for most small ponds. Some aquatic plant species (milfoil, elodeas, and coontail, for example) are hard to collect once cut, and fragments left behind give rise to new plants. Chara is particularly troublesome in this respect and re-establishes itself swiftly. Removal is best done at the height of the summer growing season, when your efforts will result in the maximum amount of aquatic plant material removed and full enjoyment of the results. Make sure to dispose of the harvested plants carefully, as some bottom material will be anaerobic, and likely, bacteria-laden. The best policy is to bury it.

Dredging and Deepening the Pond or Lake

The cost of dredging a pond or lake can be prohibitive, but it is effective in increasing the volume of your pond, its ability to handle nutrient load, and to create deeper habitat for many fish species. Depths of 18 ft. (6 m) or more will most certainly rule out nuisance growths of aquatic plants—excepting Eurasian water milfoil, which will grow in depths up to 20 ft. (6.3 m). Dredging will also create steeper side slopes, discouraging most plants from growing around the perimeter. The removal of shoreline organic deposits in the muck and perimeter soils will also remove nutrients from this area, depriving plants of this essential growth accelerator.

A rough access road to your pond is imperative, as a dragline unit's steel track will quickly ruin a typical asphalt entry road. Some contractors use old rubber tires as cushions under the tracks as the machine proceeds; these make a good barrier between treads and asphalt, but it is tough work to throw them from back to front as the machine crawls up your road. The remaining problem will be the chewing up of your lawn or the grassed perimeter of the pond as the contractor works around it. You are guaranteed to end up with piles of muck, peat, dead aquatic weeds, and tread gouges all around your pond. Weeds and anaerobic muck must be removed, and the excavated soils distributed by bulldozer all around the perimeter, returning the banks to some degree of their original state. All this disturbance also results in the loss of many invertebrates, fish, shoreline shrubbery, and possibly those trees hanging too close to the dragline boom swing that may inhibit the operator from achieving full excavation.

Essentially you start all over again with this process to create a better pond environment, with all the associated work—planting shrubs or trees, raking the banks and tread-tracks smooth, and seeding all disturbed areas.

Conventional methods using draglines elevate costs about 50 percent or more above simple sediment removal. Dredged benthic-layer muck and ooze, along with dead aquatic weeds, must be disposed of properly and are best buried on site far away from the pond. Although it may seem convenient to grade the muck around your perimeter, this invites disaster as nutrients, seeds, roots, and tubers find their way right back to where they started—in your pond!

Hydraulic Suction Pumps

Hydraulic suction pump dredges are often very useful in removing organic soils and aquatic weeds from the periphery of your pond. Because of the weight of the water-filled suction hose, the units are very difficult to manhandle around the pond perimeter. Similarly, the discharge-hose line is not any easier to control as it deposits muck, detritus, plants, and ooze as far from the pond as possible. Hydraulic dredging however proves to be the most effective method used in the majority of projects undertaken. The dredge is essentially a pump and a collection system mounted on a small boat or raft built for the purpose of dredging, and is usually operated by a diesel engine. The pump pulls material from the bottom and pumps it through a pipe to a distant location. The repository must be far enough away to assure that no run-off will re-enter the pond or lake. Usually this material is pumped into a specially excavated settling basin to contain it.

Natural depressions also offer the opportunity to utilize an existing basin. And some method must be devised to return your pond water to the dredge location, since it is only used as a carrier to move material (adhering to good water conservation practice). Usually this water can be returned after several days of settling and evaporation. If you wish to dispose of the spoils further, try contacting various nurseries in your area to see if they might buy your peat and muck as a garden-soil amendment.

Some smaller suction-pump models may be used less effectively on a sled hauled by tractor, and moved about the pond. The discharge pipe and inlet (suction) pipe need to be pulled out, moved to the next site, and reassembled, requiring a fair degree of manpower.

In some sites, where there is limited opportunities to dispose of dredged material, the use of geo-textile bags may prove convenient as temporary storage containers. Sediment is pumped into large bags which can be as long as three hundred feet (90 m). Once the material in the bag has dried out, it can be trucked away or spread out on site—as long as any drainage from it does not enter the pond. Some pond-cleaning operators filter the material sucked up through a filter box, separating weeds and other debris from the pond water which is clarified and returned to the pond. In this way, they can meet provincial or state regulations often permitting pond dredging without a permit.

Partial Draw-Down

Lowering the pond- or lake-water level to expose much of the pond bed to air has several favorable effects, and costs little. Many species of aquatic plants and some fish will be killed; however, some plants, such as cattails, are actually stimulated by summer draw-down, and it is equally ineffectual on plants such as coontail and elodea, which survive as free-floating fragments to germinate again. Winter draw-down does not adversely affect wild rice and other emergent desired at the pond or lake margin. Soft organic sediments consolidate when dried out, and you may gain several inches or even feet (centimeters or meters) of pond depth. If your pond has a properly designed dam with a control valve or gate, draw-down is easy, but possible adverse effects on downstream waters must be considered. Always seek help from your natural resources agency before doing this, as it may be illegal without a permit.

Remember, it is the owner's responsibility to release water in a "judicious, reasonable and prudent manner," as downstream waters or property can be destroyed by flooding, erosion, or sedimentation.

To draw down a pond without a drain, employ a lowhead, high-volume pump or a siphon rig but consider the length of time needed for your pond to refill. Carefully evaluate whether there will be increased danger of oxygen depletion and fish die-off during partial draw-down. Draw-down will also facilitate dredging, since the littoral edge of the pond will be exposed. This allows more efficient removal of sediment with little or no water carrying suspended solids back out of the bucket into the pond.

Draw-downs should not be done in warm weather or in shallow ponds containing fish populations that are to be sustained. Be aware that a draw-down leaving shallow water for many days in the bottom of a pond which was too deep for rooted plants might encourage seeds or plant fragments to take root in a newly sunlit environment.

After sufficient drying has taken place, raise the water level as quickly as possible, raking out any newly established plants as levels rise. Collect and dispose of all dead plants at least three hundred feet (90 m) away.

If you have outlet facilities on a dam structure that can discharge water from selected levels (i.e., a gate structure), then it is possible to reduce the pond's nutrient load from levels where they are concentrated. This occurs at certain times of the year when dissolved nutrients are collecting at these levels. Again, be aware of the effect of these nutrients on downstream waters.

Reducing Light Penetration

The reduction of light can shade out aquatic plants early in the spring before they get a chance to establish themselves. Two methods are commonly used to achieve this result:

- the use of black plastic sheeting
- water-soluble dyes

Floating black plastic attached to Styrofoam floats will prevent light from reaching small areas of the pond, but is entirely impractical for a large pond or lake. It is very difficult to install without getting into the pond yourself, and it is almost impossible to avoid snagging and puncturing the sheeting on emergent plants around the pond while installing it.

Water-soluble dyes such as Aquashade will screen out specific wavelengths of sunlight for up to two weeks, but can only be used on a closed-pond system. The duration of treatment should be at least four weeks to be effective, so several applications may be necessary.

Addition of Barley Straw

Barley-straw bales have been used to reduce algae (chara and nitella along with the filamentous algae cladophora and spirogyra). The straw has no adverse effect on established aquatic plants (submergent, emergent or floating aquatic plants), nor on invertebrates, which seem to grow well in the protected environment it forms. As the straw decomposes, the creatures thrive on the decomposed organic matter produced and increase in numbers, overall improving the health of your pond. Barley straw is a partner in producing peroxides, which prevents the growth of algae. As the straw decomposes, lignins are released and oxidize into humic acids. When the humic acids are combined with dissolved oxygen and sunlight, they convert to hydrogen peroxide. The low levels of peroxides keep the algae population down, but will not remove the algae presently occupying the pond. That is why this technique only works well if applied in the spring before any algae appears. The barley straw must be replaced within six months, allowing a new batch to decompose. Application is best achieved by bundling up the barley straw in potato sacks and placing them at intervals around your pond to float just immersed at the water surface. Attach a float such as a plastic jug to each barley-straw bundle to prevent it from sinking, and a weight to keep it in place. Place the barley straw in your pond or lake early in the spring, as it requires about a month to become effective. The process is temperature-dependent, so, as temperatures increase, the reaction proceeds faster. If you live in more southern climates where algae grows year-round, place the straw in the pond in the early fall before the existing straw bundle has rotted away. Remember that existing algae (chara, nitella, cladophora, or spirogyra) must be removed before treatment, as the barley straw bundles will keep any new growth at bay. This may mean the application of some sort of algicide first and then physical removal. Average dose for ponds is approximately three bales per acre (eight per hectare), requiring 3 to 4 ppm of oxygen in the water to be effective.

Biological Control

Increasing the zooplankton population is another avenue toward cleaning up the pond, and zooplankton collected from a healthy pond can be injected into your ailing pond. This is achieved by dragging a nylon stocking through a healthy zooplankton-populated pond and releasing them later by reversing the stocking and pulling it out over the surface of the pond requiring treatment. The zooplankton eat up the algae in the daytime, sinking to the bottom at night. In some ponds heavily infested with chara, the algae have killed off all the zooplankton and will continue to do so. Commercial products are available. Zooplankton require habitat to thrive and reproduce, so maintaining a margin of aquatic plants to foster their growth is not a bad idea.

Planting lilies and marsh marigolds around the perimeter of the pond will at least offer a jungle of narrow stems for the zooplankton to hide in and multiply, and in any case, this measure beautifies the wildlife-type pond.

Pond Aeration

Because the process of thermal stratification drastically reduces dissolved oxygen in a pond, the most logical attack is to re-introduce oxygen, thus stimulating natural convection through the water column. This involves aeration. Also, oxygen deficiency is usually due to a lack of water circulation throughout the pond. As water near the pond bottom becomes oxygenated, the surface of the pond's benthal layer (the mud and ooze) is kept oxidized, holding phosphorus in an insoluble form and less available for aquatic plants. In extreme cases, dredging can be undertaken to remove the toxic benthal layer, but this dislodges seeds and roots from the offensive underwater vegetation, dispersing them throughout the pond. Resulting most often in a regrowth of aquatic vegetation only a few weeks after initial treatment.

One of the two following methods (fountains or propeller-driven surface aeration) both of which circulate and aerate water could very well become your solution to treat aquatic weed growth along with thermal stratification.

Propeller-Driven Surface Aeration

A propeller-like device creates waves and currents in a duplication of natural action. One such tool called the Algae Mill, manufactured by Environ Mills International, Inc., in Ontario, Canada, has a patented wavemaker float system that creates a new wave every three seconds. It has a propulsion system that creates a powerful river-flow current. Resultant waves will cover up to one and a half acres (0.5 hectares) of pond surface while the current created by the device drives all the surface water around the pond in the fashion of a river flow. Nutrients are dissipated, nitrates and algae blooms broken down, while new generations of algae are prevented from forming.

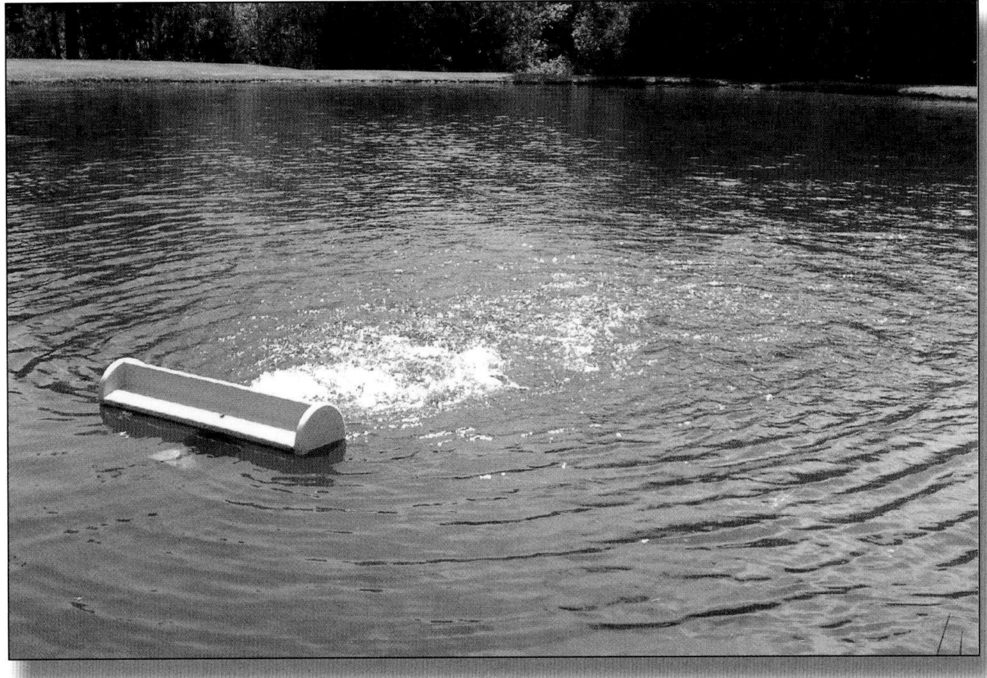

The Algae Mill device creating desired turbulence in surface water [Courtesy of Courtesy of Basil Leonard]

Fountains move water in one direction only (usually vertically), as the distribution area on the fountain's surface is usually confined to the circumference of the fountain spray: waters only a short distance away remain somewhat motionless and stagnant.

The Algae Mill also effectively controls ice build-up around docks and boats.

Critics of the propeller and fountain aerators claim penetration of oxygenated water only reaches limited depths, as these deal primarily with surface waters. They claim that the deeper hypolimnion and benthic

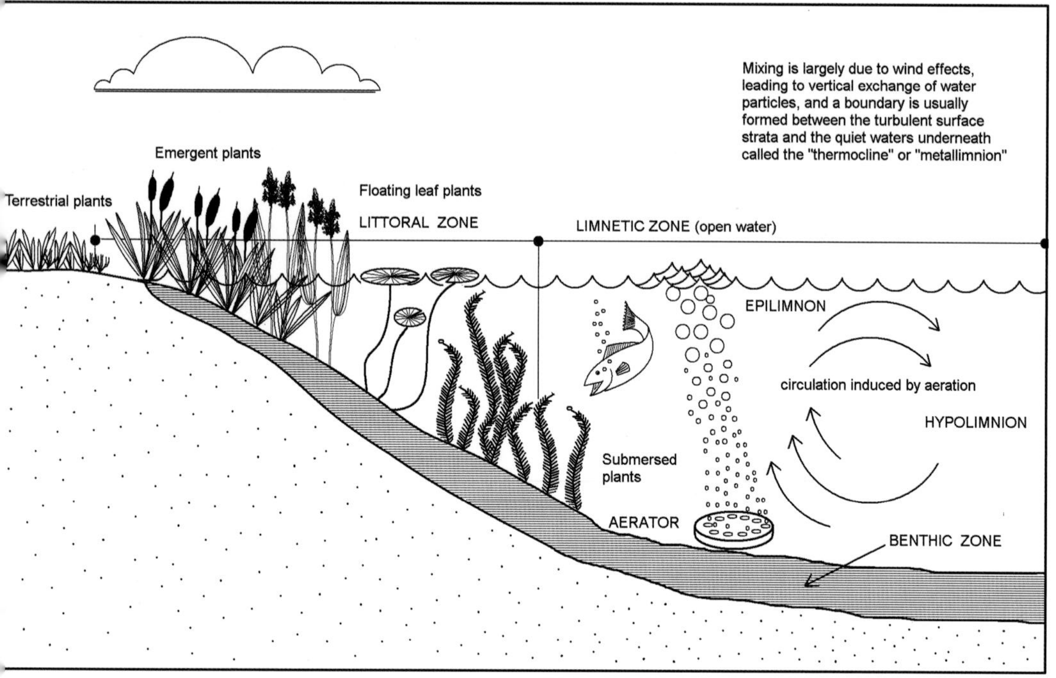

Figure 11.1 Diagram of improved natural convection throughout the water column by aeration from the pond bottom.

layers receive little or no benefit. There is some evidence through testing that the Algae Mill does, in fact, create an inverted vortex and may also pull water up from the bottom of the pond or lake. In waters at a local marine that I have visited where the Algae Mill is operating, noticed a distinct clarification of surface waters, and can be quite prepared to try out this system on my own pond where the wave action alone would be most attractive. Fountain and surface aeration devices are less effective at adding oxygen to deeper layers of the pond. They also increase water loss due to evaporation, particularly if the water is dispersed as a fine spray. Other drawbacks, according to some authorities, are the large amounts of power consumption required to run the fountain systems effectively, and their noise, although the sound of falling water is considered pleasing by some owners.

Air Injection Through Release of Fine Bubbles

Another method of oxygenating water is often used with air injection. The system employed can operate on low power with as little as a half-horsepower compressor. The equipment, developed by EP Aeration, Inc., in San Luis Obispo, California, forces air through a special hose laid on the pond or lake bottom. Specially sized apertures at precise intervals along the hose release fine bubbles of air that rise through the thermal zones to the surface. This stimulates natural convection of water through the thermal layers while also introducing oxygen—satisfying both criteria for a healthy water column. It has also demonstrated the ability to lower the surface water's temperature, thereby reducing evaporation and helping to eliminate the primary cause of thermal stratification. The bubbler system, like the propeller system, also reduces icing on ponds during winter.

Ozone can be injected into a fine-bubble, bottom-laid aeration system. It is a powerful oxidizer of many organic and inorganic materials, including bacteria, viruses, and mold spores. Ozone keeps pumps and other components of the bubbler system from fouling, and precipitates suspended solids out of solution, helping to clarify the pond or lake water. Ozone also

Photo of our own pond after we employed a self-built air-injection system. Inside the pump house on the dock, a vacuum pump supplies air to a perforated lawn-sprinkler-head on the bottom of the pond. The vacuum intake is kept open and the air pressure port is simply connected to a half-inch (12.5 mm) hose line leading to the sprinkler head at the bottom of the pond. Notice the absence of floating algae.

Above left: Photo of the hose line and sprinkler head assembled on the dock before insertion into the middle of the pond. A small section of steel plate wired to the sprinkler head serves as a weight to keep the unit on the pond bottom. (A cement block section would serve the same purpose.) Make sure you use plastic-coated electrical wire to connect the two or corrosion will soon separate them in the acidic benthal layers formed at the bottom of the pond.

aids in the breakdown of hydrocarbons, chlorinated hydrocarbons, PCBs, and other toxic chemicals into less hazardous compounds. Being an unstable gas, ozone quickly reverts back to oxygen, adding to the dissolved oxygen already in the water. Some engineered bottom-installed aeration systems, however, produce large bubbles which are not as suitable for aeration, and also stir up the bottom sediments, dispersing them and their gas products (methane) throughout the water column above the air injector. These inadequately engineered systems may actually launch algae blooms immediately following installation, but they are usually short-lived growths.

Whatever method you choose to employ, it is most critical to collect as much information about your pond or lake as possible. This will involve a complete water analysis along with an analysis of the pond's natural surroundings and its watershed. It helps to consult a pond expert who has good references, particularly one in your physiographic region, one familiar with similar soils, geology, and climatic conditions. If these criteria are satisfied you are bound to get some good solutions for your pond or lake problem.

Many pond managers treat their problem symptoms without understanding the causes. One immediate reaction is to kill off the algae with an algicide.

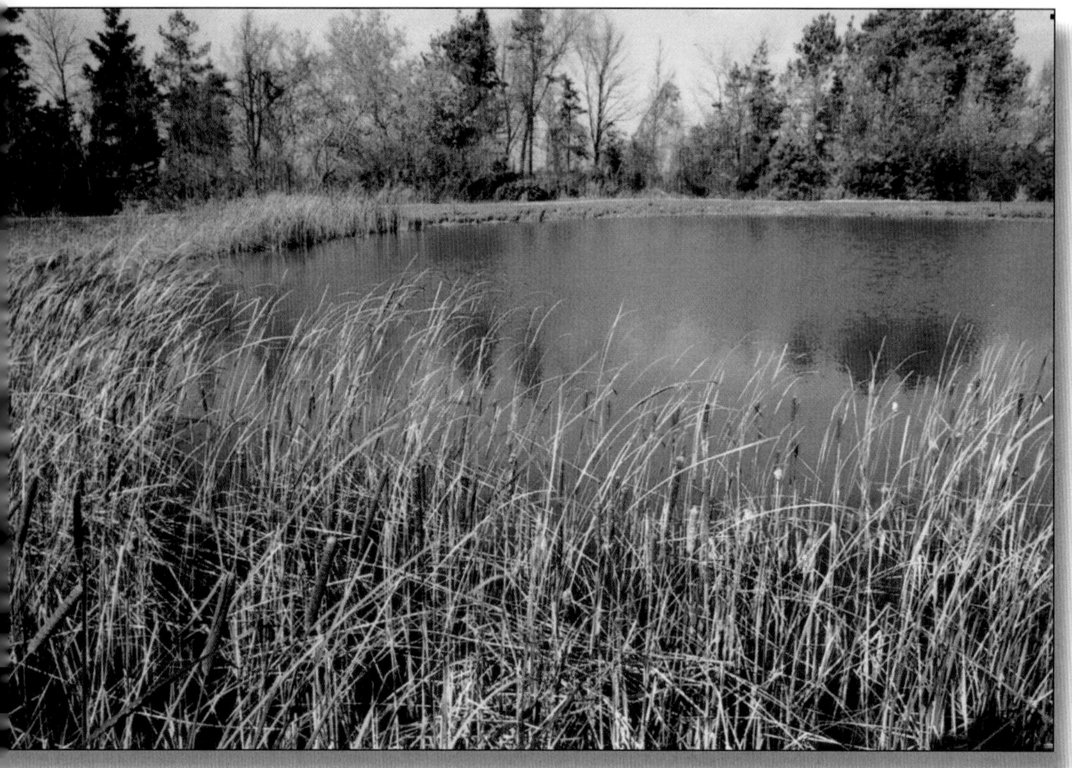

Photo of a healthy, well-circulating pond serving as an irrigation reservoir and beneficial wildlife habitat. Its marginal cattail vegetation is growing only in shallow water, and unless slumping or siltation occurs it will maintain its present state [Orchard Beach Golf and Country Club, Keswick, Ontario, Canada. Photo by John Hicks].

Having done so, they are surprised by a second algae bloom within a week, while the algicide (copper sulphate, simazine, gramoxone, dalapon, reglone, etc), and its byproducts sink to the bottom of the pond and contaminate the benthal layers. The chemical decomposition consumes more oxygen and provides extra nutrients for future algae blooms. None of these chemicals should ever be applied to ponds used for irrigation, and the downstream effects must always be very carefully considered. Legislation requires that a permit be obtained by any person applying herbicides to water or a water course. Many municipalities in North America are now banning herbicides outright unless proof can be offered that an infestation has occurred. Chemical treatment will not eliminate the causes, and the solution to the problem must be to treat the conditions that precipitate algae formation, algae blooms, and excessive aquatic plant growth. I have therefore eliminated the use of chemical additives from the book preferring to describe physical and biological methods of control. Besides, I value all the living organisms in my pond, and my objective is to provide a sustainable environment for them to live in for as long as I am their keeper and guardian.

Fish Diseases and Parasites

A wide variety of diseases and parasites attack fish, including viruses, bacteria, fungi, grubs, lice, and tapeworms. It is common to find a few fish with parasites, but not in large numbers. Organisms that cause disease do not often reach epidemic levels or cause large fish kills in most ponds, but some parasites can prevent fish growth and survival. Man is not normally affected by fish diseases and parasites if the fish is properly cooked before consumption.

Parasite and disease indicators include:

- Large numbers of dead and dying fish.
- Fish swimming habits that appear frantic or erratic.
- Abnormal positions or mannerisms, such as fish resting on their sides, upside down, or repeatedly rubbing their body against submerged objects.
- Blood in the fins or other areas of the body.
- Tumors, swollen areas or wounds on the body.

FIGURE 11.2 TABLE OF FISH DISEASES AND PARASITES

[Adapted from *Landowner's Guide to Managing Fish Ponds in Ontario*, Jan Gray, Ministry of Natural Resources]

DISEASE	FISH AFFECTED	CAUSES	INDICATIONS
Black spot or black grub	Warm-water and coldwater fish	Parasitic worms Strigeoid trematodes	Small black spots just under the skin and tissue. Spots are cysts containing a microscopic fluke
Yellow grub	Warm-water fish	Strigeoid trematodes	Cysts under the skin, especially at the back and tail: when squeezed from cysts, living worm is yellow
Eye fluke	Warm-water and coldwater fish	Strigeoid trematodes	Fish eyes are white or Opaque; fish become partially or totally blind
"Ich" or white spot	Warm-water fish; occasionally, trout	A protozoan, Ichthyophthirius multfifilis	Tiny grey-white spots on body
Skin fungus (water mold)	All fishes	Saprolegnia fungus (often results from injury)	Tufted growths of white or grey threads that radiate 0.5 in. (13 mm) or more from the body
Columnaris	All fishes	Chondrococcus columnaris bacterium	Grey-white spots surrounded by red on parts of head, gills, fins or body
Red sore	Northern pike	• Aeromona liquefaciens bacterium	Open bleeding sores from which scales are lost
Furunculosis	Trout and salmon	• Aeromonas salmonicida bacterium	Boils or furuncles on skin, inflammation of inner body walls, many small intestinal hemorrhages, bright red spleen and swollen kidneys
Fish or gill lice	Warm-water and coldwater fish	Parasitic copepods	Light-colored, wormlike body attached to fins of fish
Tumors and other deformities	All fishes	Injuries, dietary problems, genetic causes etc.	External and internal tumors of various sorts, spinal deformities, shortened or flattened heads

- Growths on the head, body, or fins.
- Visible parasitic organisms.
- Small black or white spots.
- Skin discolorations such as spots and blotches in places where they should not naturally occur.

Treatment and Help

- If parasites are found on fish, seek professional assistance immediately.
- Identification may require microscopic examination by a specialist.
- Contact your local Natural Resources District Office or Fish and Wildlife Service Department for positive identification. They may, in turn, contact a fish pathology lab for assistance.
- There is little you can do to treat diseased or parasite-affected fish unless you drain the pond, dry it out, and disinfect the pond bottom.

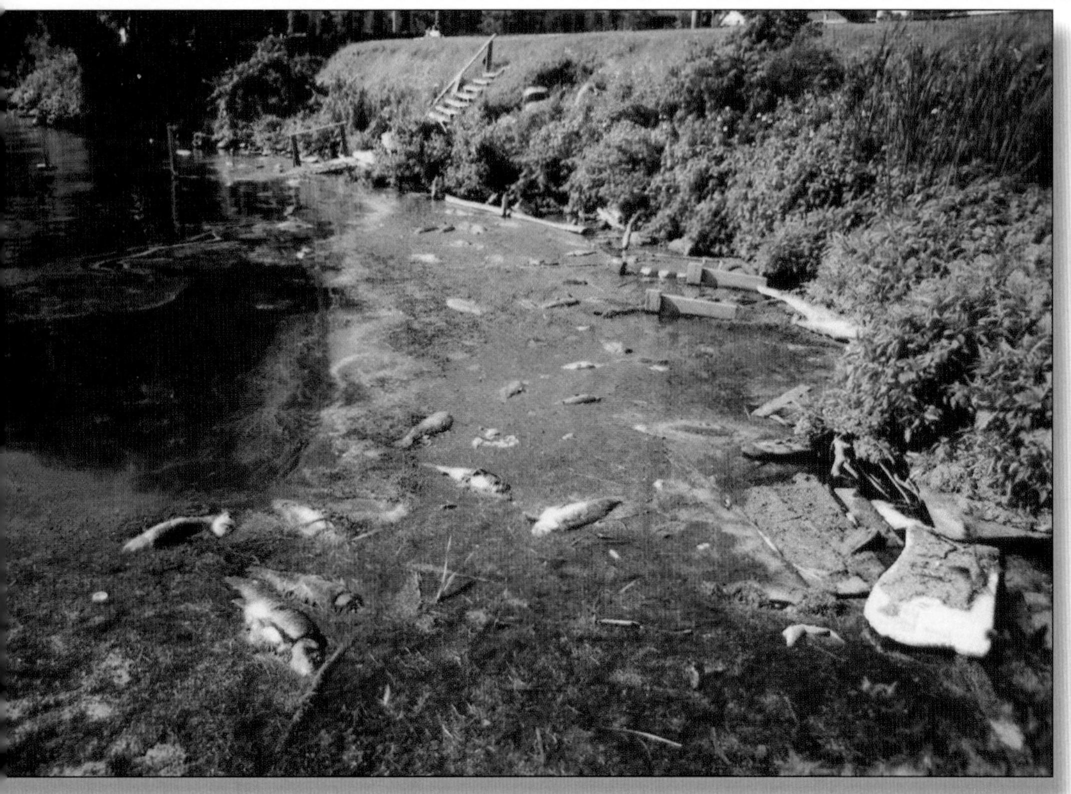

Dead carp floating on the surface of a bay in Lake Simcoe. They were killed in large numbers around the lake by a virus that attacks primarily the carp species. Fish and Wildlife authorities were powerless to prevent the infection from spreading throughout several of the Kawartha lakes in Ontario.

Prevention

Parasites may be more numerous on those fish that live in shallow, weedy ponds. Fish from deeper ponds with fewer weeds generally have fewer parasites. This is because many of the parasites infecting fish live part of their life cycle in host animals such as clams and snails that dwell in shallow water or on plants. If you make your pond deeper and less weedy, you have taken preventative action to eliminate many of these parasites. Disease is also likely to happen when the fish are under stress due to unfavorable temperature, low oxygen, or other water-quality problems. Follow recommended stocking rates and do not overcrowd your pond. Carefully examine the fish you intend to stock: if they exhibit any sign of stress, parasites, or disease, do not stock them, as they may infect the rest of your fish population. Under no circumstances should you release diseased fish into public waters. In fact, no fish can be stocked in public waters without a permit.

Nuisance Animal Control

While most wild animals, birds, reptiles, and invertebrates are invited into your pond environment through plantings and wildlife-management techniques, some of them may conflict with your interests and goals. Described here are various control methods that may reduce or eliminate nuisance animals temporarily, although these may have to be repeated. Check with your local natural resources or state law-enforcement office for regulations and permit requirements for animal control.

Muskrats

Muskrats burrow into pond embankments, weakening dams and resulting in serious leaks. Their preference for home sites involves digging into any inclined slope such as your pond embankment. The burrow usually begins about 6–18 in. (15–45 cm) beneath the water surface and runs an average length of 5–6 ft. (1.5–1.8 m). The resultant tunnel leads to a dry nest chamber above water level. Keeping the earthen embankment mowed will help to discourage these animals as they prefer cover. Armoring the face of your dam or embankment with rock or steel mesh will discourage burrowing. Trapping and shooting require a licensed trapper in most provinces or states; besides, killing muskrats is grossly unfair since you have just created their perfect habitat. Be aware that any trapper you hire to eradicate the animals will likely drown them in your pond. If you are in close proximity to other wetlands or waterways, more muskrats will invade your property. It is better to control muskrat damage by reinforcing your embankments. The pond shore can be reinforced by any one of the following techniques:

- Line the area from 3 ft. (1 m) below the water line to 1 ft. (0.3 m) above the normal water line with a foot-thick layer of rip-rap rock at least 6 in. (152 mm) in diameter.
- Use soil cement applied in the top 6 in. (152 mm) from 1 ft. (0.3 m) above normal water level to 4 ft. (1.2 m) below normal water level.
- Line the embankment with hardware cloth (heavier than chicken wire) of 2 in. (5 cm) mesh or less, within the same zone as above.

Beavers

Landowners have two choices when confronted with beavers on their pond site: they can share the pond with these animals or they can take measures to remove them. Again, it is grossly unfair to the beaver, since they are merely taking advantage of the perfect habitat you have created. Beavers can, however, become a nuisance by flooding large areas of agricultural land and forest and access roads. Their tree-felling can often be hazardous and unsightly, and this coupled with the loss of pondside trees makes these animals undesirable residents in a manicured pond. Their intrusion is much more acceptable in a wildlife pond, although measures must be taken to discourage them from damming the pond beyond its design height.

One effective method for discouraging beavers from using your pond is the beaver baffle. This uses two large-diameter drain pipes—at 3–4 in.

A large beaver house on the edge of a shallow lake. Often, beavers will leave the pond or lake level intact, content with the depth and conditions at their chosen home site.

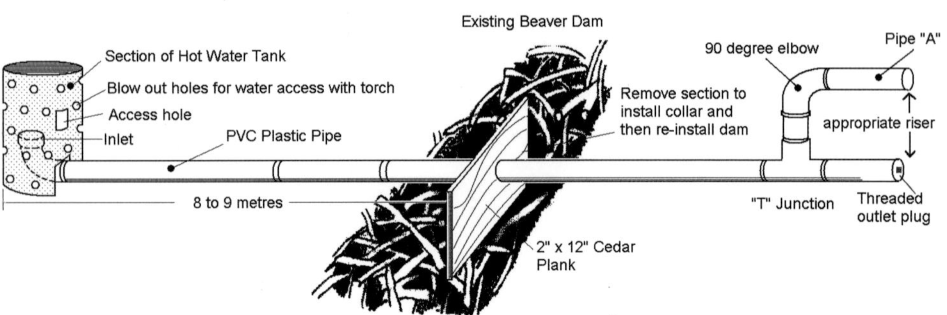

Figure 11.3 Diagram of a beaver baffle. One must disassemble part of the dam to insert the baffle through it, which is disturbing to the beaver, but it's a lot more respectful of their home and ecological benefit than trapping them outright.

(7.5–10 cm)—and is a long-term solution. The drain pipes are installed through the beaver dam, which necessitates temporary dislodgement of branches and debris that form the portion of dam the pipes are piercing. One drain pipe is installed in the deep part of the pond and the other downstream, far away from the dam. The further the distance from dam to outlet the greater the success, since beaver are attracted to the sound of running water and will try to dam it up. Rather than creating a pond upstream of the dam, the water flows through the dam and downstream. Because the drain is under the surface of the water, the beavers are not likely to discover it. Eventually they become discouraged with the situation and move on, leaving behind a small pond.

This arrangement is only required in a by-pass pond or on-stream pond where beavers might try their own impoundments on the water source above your pond.

Local stewardship councils or hunter's associations, which have an interest in maintaining ponds as wildlife habitat, can assist in installing and maintaining the beaver baffle.

If your pond is a wildlife-type design, you might be willing to let beavers create a lodge within your site along the bank, although the mess of branches and twigs may become so large as to occupy a large portion of your pond.

Trees that might be targeted for cutting by beavers can be protected by wrapping them with heavy-mesh hardware cloth or sheet metal to a height of 3 ft. (1 m). Some repellants with an offensive smell or taste can be applied to the tree boles. If beavers become a real nuisance, they can be trapped during the open season (winter) and their pelts used. Unless you are a farmer, trapping on private land must be done by a licensed trapper. Contact your local Natural Resource Agency or state Fish and Wildlife Service for the names of licensed trappers in your area. Shooting beavers that have become property-wrecking nuisance animals is allowed on your own property under the Game and Fish Act.

Trapping and shooting are, however, temporary measures. If you are offering suitable habitat, other beavers will quickly move in. It is wise to consider this before constructing your pond if you know that the beaver inhabit your surrounding area. It may be that your only recourse is to create a wildlife pond and put up with the creatures.

Moles

Mole burrows can undermine and destroy patches of sod on dams or pond banks, resulting in erosion. Control moles by trapping, or with burrow fumigants, if these are available and not considered a restricted substance under the Pesticides Act. To determine if a burrow is still in use, flatten it gently. If in use, the ridge will be raised again within 24–48 hours.

Regulations and Permits Required for Applying Herbicides or Algicides

If you plan to use any herbicide or algicide to control aquatic plants in your pond you must gain approval from the Department or Ministry of Environment or the local pesticide control agency.. Note that in some Canadian municipalities your pond/lake site may fall under the Cosmetic Pesticides Ban Act where any application of herbicides or algicides is not permited. Several other Acts directly affect the aquatic use of pesticides and algicides:

- The Ontario Water Resources Act (controls the discharge of specific waste from fish farms)
- The Pesticides Act requires a permit to purchase and/or perform a water extermination from the Ontario Ministry of Environment (a Water Exterminator's Licence may also be required)
- Pesticides must be registered under the Federal Pest Control Products Act

Always check first with your Environment agency.

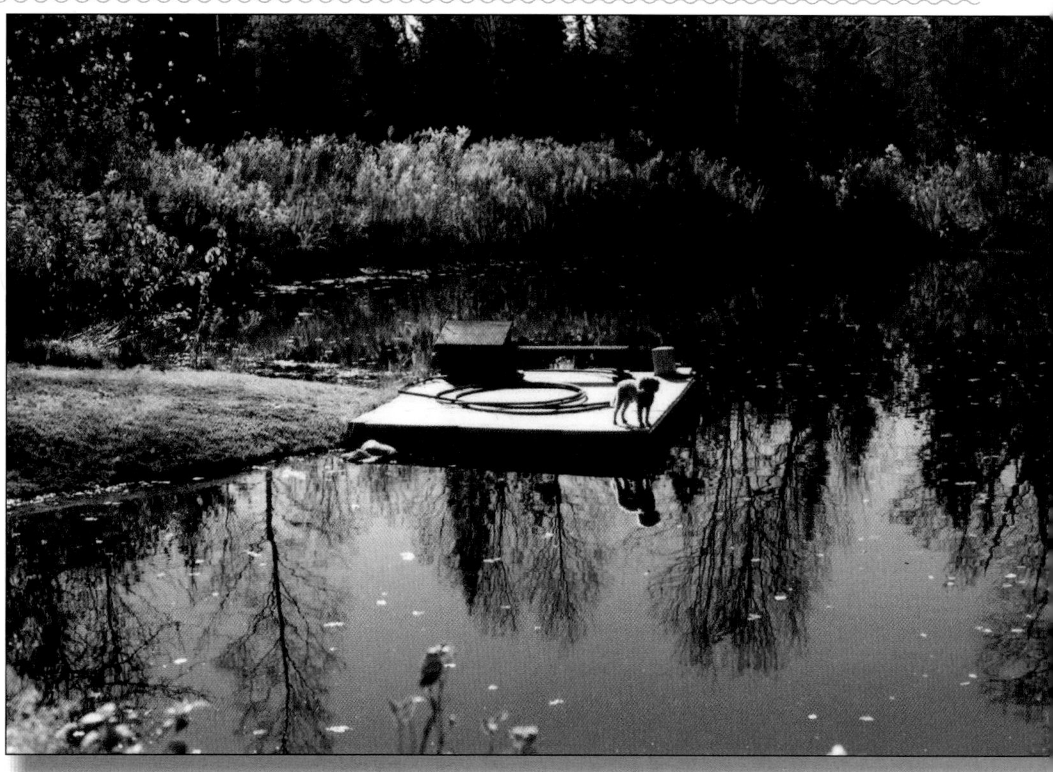

All animals appreciate a pond. Our little poodles spent a large part of their lives around it, and in it. Though they're long gone now, their memory is forever a part of the environment of this little heart-shaped pond.

The Northern forest and lake district is an inspiring and complex landscape, with great biodiversity.

AFTERWORD

As pond managers, we can promote and maintain our biological heritage and encourage its survival. We can assist the biodiversity of earth by maintaining a wildlife or fish pond.

"Biodiversity is all around us—it's the variety of life on Earth, from the tiniest insect to a vast northern forest. Maintaining biodiversity is also about being connected—no species, including people, can live without others to provide it with food and habitat. All living things are connected."[2] The world is home to an assortment of ecosystems, including lakes and ponds. It is one of our responsibilities to care for living systems and be a steward on this planet, and creating a pond ecosystem is a good beginning.

[2] Adapted from *Algonquin Information Guide*

Acknowledgements

As are many books, *The Pond Book* is the result of advice and assistance from various individuals and organizations. Assistance has come from the following agencies in both Canada and the United States of America:

Ontario Ministry of Natural Resources
Ontario Parks
Ontario Ministry of Agriculture, Food, and Rural Affairs
Ministry of Environment and Energy Ontario
Canadian Wildlife Service
Landowner Resource Centre
Royal Botanical Gardens Ontario
Toronto Zoo
University of Toronto Press
United States Fish & Wildlife Service
United States Department of Agriculture, Soil Conservation Service
Smithsonian Institute
Washington State Department of Ecology
Universities of Ohio State, Michigan State, and Minnesota
Florida Fish and Wildlife Conservation Commission
Lake Simcoe Region Conservation Authority, Ontario
Toronto and Region Conservation Authority, Ontario
Agrilife Extension Services
EcoMetrix Incorporated

Material and Information was provided by the following companies:
EP Aeration Inc.
Otterbine
Environ Mills International
Maccaferri Canada Ltd.,
North American Green Inc.
Risi Stone Inc.
Turf & Recreation Magazine

Societies and councils that supplied data toward the production of this book are:
The Friends of Algonquin Park
Connecticut Botanical Society
Save the Maskinonge
York Environmental Stewardship

Special thanks are due to the following individuals whose assistance or photographs helped to enhance the book:
George and Roland Peacock
Ivan Foster
Robert J. Eakins
William Heyd
Basil Leonard
Jerry Smitka
Brian Peterkin
Paul Kirby
Wil Wegman, OMNR
Valorie Levens
Dorothy Saffarawich
Mike Jiggens
Ron & Reese Arnold
Gabbi Liddle
Christa Sharp
Mary Jane Moroz
Lorraine Hicks
Mike Campese, OMNR
Ron Allen, OMNR
Calvin Knaggs

And many thanks to Thomas R. Biebighauser (*A Guide to Creating Vernal Ponds*) whose original script was adapted to fit this manual. Similarly, the use of information published by the Soil Conservation Service, U.S. Department of Agriculture, has contributed immensely to the success of this book, supporting much of the mechanical details associated with construction and operation of dams, spillways, and ponds in general.

And finally, last but not least, my lovely wife, Lorraine, who accompanied me on the many field trips throughout Ontario and Florida to photograph lakes, ponds, and the life around them. Without her, the book would never have been possible.

Bibliography

Chapter 1: Reasons for Constructing a Pond

Henry David Thoreau, 1854, *Walden*

Ohio Department of Natural Resources, 2008 Ohio Pond Management, *Wildlife Habitat Enhancement around the Pond*

Slemming, Brian, June, 2006, "A Dip in the Pond," *Landscape Trades,* Volume 28, No. 5

Soil Conservation Service, U.S. Department of Agriculture, 1971, *Ponds For Water Supply and Recreation*, U.S. Government Printing Office, Washington, D.C.

"Construction of Natural Swimming Pools," *The Garden Landscape Guide,* GardenVisit.com

Rawhide Fire Hose, Orrville, Ohio

Chapter 2: Planning the Pond

Ohio State University, Ohio Pond Management Extension Services, Bulletin 374-99

Soil Conservation Service, U.S. Department of Agriculture, 1971: *Ponds for Water Supply and Recreation,* U.S. Government Printing Office, Washington, D.C.

Breed and Hosmer, *Elementary Surveying,* MIT, 1919: John Wiley & Sons, Inc., New York, N.Y.

Ontario Department of Energy and Resources Management, Conservation Authorities Branch, 1968: *Rideau Valley Conservation Report*

Otterbine, Emmaus, Pennsylvania, *Otterbine News,* Summer Edition

Shrouder, John D., Charles M. Smith, Patrick J. Rusz, Ray J. White, 1982, *Managing Michigan Ponds for Sport Fishing,* Cooperative Extension Service, Michigan State University Extension Bulletin E 1554

Ayers, H.D., H.R. McCrimmon, A.H. Berst, *The Construction and Management of Farm Ponds in Ontario*

Chapter 3: Regulations, Permits, Approvals and Liabilities

Fisheries and Oceans Canada and Parks Canada, Fact Sheet #1, *Working Around Water*

Ontario Ministry of Natural Resources, 1997: Fact Sheet, *Working Around Water? What You Should Know about Fish Habitat and Controlling Aquatic Plants.*

Ohio State University Extension, Ohio Pond Management, Bulletin #374-99, *Laws and Regulations* (http://ohioline.osu.edu/b374/b374_17.html)

Chapter 4: Natural Pond succession

Shrouder, John D., Charles M. Smith, Patrick J. Rusz, Ray J. White, 1982, *Managing Michigan Ponds for Sport Fishing,* Cooperative Extension Service, Michigan State University Extension Bulletin E 1554

Ohio State University Extension Services, *Ohio Pond Management,* Bulletin 374-99

McGee, Mike, President, EP Aeration, Inc., San Luis Obispo, CA (September 1997), "Managing Thermal Stratification With Aeration", *Water Technology magazine.* (www.watertechonline.com)

McGee, Mike, Frank Gardner, (Steven Green), 1992: *Thermal Stratification—Destroyer of Healthy Pond and Lake Ecosystems,* EP Aeration, Inc.

Otterbine, Emmaus, Pennsylvania, *Otterbine News,* Summer Edition

Krichik, Vera A., Raymond M. Newman, and John F. Kyhl, 2006: *Managing Aquatic Ponds in Minnesota Lakes,* University of Minnesota

Ruttner, Franz, 1963: *Fundamentals of Limnology,* English translation of third edition, University of Toronto Press, Toronto, Ontario

Chapter 5: The Pond Ecosystem

Toronto Zoo, 2007, *Amphibian Declines* (http://www.Torontozoo.com/adoptapond/GlobalAmphibians.asp)

Gosselin, Heather M., and Bob R. Johnson, *The Urban Outback—Wetlands for Wildlife:A Guide to Wetland Restoration and Frog-Friendly Backyards,* 1995, first reprint 1996: Metro Toronto Zoo, Adopt-A-Pond Wetland Conservation Program

Choi, Charles Q, "Saving Kermit", *Scientific American,* July 2008

Dees, B. M. and John Jackman, *Field Guide to Texas Insects,* 1999: Gulf Publishing Company, Houston, Texas

Agrilife Extension, TAMU College Station, Texas

Canadian Wildlife Service, Environment Canada, reprinted 1993: *Wetlands,* Catalogue No. CW69-4/75E

Lamoureux, John W, 1970: *Aquatic Plants for Fish and Wildlife,* Royal Botanical Gardens, Technical Bulletin No. 1

McCafferty, AgriLife Extension, Texas A&M System, 1981: (http://insects.tamu.edu/fieldguide/bimg134.html)

http://en.wikipedia.org for information & photos on various beetles, turtles, damselflies, leeches, and crayfish

Solski, Ruth, 1986, *Sammy Snail's Information,* Card 5

http://www.squidoo.com/L-for-Leech for information on leeches

Baker, Patrick J., MS. *New World Pond Turtles,* second edition 2004: Gale, Detroit

Ernst, Carl H., Roger W. Barbour, and Jeffrey E. Lovich, 1994: *Turtles of the United States and Canada,* Washington: Smithsonian Institution.

Dillon, C. Dee, 1968: *Tortuga Gazette*

Palmer, Lawrence E., 1949: *Fieldbook of Natural History,* McGraw-Hill, Inc

Strickland, Dan, illustrated by Howard Coneybeare, 1990: *Peck Lake Trail, Ecology of an Algonquin Lake,* The Friends of Algonquin Park, in cooperation with Ontario Parks

USDA – NRCS, Plants Database (http://plants.usda.gov)

Common Native and Exotic Aquatic Plants in Lakes and Ponds of Pennsylvania (http://www.esu.edu/~jjewett/)

Washington State Department of Ecology: Water Quality Program, *Aquatic Plant Identification Manual for Washington's Freshwater Plants,* Plant Species Index (http://www.ecy.wa.gov/programs/species_index.html)

Connecticut Botanical Society, *Plant ID Guides* (http://www.ct-botanical-society.org)

Smith, Howard G., *Tracking the Unearthly Creatures of Marsh and Pond,* 1972, Abingdon Press, Nashville, New York

Thoma, Roger, F. Midwest Biodiversity Institute

Chapter 6: Pond Design and Construction

Soil Conservation Service, U.S. Department of Agriculture, 1971: *Ponds or Water Supply and Recreation,* U.S. Government Printing Office, Washington, D.C.

Robert Matthews, Forest Owner, Roches Point, Lake Simcoe

The section on vernal ponds has been adapted with permission from *A Guide to Creating Vernal Ponds* by Thomas R. Biebighauser.

Chapter 7: Spillways, Water-Control Devices, and Erosion-Control Materials

Soil Conservation Service, U.S. Department of Agriculture, 1971: *Ponds for Water Supply and Recreation,* Agricultural Handbook #387, U.S. Government Printing Office, Washington, D.C.

Extension Notes, *Building a Pond,* Landowner Resource Centre with support from Ontario Ministry of Natural Resources

Ohio Pond Management, *Extension Bulletin # 374-99,* Ohio State University

Strom, Steven ASLA, and Kurt Nathan, *PE, Site Engineering for Landscape Architects,* third edition: John Wiley & Sons Inc., New York, NY.

Ontario Ministry of Natural Resources, Southwestern Region, 1981, revised 1989: *Guidelines for By-Pass Pond Construction*

Schrouder, John D., Charles M. Smith, Patrick J. Rusz, and Ray J. White, Co-operative Extension Service, Michigan State University, 1982: *Managing Michigan Ponds for Sport Fishing,* Extension Bulletin E 1554

USDA Natural Resource Conservation Series (NCRS) Agricultural Handbook #590, Ponds—Planning, Design, Construction

Maccaferri Canada Limited, 400 Collier-MacMillan Drive, Unit B, Cambridge, Ontario, NIR 7H7, 1-800-668-9396 Canada (1-800-638-7744 USA)

Matson, Tim, *Earth Ponds: The Country Pond Maker's Guide to Building, Maintenance and Restoration,* 1991, second edition: Countryman Press, Woodstock, Vermont, USA

Risi, Angelo, Risi Stone Inc.

Chapter 8: Ponds for Fish

Schrouder, John D., Charles M. Smith, Patrick J. Rusz, and Ray J. White, Co-operative Extension Service, Michigan State University, 1982: *Managing Michigan Ponds for Sport Fishing,* Extension Bulletin E 1554

Ayers, H. D., H. R. McCrimmon, A. H. Berst, *The Construction and Management of Farm Ponds in Ontario,* Ministry of Agri-culture and Food, Publication 515

Knap, Jerome J. and Michael Pembry, 1979: *Country Living,* Pagurian Press, Toronto, Ontario, Canada.

Borwick, Jason, Ontario Ministry of Natural Resources, Aurora, Ontario

Wegman, Wil, Ontario Ministry of Natural Resources, Aurora, Ontario

Campese, Mike, Ontario Ministry of Natural Resources, Aurora Enforcement Unit (GTA), Aurora, Ontario

Chapter 9: Fish Biology Profiles

Raver , Duane and Tracy Lee, Duane Raver Art, U.S. Fish & Wildlife Service, Freshwater Fish Collection

Eakins, Robert J., Ecometrix Incorporated

Wegman, Wil., Ministry of Natural Resources

Chapter 10 : Managing the Pond for Wildlife

Gosselin, Heather M. and Bob R. Johnson, *The Urban Outback—Wetlands for Wildlife: A Guide to Wetland Restoration and Frog- Friendly Backyards,* 1995: Metro Toronto Zoo, Adopt-a-Pond Wetland Conservation Program, first reprint, 1996

Landowner Resource Centre, *Buffers Protect the Environment—Extension Notes,* LRC 77, Queen's Printer for Ontario

Ontario Ministry of Agriculture, Food and Rural Affairs, *Agriculture and Agri-Food Canada, Best Management Practices, Fish and Wildlife Habitat Management,* 1996

Chapter 11: Common Pond-Management Problems

Schrouder, John D., Charles M. Smith, Patrick J. Rusz and Ray J. White, *Managing Michigan Ponds for Sport Fishing,* 1982: Cooperative Extension Service, Michigan State University, Extension Bulletin E1554

Ministry of Environment and Energy, Science and Technology Branch, Aquatic Science Section, *Barley Straw for Algae Control in Ponds,* 1996

The Friends of Algonquin in cooperation with Ontario Parks, *Algonquin Information Guide,* Spring 2010 to Winter 2011

Gray, Jan, *Landowner's Guide to Managing Fish Ponds in Ontario,* Ontario Ministry of Natural Resources

Landowner Resource Centre, *Protecting Fish Habitat from Sediment,* Extension Notes, LRC 75, Queen's Printer for Ontario

Landowner Resource Centre, *Options for Controlling Beaver on Private Land,* 1994, Queen's Printer for Ontario, Bulletin 50515

Lopinot Al, *Winterkill—How to Prevent it,* 1976: Farm Pond Harvest

Ministry of Environment and Energy, *Ontario, Permits for Aquatic Weed Control—Application Information Guide,* 1995

http://en.wikipedia.org/wiki/Red_algae, for information on red algae

http://dnr.wi.gov/lakes/bluegreenalgae, for information on blue-green algae

PCI Dredging, Sediment Removal and Dredging Services, for information on dredging

Water Gardening magazine, "Barley Straw: Nature's Way to Rid Your Pond of String Algae", March/April 1999

Florida Fish and Wildlife Conservation Commission, Fish and Wildlife Research Institute, "Sea Stats—Red Tide, Florida's Unwelcome Visitor", June, 2005.

Sinkler Pond Cleaning, King, Ontario, for information on cleaning

Index